The Art of the
South African
Insult

Published in 2006 by 30° South Publishers (Pty) Ltd.
28, 9th Street, Newlands,
Johannesburg, South Africa 2092
www.30degreessouth.co.za

Design and origination by 30° South Publishers (Pty) Ltd.
Printed and bound by Pinetown Printers (Pty) Ltd.

ISBN 1-920143-05-X (9781920143053)

The Art of the
South African
Insult

Sarah Britten

"Shit!"

Contents

Introduction

"The art of the South African insult," you say, sounding sceptical. Is such a thing possible?

South Africans, as we know, are not known for their appreciation of wit or irony or, in fact, anything requiring too much mental effort. As Lin Sampson once noted, "It was a South African who came up with the stunning riposte: 'Is it?'"

> "You can't have humour without offending somebody. Every joke offends somebody down the line. Humour that didn't plunge the knife into somebody's ribs would be terribly pale, vapid, weak." Robert Kirby.

Granted, South Africa may not possess an Oscar Wilde, but our insults measure up to the most devastating the world has to offer. We have a rich vocabulary of rude words; our public life is filled with *moegoes* and foot-in-mouth disease rages through the land. We have Zapiro and David Kau and the *Daily Voice*. '*Jou ma se*' is as authentically South African as *imbizos* and biltong.

Our languages are rich and expressive. Zulu and Afrikaans are the best languages to use for insulting, says Fred Khumalo. "Only in Zulu (and possibly in Afrikaans) can you swear in a manner that drives the fear of God into your adversary's heart."

English is certainly no match for Afrikaans. Mosibudi Mangena, president of Azapo, describes a 'swearing duel' between Kamteni, a political prisoner on Robben Island, and one of the Afrikaans prison warders. Kamteni "did not start too badly, but as his dirty-word ammunition quickly ran out, his opponent was gathering momentum, spewing one sordid salvo of insults after another."

> His position was further undermined by the fact that he was fighting through the medium of English while his opponent employed a language in which obscenities could sound a lot more devastating—the guttural Afrikaans. When his swear vocabulary was completely depleted and he could only respond by producing

clicking sounds with his tongue, the gaoler laughed triumphantly and said, "*Laat ons maar los, jy kan nie vloek ni*e (Let's leave it, you can't swear)."

So, in part, this book may offer a solution to those who, like Kamteni, feel that perhaps they are lacking in the vocabulary of profanity. May you find inspiration in these pages. (If you do choose to use anything you find here on your fellow South Africans, please note that we do not take responsibility for any consequences of your actions. So, if somebody *moers* you, that's your fault for being a doos.)

"Humour is one of the great solvents of democracy ... It is an elixir of constitutional health." Albie Sachs.

May you also be reminded that insults are our most accurate barometer of democracy. Beware those in power who reserve the right to insult others, while denying it to the ordinary citizens in the street.

Mainly, though, the point of reading this book is that, whether you're laughing at others or laughing at yourself, insults are funny, and laughter is at least good for you as are garlic and beetroot.

"People who earnestly believe they are better than someone else are sick, evil, unhealthy and must be zapped." Chris du Plessis.

Chapter 1

Yo! Yo!
The national character

"We are a nation of pea brains with 30-second attention spans." *Sunday Times*.

What can be said about the country that Bafana Khumalo once referred as "God's armpit"?

Many observers have offered up opinions. "By and large," writes Charlotte Bauer, "our national temperament is rude, anti-intellectual and hangs by an extremely short fuse." "We like our violence graphic, our emotions simple and our heroes one-dimensional," the *Sunday Times* argues. "Anything more confuses us."

"You know as well as I do that given the choice between *Boesman and Lena* and *100 Kak Jokes That Will Make Your Poephol Sting*, most people will opt for the poephol," Tom Eaton, channelling *Liewe Heksie*, points out. "*Skuus dat ek so vloek*."

The most popular show on South African TV after *Generations* is *WWE Raw*. Who votes for whom on *Pop Idols* and *Strictly Come Dancing* is the subject of more national debate than who votes for the ANC or the DA.

"South Africans, as a rule, do not frequent museums and public art galleries except to steal large public sculptures." *Sunday Times*.

We have an apparently insatiable appetite for stories about Advocate Barbie, transvestite hookers and gay tokoloshes who sleep with both a husband and his wife, thus accounting for why the wife is HIV+ but the husband is not (he knows for sure, so he doesn't need to get tested).

When we do read books, they're by Robert Kiyosaki or Dan Brown. "God, South Africans have a terrible weakness for clichés," Breyten Breytenbach sighs.

Culture, in South Africa, is an alibi.

"Our predilection for settling things with a quick *klap*, physical or metaphoric," Charlotte Bauer reflects, "is one instance where the 'cultural differences' we call upon to explain anything we don't understand about each other's lifestyle preferences—ritual cow killing, gefilte fish, Jeremy Mansfield—just melt away."

> "[It's] the kind of film you're gonna see twice. Somewhere between the analytical insight of Leon Schuster and the tremendous gut-wrenching humour of J. M. Coetzee." Aryan Kaganof on his own project, the first movie ever to be filmed entirely on cellphone.

We like everything to be easy, to not to have to think too deeply.

Beyond agreeing that Nelson Mandela is a hero and all-round lekker guy, we are not entirely sure what we stand for. When called to rank the greatest members of our nation, we place Leon Schuster above Oliver Tambo, Steve Hofmeyr before Walter Sisulu and Beyers Naudé, Jeremy Mansfield ahead of Cecil Rhodes and Eugene Terre'Blanche and Brenda Fassie above all of them.

We are held hostage by history, though we try to forget it. Some of us are still trying to deal with the kid who picked on us from Grade One to Standard Five, the boy who said we needed Clearasil when we were thirteen, or the sergeant who yelled, "*Troep, jy is laer as slangpoep!*" at us during Basics, when he wasn't yelling, "*Troep, ek sal jou blindederm by jou hol uitpluk dan gat ek jou in daai doringboom hang!*"[1]

Quite frankly, we are confused. In the past decade and a half or so, we've gone from arsehole of the world, to shining apple of the everybody's eye, to something like the global fourth toe of the right foot: not particularly pretty, somewhat hairy, and can be ignored unless you stub it against the chest of drawers in the bedroom, in which case it hurts like hell.

> "Fancy, a whole nation of lower-middle class Philistines, without an aristocracy of blood or intellect or of muscular labourers to save them!" Olive Schreiner.

But there is hope for the country that Michelle Constant describes as "a bobby-socked

---

[1] "Troopie, I'll rip out your appendix through your arsehole and then I'll hang you in that thorn tree."

meisie from the platteland". For a start, we have a tremendous capacity to overlook the faults of people we like, no matter how obvious they are. We are in touch with our emotions. We can go from worshipping the ground our sports people jog over, to suggesting that they should be fired, in the space of two games.

We are inventive and resourceful. Anybody who has seen a taxi steered by a spanner and held together by wire can be in no doubt that the philosophy of *'n Boer maak 'n plan* is alive and well across the land.

> "We see a nation descending into stupidity." Mondli Makhanya.

We have an innate ability to adapt to new conditions. Like bacteria down a borehole in Delmas, the language of the streets is always evolving. So a low-maintenance girlfriend becomes an 'Mzansi Account' (her high maintenance equivalent is a 'Talk 1000'). We demonstrate our familiarity with global geopolitics by calling a woman with a flat bum 'Afghanistan' because a well-endowed woman is 'Pakistan'. The average bergie in Cape Town comes up with better lines during one morning of sorting through the dustbins in Obs than a star on the bill at the Montreal Comedy Festival does in a month of snorting coke in Hollywood.

Even Afrikaans has poked its head outside the laager. "I think that Afrikaans," says *Idols* judge and the man the *volk* love to hate, Deon Maas, "is like an abused wife who's finally decided to divorce the husband who kept beating her up."

In the end, we will always find plenty to distract ourselves: shopping, complaining, worrying about the kids, braaing on a Sunday, yelling abuse at our team on the TV screen, hoping Tito doesn't put interest rates up again because that's going to make the car repayments even tougher, buying a R28 Quickpick because it's a R20 million draw and *somebody* has to win, right?

We are South Africans, just doing our thing, and if you don't like it, we'll bliksem you, my china.

> "Many of us go through the swamplands and deserts of life swathed in a glossy kaross of self-delusion." Credo Mutwa.

Chapter 2

Between a rockspider and a hard place:
ethnic insults

"I'm prejudiced because it's good for survival." Eric Miyeni.

When the honourable Cape Judge President John Hlophe denied telling attorney Joshua Greeff in 2005 that he was a piece of white shit and it was time he went back to Holland, he may or may not have been continuing a proud South African tradition.

We may not be very good at soccer. Or cricket. Or sticking to the speed limit. (In fact, if we are going to be honest with ourselves, it does seem, from time to time, that we are not very good at anything except inventing automatic pool cleaners, perfecting chutney recipes and carrying out cash-in-transit heists.) But, at any given point in time, we are very good at calling each other names.

South Africans are, after all, a bunch of Dutchmen and Souties, Charras and Hotnots, Shangaans and the Xhosa Nostra, Bushies and Afs, Goms, Porras, Lebs, Crunchies, Zots, Mlungus, Japies, Boers, Chinamen, Makwerekwere, Rooineks, Rockspiders, Makwankies, Hanskhakis, and yes, even though we know of course that nobody except Australian cricket supporters use it, Kaffirs.

It's what defines us as a nation.

1488 and all that

If we're going to get down to technicalities, of course, it must be said that for millennia, large parts of South Africa were the domain of charmingly artistic people who now, for the most part, arrows on back and bows in hand, prance across flea-market placemats, hotel staff uniforms and duvet sets from Mr. Price Home.

But we all know that history only starts when men show up in boats.

Despite the prevalence of the K-word in our geography in the years preceding (and in some cases, extending into) the New South Africa, the early years of European exploration were disappointingly restrained in their descriptions of their encounters with the locals.

There was that unfortunate incident at Mossel Bay, where Bartolomeu Dias fired a crossbow at the gathering crowd and killed someone, thus setting the tone for some of the 1600s and the 1700s as well as a large part of the 1800s in addition to the 1900s. Nonetheless, we have to wait until the arrival of the Dutch to see some good quality nastiness.

And the Dutch, efficient as they were back then in the days before they became limp-wristed liberals who decriminalized hashish and embraced various forms of loose living, wasted no time. According to a book compiled in 1652:

> The local natives have everything in common with the dumb cattle, barring their human nature ... [They] are handicapped in their speech, clucking like turkey-cocks ... They all smell fiercely, as can be noticed at a difference of more than twelve feet against the wind.

The smell must have been impressive, given that the European visitors themselves back then were hardly poster boys for personal hygiene. As we all know, the world would have to wait 350 years for Jacques Kallis to tell us all about the importance of using antibacterial showergel.

By 1653, van Riebeeck, the man with the long hair and chiselled cheekbones who used to smile mysteriously from our bank notes back when it was £2 to the rand, was begging the VOC (Dutch East India Company) to remove him from the company of the "dull, stupid, lazy, stinking people" at the Cape and send him to Japan instead.

Laziness was a big problem at the Cape. The laziness of the locals became the third-favourite obsession of the Europeans, after the difficulty of finding a good slave and the challenge of driving the Bushmen and the local wildlife to extinction.

In 1654, Johan Nieuhof declared:

> They are lazier than the tortoises which they hunt and eat.

In 1667, a man by the mildly Harry Potteresque name of Volquart Iverson observed:

They are a lazy and grimy people who will not work.

William Dampier in 1691:

They are a very lazy sort of people.

By 1719, nobody had thought of anything new to say, but Peter Kolb said it anyway:

They are, without doubt, both in body and mind, the laziest people under the sun.

And, in 1801, a dazzling display of originality from C. F. Damberger:

Perhaps the laziest nation on earth.

In contrast, Governer Wagenaar, who replaced van Riebeeck, was very worried about the laziness of the burghers, who exhibited "indolence" and led "irregular and debauched lives". This was 1663. How comforting to know that nothing has changed.

I'll throw you with 1836 tomatoes

"Voortrek, draadtrek, saamtrek," ("Trekking, wanking and coming together") as performance artist Peter van Heerden sums up Afrikaner history.

If you were to sum up South African history in general, you would probably only require two words instead of three, namely stealing and killing. Most of our history up to and including 1902 involves grasping British imperialists, backward Boers and savage Natives. None liked the other very much. The American historian Stephen Crane summarized the situation that led to not one, but two wars:

To the Boers, the English seemed prejudiced and arrogant beyond mortal privilege; the English told countless tales of the Boers' trickery, their dullness, their boasting, their indolence, their bigotry.

Certainly, Crane noted, the Boer was not exactly a fun-loving party animal. "But in spite of his dour sanctimoniousness, he was not a perfect person, any more than his brother Briton." When the Great Trek started in 1836, the British seemed to think it was good riddance. Lord Glenelg, the Colonial Secretary at the time wrote, "I can hardly suppose it serious … if reports be true, they are no longer useful citizens but freebooters."[1]

Then followed lots of battles in which Boers, British and Natives took turns to slaughter each other. Even God got involved, stepping in to help the Boers at Blood River but apparently deciding to sit out the rest of the nineteenth century. The ancestors weren't going to be left out either, sending messages to Nongqawuse, who told the Xhosa that if they slaughtered their cattle and burned their crops, the white man would be driven into the sea. (It turned out the ancestors were actually a third force and secretly conspiring with the white man.)

> "Beards are the only crop the Boers have ever grown without a government subsidy." Roy Campbell.

Not one, but two Anglo-Boer wars ensured that Blerrie Rooinekke would never get on with Stupid Dutchmen. "I have fought against many barbarous kaffir tribes," declared Paul Kruger, "but they are not so barbarous as the English, who burnt our farms and drove our women and children into destitution." In 1927, the *Sunday Times* pleaded for greater racial harmony:

> Cast aside suspicion, distrust and racial prejudice, and grasp your Dutch or British fellow-South African by the hand. You will be surprised and delighted to find what a good fellow the average representative of the other race is at heart.

This was back in the old days, when the Rainbow Nation was still in black and white.

We didn't invent racism. We just perfected it

"We Afrikaners are too lazy and too stupid to have thought up something so successful,"

---

[1] "An Afrikaner," sniffed an anonymous nineteenth-century official, "is a person of Dutch extraction who believes in the expansion of the brandy market, the promotion of the corn market and the suppression of the native."

Evita Bezuidenhout once said. "Apartheid was brought to us by a Dutchman."

And she was right. Apartheid could be very confusing.

In 1959, Jan Smuts Airport was forced to change its signage to 'Whites' and 'Non-Whites' because 'Europeans' and 'Non-Europeans' confused the foreigners. Apparently, the Americans kept trying to use the 'Non-Europeans' exits.[2]

Then there were the unfortunate municipal employees tasked with patrolling Port Elizabeth's beaches in 1976, when the city divided access to the sea, not only between Europeans and Non-Europeans, but between whites, coloureds, Indians, Chinese and Malays. (Black beachgoers, in case you were wondering, were banned completely.) The rangers, whose job it was to make sure that no group crossed another's line, found enforcement unexpectedly challenging. Sometimes it was hard to tell the difference between one group and another, especially the Malays and coloureds. "In that case," explained a city official, "they look for liquor. Where they find it they know the people are Coloured—because Malays do not drink."

In light of the ever-present need to clarify matters, a helpful little manual was produced for use as a textbook in a police training college.[3] Indians, explained the book, were an "unhygienic health menace". Jews were sly, liable to be guilty of "fraud, embezzlement and swindling". Portuguese and Greeks "were hot-blooded and prone to crimes of passion". Blacks were "primitive" and needed firm but kindly guidance from their noble Aryan superiors, who were of course better behaved than anyone else, and, if occasionally you had trouble remembering that, they'd bliksem you to make sure that next time you did.

"I have sought to recruit many competent black people, and no sooner have we recruited and trained them than they leave. I get so upset … I am stopping this recruitment of black people. I am okay with my Afrikaners. They stay and do the work, and become experts." Reserve Bank governor, Tito Mboweni at a Joburg business breakfast, September 2006.

---

[2] More than forty years later, Chris Forrest described the strange experience at Heathrow Airport of having to choose between a Europeans and a Non-Europeans queue. "For the first time in my life, I went to the Non-Europeans queue. And I thought, so this was what all the fuss was about."

[3] A copy was leaked to Rian Malan who, long before he became a famous journalist, poured scorn on official Aids statistics and had videos of his latest *liedjie* shown on *Pitstop*, worked as a crime reporter for *The Star*. He describes the book in *My Traitor's Heart*.

Ah, you had to love apartheid. You might be in the camp that argues we should 'move on' and pretend it never happened, or you might hold firm to the belief that apartheid should be blamed for HIV/Aids, persistent power failures and the impending catastrophe that is global warming, but when it wasn't making things complicated, sensible people knew that apartheid was wrong, and that made things simpler and there's something to be said for that.

As Nowell Fine, aka Pieter-Dirk Uys once said, "There are just two things I can't stand about South Africa: apartheid and the blacks!"

The happy, singing, dancing race

In 1948, Mr. H. Oost of the Afrikaner Party complained to the House of Representatives that the Natives were both idle and restless, a most worrying state of affairs.

> The Native has lost all the respect he should have for his master. The Native's philosophy is not to work more than is absolutely necessary for him to keep body and soul together on mealie pap, and the biggest complaint today is that Natives are indolent and disobedient.

The Dean of Bloemfontein, the Very Referend C. C. Tugman, was more generous. "The Bantu is not lacking in intelligence," he allowed in 1949. "What he lacks chiefly is ambition." A year later, Mr. M. C. de Wet of the National Party offered the following insight: "They are by nature a cheerful race; if you make their souls happy they are a dancing, singing, happy race."

The passing of time did not lead to much apparent progress in inter-racial understanding. During a commission set up to investigate the causes of the 1976 Soweto riots, a Mr. Ron Stephenson of the National Forum explained that the brains of blacks and whites were so different that ethnologists no longer considered them the same species.

Damp summer biltong

Around about those halcyon days of white South Africa, the mid-seventies, in a book with the intriguing title of *Agter Die Mielies*, Bertus de Beer explained that black and white South Africans found one another smelly. Black people likened the smell of whites to a sheep, while the smell of a black man was very much like "damp summer biltong which is unsuitable for human consumption". (One can only assume that interesting things were going on behind those mielies.)

The issue of smell was one that appeared to fascinate many white South Africans. Describing the morning ablutions of his protagonist in *The Suit*, Can Themba wrote, "This ritual was thorough, though no white man a-complaining about the smell of wogs knows anything about it."

Mrs. Betsie Verwoerd stated in 1973 that she had raised her children without the help of black nannies and their "characteristic odour". "If white children of working mothers were cared for by blacks," she wrote:

> it is natural that the white child would develop an attachment for his black 'mother'. Even the characteristic smell which is normally repulsive to a white person will become associated in the child's mind with the person with which he spends most of his time. Can this later repel him when he is grown-up?

Nannies, as most white South Africans will recall, smelled of either Lifebuoy or Sunlight soap. Was Mrs. Verwoerd suggesting that the smell of soap was repulsive to whites? In a hot climate like that of Orania, attitudes like this should be guarded against.

The baboons are back

Thirty years later, black and white South Africans are no longer considered different species, and we all use the same brands of deodorant. Nonetheless, in the spirit of Marxist dialectical materialism—which was so important to the comrades before they discovered the delights of plain old materialism—it is entirely appropriate that the pendulum should begin its inexorable swing in the opposite direction.

> "A lot of people are going to be shocked when they die and come before a black God. They will have to answer for a lot of hate." Pauline Shapiro, letter to *You* magazine.

"Black people are also racist; they aren't angels ... People like you who bring out the racism thing make me sick ... Maybe you'll be just as shocked when you get to heaven and find out God is a she." Celeste from Windhoek, in a response to the letter above.

In 2005, Professor Malegapuru Makgoba, the Vice-Chancellor of the University of KwaZulu-Natal, turned his considerable intellect to considering the similarities between white South African men and baboons or bonobos. The "dethroned white male in South Africa," he wrote, "is playing the same role as dethroned baboon troop leaders."[4]

The dethroned male becomes depressed, quarrelsome and a spoiler of the new order until he gets ostracized from the colony to lead a frustrated, lonely and unhappy life.

This was not the first time that white men had been likened to baboons. P. W. Botha once said, "There is only one element that can break the Afrikaner in this country and that is the Afrikaner himself. It is when the Afrikaner, like a baboon shot in the stomach, pulls out his own intestines." Admittedly, PW had a slightly different agenda in mind.

The good professor felt that "The white male should ... be excited by the new prospects of imitating Africans." White men should learn to "speak, write and spell" in an African language. They should be like Johnny Clegg and learn to dance like Ladysmith Black Mambazo:

He should learn kwaito, dance like Lebo, dress like Madiba, enjoy eating 'smiley and walkies' and attend *lekgotla* and socialize at our taverns.

It must be said that it seems a little unfair of Makgoba to expect white men to be

---

[4] For left-wing academic Ashwin Desai, who was involved in a very public dispute with Makgoba in 2005 and 2006, the baboon article featured among a body of evidence of Makgoba's "well-worn deck of race cards". "There is a racist pong hanging over UKZN," Desai wrote, "... but for the fact that Makgoba is African and employs this as pre-emptive cover for his mismanagement of the institution, he would have been laughed off campus long ago." Makgoba had also dismissed striking workers as "mindless Zulus" and suggested that an Indian cabal was ranged against him. In that case, wrote Desai, "Put me with the coolie and the squatters, professor."

able to dance—like a professional no less—to Zola's latest hits when we all know they have no rhythm. And though compulsory attendance at taverns and *lekgotlas* sounds reasonable enough, forcing people reared on *ribbetjies* and macaroni cheese to develop a taste for chicken faces raises questions about whether Makgoba is in fact moonlighting as scriptwriter for South African *Fear Factor*.

"White South Africans have to be the most spoilt race in the entire universe," adman Peter Vundla has complained. So it is perhaps unsurprising that people like Makgoba want to exact revenge by making white people look like complete arses. At least he is prepared to put in some effort into making them change. "I am no longer prepared to waste my time on white people," Winnie Mandela said in 1987.

"Most white South Africans are not nice people." Eric Miyeni.

Motsweding Radio DJ Peter Manzana was more charitable about whites, who, in his view, merely took advantage of the inherent untrustworthiness of black people. "Black people," Manzana informed his listeners one fine Saturday morning in October 2005, "are sell-outs and backstabbers and they can kill you."

For democracy to take so long, it is not because of the Boers but our people. You know! Boers use the very black people to spy amongst themselves … For Mandela to spend 27 years in prison; it is because he was sold out by black people. If I see a black person with a person of another race i.e. Coloured, Indian or White, I just think of spying. *Jissus! Nee man!*

Presumably Mr. Manzana had recently been the victim of crime; as he went on to complain about the stealing of cars. "Do you know a black person can steal your R200,000 car and sell it to whites for R200? They will give him R200 and he will say 'Thank you boss.' He will go to the white person and say 'Boss, I've got a parcel' and they are afraid of whites; that is why whites are taking us for granted."

"I refuse to accept that black people can be racists." Jon Qwelane.

Still, "Black culture and Afrikaans culture have more in common than you think when just looking at the political buggerup," Nomavenda Mathiane, writing during the apartheid years, quotes a (black) friend.

And she has a point. Think about it. Both fond of pap and charred beef fresh off the braai, most black and Afrikaner South Africans consider themselves Christian; both write letters to the press about the impending apocalypse brought about by gay marriage.

Go into your average middle-class black or Afrikaans home and you will see the same things: a love of klinker brick (it's practical) and a fondness for show-wood lounge furniture and sentimental bric-a-brac. Wouldn't it be wonderful if black and Afrikaner South Africans could realize that underneath it all, they want the same things, namely an Isuzu double cab and a 54-inch plasma screen for the den in the facebrick Tuscan in Roodepoort?

> "That should be a lesson to black people to vote only for each other." Sundowns lead cheerleader Babalwa Mneno, after being voted off *Strictly Come Dancing*.

White people can't dance, black people can't swim

Where would we be without tired clichés? For example, it's not fair that we only have Great White Sharks, argued John Vlismas. "I think we should have a Great Black Shark. The thing is, it would hardly get you because it's battling to swim."

Even black people make jokes about how black people can't swim.

"Black people have accepted that they can't swim," admits Judy Jakes. "We sit on the beach at Durban and watch you white people swim. So, I think it's about time you white people also accepted the things you can't do. So, next time at the club, you sit at the bar and watch black people dance."

"Black people don't like water," David Kau agrees. "Think about it. How many people tried to rescue Madiba from Robben Island?"

Tshepo Mogale freelances as a lifeguard in December. "It can happen—they have got to fill the quota system. I was taking chances—I can't swim myself. So I figured the best thing to do is to keep all the black people out of the water. Can't drown on my shift man, it makes me look bad!" There are other clichés. "Black people are not reliable," says Judy Jakes. "They have funerals to go to." There are advantages to being a black guy living in the suburbs, as Tshepo Mogale points out. When a TV licence guy knocks on your door, you tell him, "*Jammer, die baas is nie hier nie.*"

Why is it, wonders David Kau, that when you're black and you start coughing, people say quietly to themselves, "Oh fuck, another undisclosed illness." And when you go to the doctor, the doctor suggests that you "get tested". Whereas if you're white, your lungs can be falling out, and the doctor says, "It must be stress!"

Even the government makes use of clichés. "How do black people spend their recreation time?" KwaZulu-Natal premier S'bu Ndebele asked a conference on sport and recreation in April 2005. "It's SA Breweries and sex, that's it ... that's what blacks are about—no, no, it's wrong."

> "You know, it's the first time in my life that I've done it with a bantoe." Sy Makaringe, quoting a coloured woman who spent the night with a young black journalist.

Some blacks are not considered black enough. "We have real blacks, not like Egypt and South Africa," a senior Nigerian official said in 2005, arguing that her country should be given a seat on the United Nations Security Council. Blacks who get too friendly with whites are liable to be dismissed as coconuts by people like Jon Qwelane. This rant, vintage JQ, dates from 2006:

> The hypocrisy and downright laggard racism of certain sections of especially our white community and their coconut sleeping partners—colourless lackeys if you ask me, to borrow the late Steve Biko's term for these so-called blacks—is mindboggling.

The language club

Rockspiders, rocks, Dutchmen, crunchies, boers, planks, goms, gawies, japies—in the ethnic epithet stakes, Afrikaners are far ahead of any other group in South Africa. "Some of them are just downright thick," Cape Town DJ Nigel Pierce commented on the high percentage of Afrikaners in the Springboks. "What we need to do is we need to get rid of these thick Dutchmen within the squad. Seriously."

Barry Ronge, interviewing the organizer of a rock concert at the Voortrekker Monument in 1998, speculated "how the rocks that built it will feel about a rock concert being held at the Voortrekker Monument." Darren Simpson, mocking people from Brakpan during *The Rude Awakening* show, told listeners:

> If you buy the White-Trash Noise CD today, you'll also get these soothing white-trash sounds; the sound of a Ford Cortina falling off the bricks, a fly swatter, and every song from Steve Hofmeyr.

"Can people get away with hate speech as long as it is aimed at Afrikaans?" complained a writer to the Broadcasting Complaints Commission. Certainly, it's hard to imagine John Vlismas saying, "I can't wait until Afrikaans people are extinct" about Muslims or Xhosas to an audience at Sandton Convention Centre and getting away with it.

Much like the English, Afrikaners are a mongrel collection of the descendants of various European adventurers, nonconformists and miscreants united by a language borrowed from the servants. Over the years, Afrikaners developed a reputation for being *verkramp*, but, in their defence, it's worth asking how long a band called Fuckoffpolicecar would last in this country.

> "The lost raisin in the white bread." Mohamed Shaikh, spokesperson for the University of Stellenbosch and one of its first non-white students, describes his experience.

So why all the plank jokes? Perhaps one Dr. Koot Vorster can offer a clue. In 1980, he said, "Nobody can be a good South African if he is not first an Afrikaner."[5] You can't go around telling everyone who cares to listen that you are God's chosen people without somebody wanting to take you down a notch or two.[6] Rian Malan, reflecting on Afrikaners and apartheid, wrote: "We shit on the altars of Western Enlightenment and defy the high priests who would have us behave in accordance with its moral tenets."

Like Malan, J. M. Coetzee grew up English-speaking despite his Afrikaner background. Describing his childhood in *Boyhood*, the twelve-year-old Coetzee acknowledges that he has an Afrikaans surname and speaks Afrikaans without an English accent. But he considers himself English. The Afrikaans boys are too different. He is not one of them:

---

[5] The more things change, the more they stay the same. Sort of. Take this comment that appeared on the Friends of Jacob Zuma website 25 years after Vorster's statement: "Zulus alone are South Africa itself".

[6] On this point, doesn't it strike you as strange that every second group—Afrikaners, Rastafarians, white Aryans—claims to be a lost tribe of Israel? Especially as half of them are, well, not exactly fans of the Jews and being a tribe of Israel must imply at least a *distant* relationship to the orchestrators of the one-world government?

There is a manner that Afrikaners have in common too—a surliness, an intransigence, and, not far behind it, a threat of physical force [he thinks of them as rhinoceroses—huge, lumbering, strong-sinewed, thudding against each other as they pass]—that he does not share and that he in fact shrinks from. They wield their language like a club against their enemies.

Sometimes the enemies take that club and use it for themselves. Zebulon Dread, a self-described "fatuous fart married to a white poppie from Kempton Park", is the most offensive man in South Africa. Word for word, Mr. Dread is even better at pissing off white people than Jon Qwelane. He had lots of fun offending white people at the 2001 Klein Karoo Kunstefees. Dread had chosen to go into the "heartland of the enemy," he explained in the *Mail & Guardian*, "to raise the hackles, the roof and the enemy's ire through ribaldry and satire … I wanted to make them laugh by using their own language with such succinct and lyrical nuance that they would stand in awe of this *kaffir* who spoke Afrikaans better than most of them could dream of."

You can imagine the scenes. Dread then proceeded to inform them with "demonstrative verbosity" that they were

naaiers, fokken dom konte, varkvretende honkies and a bunch of deluded idiots for thinking that Brother Jesus even took the time to listen to meat-eating beasts who cared more for their pit bull terriers than they did for their fellow black humans.

One tannie approached Dread to tell him that he was a bad man. He just laughed and danced with her. That Dread lived to tell the story is an indication that things have improved in the new, slightly used South Africa. In the old days, the okes would have clubbed together to *moer* him.

Instead, in a disappointingly sober assessment, instead of denouncing Dread as one of Satan's lieutenants, the Freedom Front wrote to the *Mail & Guardian*: "A distinction must be made between immature touchiness about criticism of Afrikaners on the one hand, and the crossing of borders and the abuse of the freedom of the press on the other hand. In our opinion, the article by Dread fell in the latter category … He deliberately tries to shock and to offend. Such vulgar language might possibly be acceptable in a private conversation, but never in a newspaper."

Afrikaners are getting soft, it seems. In reflecting on how Afrikaners have changed since the advent of black rule, Rian Malan looks to the aforementioned Fokofpolisiekar. "These boys have long hair, loud guitars, foul mouths and one of the most offensive names in the history of rock music." In a previous era, they would have been harassed by the police and denounced in Parliament.

> Today they pull adoring crowds and get played on Radio Sonder Grense! I tell you, the local Dutchman is evolving in the same direction as his forefathers in Holland, where people are so meek, tolerant and open-minded that their brains are in danger of falling out.

Choking on broccoli

Chris Chameleon once said that singing in Afrikaans was like choking on broccoli.

Nobody seemed to mind as much, though, as they did when the Bible of global cool, *Wallpaper* magazine, described Afrikaans as "one of the world's ugliest languages" in its September 2005 edition. Johan Rupert, who is also the CEO of Richemont, responded by withdrawing millions of pounds of advertising for some of the world's most desirable brands, effectively telling this nauseatingly self-regarding bunch of ponces to stick their Philippe Starck up their Rem Koolhaas.

In our globalized society, Rupert showed us that the best way to get your own back is to use your status as a captain of industry at the helm of a huge marketing budget to further your own personal agenda. It makes more sense than writing letters to the *Sunday Times*.

Of course, it was only a matter of time before Steve Hofmeyr, having fathered half the Afrikaner nation (*Wie's jou papa?* as the jokes go), crowned himself defender of the *volk*. Thus Afrikaners now have a choice, if one can call it that, between Steve and the Don of Dainfern, Dan Roodt. At least Dan wouldn't be caught dead in a brown patchwork leather jacket.

> "I've seen the colour of the Afrikaans flag, and it sure as hell isn't Roodt."

Young Afrikaner to Chris Roper, who likened Roodt's thought processes to the Taalmonument, "grey, brutalist, and utterly lacking in nuance".

Complaining about yet another joke about planks on 94.7's *Rude Awakening* show, Steve exclaimed, "Jeremy Mansfield said stuff about the Afrikaner which he would never have got away with if he had said it about Muslims. I'm through with jokes."

He then got everyone excited by suggesting that he might take himself off into self-imposed exile. "We are being tested, and if we continue to be tested, we might go away. We've got to fight for our uniqueness." Whence 'we' would go, he left unspecified. Orania? Paraguay? Wimbledon, perhaps—three quarters of Afrikaners between the ages of 18 and 30 are there already, which would at least make the move more practical.

We will leave it to Chopper Charlie, a columnist on the website watkykjy.co.za, to bring some perspective to the language debate:

This might be news for a lot of people, [but] Afrikaans is just a language. It's not a fucking faith or an issue or a licence to be a doos.

The National Problem

Conrad Koch and his coloured sidekick Chester scan the audience for black South Africans. "Those folks aren't black, they're Indian," says Chester. "They're only black when they want a job."

"We all know that everyone has their Indian." A so-called 'Gucci revolutionary' and Jacob Zuma supporter, to *Sunday Times* editor Mondli Makhanya.

According to a Standard 9 history textbook used in 1987, the Indians were first brought to South Africa in 1860. "As the years passed," noted the textbook, "they began to create certain problems. By the time of Union they had become a National Problem."

By the time Dr. N. J. P. Steyn wrote a book entitled *Biblical Aspects of Apartheid*, the National Problem had become pressing. This was because Indians, the good Doctor explained, live in a cheap way, are no asset to any community, contribute nothing to society or the country, do not associate with natives or other races, have no access to European circles, are in general of a very low type and are of no consequence to the general interests of South Africa.

In 2002, Mbongeni Ngema expressed his particular take on the National Problem with a song entitled *AmaNdiya*. "Indians don't want to change, even Mandela has failed to convince them," went the song. "It was better with whites, we knew then it was a racial conflict." The lyrics also included the following pithy observations:

... Africans struggle so much here in Durban, as we have been dispossessed by Indians.

and

I have never seen Dlamini emigrating to Bombay, India. Yet, Indians arrive every day in Durban—they are packing the airport full.

Ngema said he was only trying to stimulate discussion. The SA Human Rights Commission said he was stimulating racist hate speech. The song was duly reclassified R18 and Mbongeni managed to stay out of the headlines until he split up from Leleti Khumalo in 2006.

AmaNdiya was something of an exception, however. If what appears on our television screens is anything to go by, the cultural compass is now pointing east. Indians are now South Africa's most fashionable minority. Forget the Year of the Rooster, 2005 was without doubt the year of the Indian. Every second ad on TV featured people who called everyone "my larney". Raj and Raj continued to flog Corsa Lites, an Indian businessman used his Kia bakkie to transport curry powder; an Indian burglar enjoyed a polite, yet amusing conversation with his Indian victims, and there was an Indian who climbed into a fridge to teleport himself to his mother in Durban. (That last one was banned for encouraging children to climb into fridges.)

Even Naas Botha turned Indian in an ad for a spicy burger from KFC, which must

have sent our cultural policemen and -women into spasms of righteous indignation at the blatant reconfiguring of historically modulated relations of domination in concert with the mediation of the visibility of minorities by consumerist capitalism.

"Ten years. Then I leaving South Africa. It all going to dogs. Too many blex," Bhavna, from India, tells Achal Prabhala while they are stranded in the airport at Nairobi on their way to Johannesburg.

"Indian people are the new black people"

Indians also featured in several high-profile criminal trials.

"Did you hear the collective sigh of relief among black people when they found out Leigh Matthews' killer was an Indian?" David Kau asked the audience at the 2005 edition of *Blacks Only*. Looking over recent news headlines—Schabir Shaik, Donovan Moodley, Ahmed Essop of Madibagate—Kau observed, "Indian people are fucking up. Indian people are the new black people."

Kreejay Govender was amazed by the revelations about Donovan Moodley as everyone else. "Flip man, we're not a violent race. Every Indian knows, if you want R50,000, you phone Schabir." (Now, if Schabir had really been clever, not only would he not have returned from his little trip to Mecca, he would have trademarked himself and charged a royalty for every joke in which he played a starring role. This would have made a valuable contribution to the Friends of Jacob Zuma Fund.)

Perhaps Indians are a source of fascination because they don't play rugby or soccer. Therefore, South Africans don't understand them. As Riaad Moosa points out, "The only time you see an Indian with a rugby ball, he's putting a price on it."

"Will these Indians ever shut up?!" Graffiti on a desk in the Commerce Library, Wits University.

Two men and a Pondo walk into a shebeen

"Pondo, a tribe famous for their foul language and excellence in witchcraft." Fred Khumalo.

In 2005, a Klerksdorp man shot dead a fellow drinker in a tavern. The reason? The dead man had called him a Shangaan.

Stereotypes in South Africa are a matter of life and death.

To call a non-Shangaan a Shangaan is considered a grave insult, because Shangaans are viewed as country bumpkins, if not actually subhuman. A substandard type of wors in the townships is known as Shangaan wors. Pedi people have bad body odour. Xhosas are ambitious, cunning and tend to look out for each other, hence the Xhosa Nostra theory, also known as the iLuminati. Zulus are dumb but strong and brave—most security guards are Zulu—and rely too much on Indians. Sothos are lazy; probe far enough into the family history of most criminals and you'll find a Sotho. And you won't get far in Durban if you're a Pondo.[7]

> "The Zulus are already pissed off because their website is zulu dot coza." Conrad Koch.

"In any society that is strong on stratifying people according to race, those at the bottom layer tend to be vicious with each other," writes Fred Khumalo, who also notes that Shangaans are said to have no fashion sense. "Zulus were dismissed as warlike and stupid."

> Sothos were cowards who spied on their black brethren on behalf of white bosses. Tswanas were stingy and mean-spirited (they'd rather drown themselves than give the enemy the pleasure of beating them up). Vendas were thick-headed but well-endowed. Historically, Swazis couldn't fight to save their lives; all they could do was insult their enemies and hope the latter would wither away under the immense power of the insults.

> Friday was known as Boesman's Christmas because of the perception that coloured people spent their money on delicacies and booze come Friday, payday, and were dirt poor by Monday.

When Zulu people want to tell you how inebriated you are they say: "You are as

---

[7] It's not all bad news though: Shangaans are reputed to have the biggest penises, while Swazi women are considered the best in bed. Maybe everyone else is just jealous.

drunk as an Indian who doesn't own a business." (This, of course, is based on the observation that serious Indians who run businesses—mostly Muslims—do not drink.)

"It's so sad to see how black people talk of how they were oppressed," writes Tsonga-speaking Sowetan Wisani Baloyi to the *Daily Sun,*

> but never think of how the Shangaans and Vendas living in townships like Meadowlands and Chiawelo were treated. Growing up in Chiawelo and surrounded by Zulus and Sothos in Senoane, Phiri and Dlamini, we were treated like rubbish.

Tsotsitaal is full of terms for the colours of our rainbow nation. *Amper-baas* is a black person light enough to pass for white. Whites are *japies, plaasjapies* or *boere.* If you come from Mozambique or Zimbabwe, you are dismissed as a *mangoro.* A Malawian is a *makiriman. Rampie* refers to migrant workers, especially those who work on golf courses. And it is best not to call a Shangaan a *makwankie,* unless you harbour an obscure masochistic urge to be panelbeaten.

Even white people noticed that not all servants were the same. In 1911, a letter writer to the *Sunday Times* advised housewives to avoid employing Basotho houseboys, "for they are incorrigible thieves".

All I want for Christmas

"Wouldn't a Great Coloured Shark be great?" John Vlismas said once. "Then I thought, it's pointless, because it's got no front teeth."

> "There are three kinds of coloureds. Those who think they're white; those who've been duped into believing they're black, against the ontological evidence of their senses; and the rest of us—the sane ones, those who know we're coloureds."
> Aryan Kaganof.

In 2005, Capetonians awoke to the ruminations of one Blackman Ngoro, the accurately, if not especially poetically named media adviser to the mayor, on the subject of race relations in the Western Cape. Tired of running a gauntlet of bergies "homeless and drunk on cheap wine", Ngoro took this as evidence that Africans were "vastly superior" to coloureds. "Coloureds have not yet realized that the time to be the cheerleaders for the white race is long past and gone."

Blackman felt that their salvation lay in the embracing of the ANC. "Coloureds must undergo ideological transformation if their race is to prosper and not die a drunken death," he wrote, somewhat ominously.

In response, the Cape-based tabloid, *The Voice*, was moved to new heights of literary virtuosity. Taking a photograph of Blackman, they Photoshopped a donkey's ears and muzzle onto his features along with the headline 'Sack this dumb ass—Demand for mayor to skop her racist toyboy'.

Coloureds had much to be proud of, averred the paper: dried snoek, the Kaapse Klopse, and the most famous geographic feature of the Cape, the passion gap (otherwise known as *tanne vir die manne*). To prove their point, *The Voice* delivered a 'Gatsby' sandwich— a concoction involving polony somewhere in its genesis and apparently the crowning achievement of coloured cuisine—to Ngoro's office, though he failed to accept it.

The paper's Elliot Sylvester pointed out that, given that Ngoro was married to a Japanese woman, their offspring were technically ... coloured.

> And from what he says about coloureds being drunk beggars, we hope he is saving some of his half-a-million-rand salary to rehabilitate his kid when his coloured genes kick in. Ngoro should be nervously watching and waiting for his kids to extract their front teeth, join a gang, develop a tik habit and randomly scream "*Jou ma se p**s*" at passing blacks.

Blackman was eventually forced to resign. Later he wrote on the same website, "If I am racist it is thanks to the white people in Africa."

It is a quite lovely irony that none of this would have happened if Blackman had not approached a foreign NGO for funding for his website. His contact at the NGO, who just happened to have grown up on the Cape Flats, was sufficiently intrigued by Blackman's ramblings to pass them on to several people to ask whether she was seeing things. And one of those people was only too pleased to share them with her fellow Capetonians.

Perhaps poor Blackman had been traumatized by the sight described by Tatamkhulu Afrika, in his poem *Trespasser*, which describes a homeless couple in Cape Town:

> She has the usual wrappings on
> stick thin, brittle shins,
> patchy-purple, quietly rotting
> methylated spirits skin:
> doekie of incongruous elegance crowns
> the scabrous, half-bald skull.
> Her man, grotesque
> as a gargoyle roused from stone

> "You guys are Indian right? You know in this light everybody looks coloured!"
> Kreejay Govender.

The issue of coloured self-esteem was one that appeared to interest the Nats, even as they took the vote away from them. Dr. J. H. Loock told the House of Assembly in 1950:

> Let me tell members that Coloured people are not ashamed of being Coloured. It is no disgrace being a Coloured person. One is not responsible for one's birth.

By 1955, opinion was starting to swing the other way. The Minister of Labour himself said that the training of 'European' apprentices by coloured artisans threatened European civilization. If our first lady of the thin lips, Marike de Klerk, (none of Tannie Elize's billowing, obtuse cheeriness for her) is quoted in future history books, it will be the following thoughts on the coloured community, circa 1983:

> You know, they are a negative group. The definition of a coloured person in the population register is someone that is not black, and is not white and is also not an Indian, in other words a no-person. They are the people that were left after the nations were sorted out. They are the rest.

Coloureds often complain that, if before they weren't white enough, now they aren't black enough.[8] This has failed to deter the ventriloquist Conrad Koch, who for a time took on Chester, a coloured sidekick, as his BEE partner. "What's with this Randall Abrahams on *Idols*? If we wanted someone to make coloured people look bad we would have phoned Alan Boesak."

"All coloureds are not skollies." P. W. Botha.

Salt dickheads

Some ethnic groups in South Africa are afflicted with a genetic predisposition toward high cholesterol levels. English-speaking South Africans have historically been afflicted by the conviction that they are better than everyone else. As Cecil Rhodes saw it, to be born an Englishman was to win first prize in the lottery of life.

"Anglo-Africans by and large squat flabbily behind the ramparts of Afrikanerdom— carping, but profiting hugely." Breyten Breytenbach.

English-speaking South Africans have always felt the burden of having to bring civilization to everyone else. "England can never be clear from the guilt of the long-continued slave trade till Africa is free, civilized and Christian," David Livingstone told the London Missionary Society in 1857. Trust a Scot to invent white guilt.

"Blah blah blah," snorted John Matshikiza, reflecting on Livingstone's ambiguous role in history. Africa would have been a lot better off if some forward-looking tribesman had shot Livingstone long before he ever encountered Stanley, because it was Livingstone who started the rot.

Here began a litany of woes for the African people ... in Livingstone's lexicon, 'civilization' went hand in hand with the imposition of and illogical, imported religion called Christianity.

So we did not shoot the geezer. We spent the next 150 years or so learning how to

---

[8] Certainly not black enough for Eskom—short for Employment Supply Kommisariat—which famously appointed a black engineer over a more qualified coloured engineer on the grounds that the coloured man had suffered less under apartheid.

walk in impractical leather shoes, wear underpants and take the bones out of ours noses in the hope that they would like us for it and leave us alone. No such luck.

The British, says Rian Malan, were the real overlords, not the Boers. With their hut taxes and mine compounds, they began what would later become apartheid, and

spent the next 90 years reaping obscene profits and laughing at all of us in their superior and condescending manner. Truly! All blacks were savage as far as they were concerned. Boers were backward. Stupid. Illiterate. Cowardly. Deceitful. "Low-grade people," sniffed Sir Whatever.

By 1949, the Boers were in power, but Africans were not considered sufficiently civilized to have the vote. "I would not give the vote to my three-year-old child," said Senator the Reverend Miles-Cadman OBE, "or to any five-year-old child, and it is nonsense to recommend that we give votes to child-like Natives."

The poet dikobe wa mogale never specifies exactly who he's describing in his poem *people* but there can be no doubt who he is referring to:

some people laugh like advertisements
with their macleans white teeth only …
some people maintain a boerewors status quo
with liberal cheese and wine dignity
with conservative rent a bakkie smiles
and braaivleis moralities
based on contraband kentucky fried threadbare race theories

David Hall-Green, the *Police File* man who later turned his penchant for hot air into a rewarding career painting steam engines, caused an outcry in the late 1980s when he said of a black woman who had been on his show, "I bet she has fourteen children and all by different men."

This comment was viewed by blacks as "typical of the English", Nomavenda Mathiane wrote in her column on behind-the-scenes life in Soweto. "Unlike the all-knowing English writing theses about the barbaric African tribes, the Afrikaner has lived and worked shoulder to shoulder with the Africans and could not throw out such an insult." Living and working shoulder to shoulder with the Africans, Afrikaners came up with words like *kaffer* and *baas* and *bobbejaan*, whereas English-speakers specialized in comments like Nigel Bruce's observation about certain black waiters who could be characterized as "truculent tribesmen with an eye on the clock and a thumb in the soup".

> "I feel it is an insult ... to speak English to an Afrikaans speaker while everyone understands Afrikaans." Mine employee Ferdinand Lubbe, who received a written warning for speaking Afrikaans to a colleague in September 2006.

"I have met the brain drain, and he's ghastly," Tom Eaton writes of a certain kind of English-speaking South African.

> He doesn't challenge his world-view by reading newspapers (or reading anything, for that matter), so I could name him with impunity, but his real name doesn't quite convey the flaccid provincialism that infects one's first impression of him.
> He could be Shane or Chad or Brad or Steve, but for now let him remain Josh, perky and noxious.
> The first thing one notices is that there is almost no brain to drain. Josh is a bundle of toned muscles, of suppressed aggression, of nursed hurts and resentment. He is an automaton dedicated to small-time hedonism and big-time conformity. His parents are terribly proud.

Before people like Josh emigrate, they live in Fourways. They resent the fact that playing hooker in the St. Wotsisface First XV isn't enough to get them that nice job at SA Breweries. They don't like blacks or Afrikaners or Jews—or anyone in fact. A lot of them end up in Australia, with J. M. Coetzee.

> "Will someone tell the racist Natal English types how disgusting and lame this habit of Afrikaner-bashing is?" Eric Miyeni.

Eaton has authored a book entitled *The De Villiers Code*, which is a pity because this is

the book that Dan Roodt (otherwise known as the Roodt of all evil) should have written. In it, he could have exposed the plan by Rooineks and their fellow travellers to undermine the Afrikaner. Instead, Roodt was reduced to writing letters to *The Argus* fulminating against the aforementioned *Wallpaper* insult. This, he wrote, was evidence of "a kind of cultural cold war brewing in South Africa with a motley alliance of English colonials, Afro-Saxon fanatics and yobbish tourists from that rainy island north of Europe moving in for the kill now that Afrikaans culture is struggling under a hostile pro-English government."

In comparison to Afrikaans, "the increasingly tatty local dialect of English has remained the vehicle of stereotype and pretence," wrote Roodt, demonstrating the use of English to express stereotype and pretence with admirable fluency.

Ag, kak man, as Chris Roper says.

The K-word

We have left the K-word for last, partly because we have been putting it off until the last possible moment, and partly because no overview of the art of the South African insult would be complete without an examination of these most politically explosive two syllables in our national vocabulary. Once, not so long ago, the K-word was everywhere and the F-word was forbidden. Now the F-word is everywhere and the K-word is forbidden.

Well, that's the theory, anyway. Like blue eye shadow and Foster and Allen CDs, the K-word can be relied upon to make unwelcome appearances at regular intervals.

Just when you think that South Africans are finally learning to broaden their vocabularies, there go a bunch expat dooses (and some local ones, according to the official investigation) in Australian cricket crowds mouthing off about *kafferboeties* and Mike van Graan is advising coloured South Africans who wish to be considered coloured Africans, to say 'kebab' if they absolutely *have* to use a K-word.

"You kaffirs are uncivilized!" Large white man in a pub, to Fred Khumalo.

Pity the poor young white Tourette's Syndrome sufferer featured on a recent episode of *Carte Blanche*. The word he used most often, noted Ruda Landman, was the K-word. "My mom has tried to change it to another word, like 'coffee'," the man explained ruefully. "But it's made no difference." Fortunately for him, revolutionary brain surgery relieved the symptoms.

Perhaps deep brain stimulation will work for the Pretoria motorist who used the K-word on Bernard Ngoepe, the Judge President of the Transvaal during a road rage incident. Or the employee of a major insurance company who was fired, hired and re-fired for using the word in reference to her colleagues. The Klerksdorp garage which labelled the keys belonging to Solly Makhele's Toyota Tazz as 'Kaffertjie' could certainly do with lessons in customer service. Hestrie Cloete's family used the K-word repeatedly during an interview with the *Sunday Times* during the 2004 Olympics, but for once it was the C-word that got all the attention. (They called Sam Ramsamy a 'coolie'.) Before that, André Markgraaff[9] famously let the K-word slip during a taped phone conversation, and Arthur Mafokate had a kwaito hit with a song entitled *Kaffir*.

Eric Miyeni, who is best known as an actor, once started an advertising agency. He had his business card printed with the words, 'Kaffir in charge'.

> "As soon as I get uppity and become a cheeky kaffir by having the nerve to criticize baas and miesies, I must be firmly put back in my place." The inimitable Jon Qwelane, responding to his critics.

The K-word has its origins in the Arabic for unbeliever, and did not necessarily refer to skin colour. In 1799, a letter noted that Tipoo Sultan wished "to drive the English Caffirs out of India". an expression, says Geoff Hughes "which seems ironic in view of subsequent developments."

It took a while for the word to evolve into the full glory of its offensive power. In the 1830s, Thomas Pringle wrote, "The Kaffirs are a tall, athletic, handsome race." But by 1842, a man named William Shaw was observing that the Xhosa regarded the word "as a term of contempt". From then on, it was all downhill. By the early years of the twentieth century, every self-respecting Johannesburg housewife employed a 'Kaffir houseboy'. In the early '70s, Fred Khumalo's Grade 1 teacher, a Mistress Khumalo, had the class repeat the phrase, "All kaffir boys eat mealie meal and do not think at all."

Perhaps the most famous literary instance of the K-word is the opening paragraph of Herman Charles Bosman's story, 'Makapan's Caves':

---

[9] In 1997, the same year that Markgraaff was caught out, a British-bred racehorse named Kaffir campaigned in Italy with some success. The colt won several stakes races and was considered good enough to keep his testicles, no mean achievement for an equine. This is generally believed to be a coincidence—the horse's name, that is, not the intact testicles.

Kafirs? [said Oom Schalk Lourens]. Yes, I know them. And they're all the same. I fear the Almighty, and I respect His works. But I could never understand why He made the kafir and the rinderpest. The Hottentot is a little better. The Hottentot will only steal biltong hanging on the line to dry. He won't steal the line as well. That is where the kafir is different.

Despite the kwaito hit, the K-word has not become part of lokshin lingo. Compare that to the American equivalent of the K-word, the N-word. Nobody really minds the N-word; we've been hearing it in hip hop hits for years. *Capitalist Nigger* has been on the best-seller lists for months.

Zingisa Mkhuma, writing in the *Saturday Star*, wondered why we stress over the K-word. Kaffir, she noted, is defined as "uncivilized, uncouth and coarse". Would it be offensive, then, if a person of another race called a white person a kaffir? And why should kaffir be only for black South Africans? "In fact, I think there are 'kaffirs', lots of them, in this world, and they come in many colours."

Just don't say it to their faces, though. They might bliksem you.

Chapter 3

The nation at war:
sport

"When South Africa plays New Zealand, consider your country at war." Springbok rugby great Boy Louw to the team before the first test against the All Blacks, 1949.

"Sorry for you Graeme Smith," Barbara of Bedfordview wrote to *The Citizen* in February 2006. "I have never been so disgusted and humiliated in my life watching you play against the Aussies."

Barbara of Bedfordview—the name has a certain ring to it: 'Barbara of Bedfordview' could be the title of a warrior princess, or the registered name of an American saddle horse competing in the three-gaited championship class at the Bloemskou—is a very lucky woman. No tripping on her dress on the way back from the buffet at the Matric dance for her; no drunken boyfriends vomiting on maiden aunts at family do's: no, the most humiliating event in Barbara's life played itself out on the 54-inch Samsung with surround sound as she issued abuse from the green leather Juan couch she bought from the Eastgate Glick's before they closed it down.

"Sports fans who don't understand sport are like Labradors that won't stop humping your leg." Tom Eaton.

Barbara is but one of the millions of South Africans for whom the "magnificent irrelevance" of sport is far more important than real life, as described by Darrel Bristow-Bovey. Sport, Frederik van Zyl Slabbert wrote back in 1985, "is more than a religion, it is a total strategy against total onslaught; it is the guardian of our national character; the barometer of our despair or hope."

"The Oom has long felt that the Aussies' reputation as a boorishly cultureless bunch of Springbok-torturers and Protea-tormentors is wholly unwarranted." Krisjan Lemmer.

Slabbert was writing about white South Africans, but the same principle now applies to South Africans of any hue. When Bafana Bafana bowed out of Afcon in January 2006, fans across the nation felt betrayed. "Our hearts are filled with pain and bitterness," wrote one *Daily Sun* reader. South African citizens, fumed another, are "confused, angry and disappointed."

"We in this country are a bunch of losers, born losers, and we seem proud of it," ranted Jon Qwelane, who had obviously taken Bafana Bafana's declining fortunes to heart.

"The nation is now gatvol." Sowetan Says column, on the subject of delays over the confirmation of Carlos Parreira's appointment as Bafana Bafana coach.

Chris Roper has suggested that it is easier to insult a South African oke's mother than it is to cast aspersions on the national rugby team. "You can walk into a South African bar on a Saturday afternoon, a bar full of big, maudlin, beer-fuelled men, and insult their mothers, and only 42% will respond ... But walk into that same bar and say 'The Springboks suck' and 97% will respond with actual physical violence."

"Sport is the South African Prozac. People who have nothing in common can discuss the cricket on Monday and pretend we're a nation." Aryan Kaganof.

Obviously, not every single South African finds sport fascinating.
"You cretinous mass of self-deluded hysteria," Zebulon Dread reprimanded South African sports fans on the occasion of the 2001 Cricket World Cup. Sport, he declared, is "pissy and inconsequential."

Has everyone forgotten that this is simply a bloody fucken stupid little sport played by mundane, middle-class, often mediocre, individuals whose only worth is that they are good batters or bowlers of a little ball flung between six sticks from one end of the field to another?

... Are we again to hear the bullshit delivered from the political domain, with its minimal successes, as to the absolute importance of this orgy of balls so that the nation can feel proud? Blah, blah fucken blah!

Dread is outvoted, though. South Africans do feel proud when their team wins. Sure, they haven't felt anything resembling pride in a while, but that's not the point.

"One nation, one soul, one beer, one goal." Castle Lager campaign song, prior to the 1998 World Cup.

The thinking man's game

South African sport is not overburdened with the presence of intellectual giants. Jacques Kallis is famous for having asked, while jogging with the team along a beach in the Middle East, how high they were above sea level. Not the brightest light on the plastic Christmas tree. Or Hershelle Gibbs who reputedly asked his teammates how many teams were playing in a forthcoming triangular tournament in Australia.

It must be said that it is rather surprising that bets have not yet been placed on which celebrity couple's offspring will be more handicapped in the grey matter department: Jacques and Cindy's or Joost and Amor's.

John 'Shoes' Moshoeu tried to break out of the mould with a philosophical voice message along the lines of, "The greatest definition of concentration is wherever you are, be there." Tsamaya found such thoughtfulness irritating. "This is confusing," they said, "because Moshoeu is never there to answer his damn phone."

Stick to football 'Shoes'.

"At least we know Joost has read one book, although it's possible he just got told what happens at the end." Tom Eaton, reflecting on van der Westhuizen's condemnation of the journalist who blew the whistle on Kamp Staaldraad as 'Judas'.

Chris Roper argues that rugby players shouldn't try to read. "It would just confuse them.

And let's face it, our Springboks are confused enough. If rugby players start reading, they'll all turn into Nick Mallet, and one clever rugby player is enough for any nation. We don't want to start playing like the French."

Roper also felt compelled to nominate Neil Andrews of *Supersport* "for a special mention in the Hall of Fame of Incredibly Strange Sport Quotes".

After the last Australia vs. All Blacks game, Andrews came out with the following gem of analysis. "You have to wonder whether, pendulum-wise, these two sides are on a different wavelength."

Perhaps Andrews had mastered some of the more arcane aspects of quantum mechanics, in which case this observation makes perfect sense. Or perhaps not.

"Herschelle Gibbs: noted cricketer and amnesiac, famous for having admitted at his book launch that he hasn't read his own co-authored biography. He has read 'most of it', though. You go Gibbers! Ah, the fruits of a Bishops education." Chris Roper.

Sporting races

Over the past decade or so, the role of sport has been, theoretically at least, to make all South Africans feel warm and fuzzy about each other. Unity through sport was something of a challenge, even when 'unity is strength' referred to the British and Boer 'races'. "It is worthwhile considering the Boer in sport, for it is there that he is seen at his worst," John Buchan, the novelist, wrote with typical Imperial sniffiness in 1903. "Without tradition of fair play, soured and harassed by want and disaster, his sport became a matter of commerce, and he held no device unworthy … [The Afrikaners] are not a sporting race …"

"You don't play an Englishman against an Englishman, you play a Boer against an Englishman." Slogan used in 1955, when Stephen Fry was chosen as Springbok captain to lead the team against the British Lions.

The Art of the South African Insult

By 1906, the Boers were demonstrating that, actually, they were quite good at sports like rugby. This was the year that a South African side toured Great Britain and won all their matches convincingly. After they defeated the Midland Counties 29–0, the *Daily Chronicle* declared, "The Colonials have met the cream of the Midlands, and have made them look like skim milk."

It was during this tour that the South Africans called themselves the Springboks, before the British press could come up with a name for them. A century later, there are those sports fans who would also like to come up with other names for the national team, but the Springboks they are.

"The Spring-Blondes." David Shapshak's nickname for the Springboks, 2004.

It took longer for Afrikaners to pick up cricket. "The Boer element is not vastly taken up with the game, although some of the papers do print reports of it in Africaans (sic)," one W. Pollock wrote in 1941. Of course, blacks and coloureds had been playing cricket and rugby all along, but nobody paid too much attention.

"We have no sympathy with your cause in any shape or form and regard you as an utter nuisance … I personally suspect your motives and your background." Prominent British sports administrator, Wilfred Wooller, to anti-apartheid sports activist Denis Brutus, in 1969.

More than thirty years later, Cape Town DJ Nigel Pierce got into a bit of trouble for suggesting on air that there were too many Afrikaners in the Springboks. "Yesterday I said that there were just far too many Afrikaners in the rugby squad. I did a count yesterday. Of the fifteen players taking to the park tomorrow at Carisbrook, ten out of the fifteen players are Afrikaans."

"When Luke Watson said Jake White should pick him for the Springboks, it was as good as tickling the balls of a lion." Mark Keohane.

Sacred scrums

"Rugby is the Afrikaner's second religion." Norman Middleton, President of SACOS, 1976.

Remembering his childhood, Max du Preez recalled a time when rugby was more important to him than the church, school or braaivleis, and how going to a Test match was "a sacred act that made you a better person". Hans Pienaar also saw rugby as central to Afrikaner culture. Rugby's complicated rules echoed the complicated apartheid politics that Afrikaners had created for themselves:

> On Saturdays the referee told them which interpretation held sway on the rugby field; dominees told them on Sundays which interpretation of the Bible to believe; on Mondays their bosses brought them the latest interpretations of the secret Broederbond masterplan.

So for many politicians, rugby was far more than a matter of life and death. It was central to the identity of the *volk*. In the early 1970s, some Nationalists were so offended that Prime Minister John Vorster allowed Maori players to tour South Africa in 1971 that they formed the Herstigte Nasionale Party.[1] In the early 1980s, the opening up of the Craven Week schools rugby tournament to all races was one of the contributing factors to the formation of the Conservative Party.

In the early 1990s, drunken rugby fans sang "*Fok die ANC, fok die ANC*" at one of the first international rugby matches to take place after F. W. de Klerk's historic speech of 2nd February and promptly threatened to send South Africa back to international sporting purgatory.

"Never have I felt more intensely the schizophrenia of being a white South African," Shaun Johnson wrote of his experiences at the match. "It seemed like a besieged tribe had gathered to take strength in their numbers and to send, from their protected citadel, a message of defiance to their perceived persecutors."

---

[1] This is the same political powerhouse that would emerge from cryogenic storage 35 years later to urge Fifa to take the 2010 World Cup away from South Africa.

"I don't suffer from dry-eye; I'm a Cats supporter." 702 listener during 'Dry-Eye awareness week'.

Now of course, you're most likely to find the latter-day equivalent of this sort of fan in Wimbledon. This is the type who likes to sing *Die Stem* when they get drunk and drape themselves in the oranjeblanjeblou. In the UK, they are known as 'Puffniks', named for the bulky clothing they wear to protect them from the northern-hemisphere cold. According to Andrew Donaldson, Puffniks resemble a "jolly green Michelin Man". "The Saffers," he observes, "always look like yokels, sporting bosveld-type floppy hats and questionable facial hair."

How do they know the Lions supporters were the ones who started the Mexican wave at Ellis Park on Saturday?
It was the only time they got to stand up.

The 1995 Rugby World Cup

"A month-long orgy of chauvinism and mime-show of war among nations." J. M. Coetzee on the Rugby World Cup. He probably wasn't very good at sport at school.

Despite such unpromising beginnings, rugby was able to deliver the heart-warming nation-building Kodak moment that everyone was looking for. George Orwell once observed that sport is "war without the shooting", and nothing brings a nation together more effectively than the prospect of an external enemy. Tokyo Sexwale's declaration before the opening of the 1995 World Cup is one of the great classics of South African oratory:

Let Samoa, Tonga and Ivory Coast know that we are not a banana republic. Let Italians realize that we don't eat pizza, but pap and wors. Regarding the French let's do to them what we do to their polony—eat them. As for the English, Carling, their captain apologized[2]—we don't. But above all, teach the New Zealanders a lesson because, whilst we are a rainbow nation, they still go about calling themselves the All Blacks.

---

[2] Carling had referred to English rugby bosses as "forty farts".

The opening ceremony was a colourful spectacle. The novelist Justin Cartwright hated it. "Hundreds of non-specific African dancers were choreographed in a relentlessly colourful process of trivialization," he wrote later.

J. M. Coetzee also hated the show. "It presented," he observed, "a de-historicized vision of Tourist South Africa: contented tribesfolk and happy mineworkers, as in the old South Africa, but purified and sanctified, somehow, by the Rainbow."

The World Cup, he wrote, was an attempt by what he called the "shadow-players" to construct a "piquant, easily digest[able]" version of South Africa for the benefit of tourists. "Today's image-makers and image-marketers have no interest in complex realities, or indeed in anything that cannot be expounded in fifteen seconds," he remarked acidly.

It was Mike Tissong, an editor at *The Sowetan*, who came up with the name Amabokoboko after witnessing a crowd of people watching the opening RWC match on TV:

I teased them that they weren't watching Amabhagabhaga, which is a Zulu nickname for Orlando Pirates. "You are watching Amabokoboko," I shouted. Everyone laughed, so I said we would use that name on the front page if South Africa won.

Louis Luyt, a man famed for his diplomacy and tact, gave a most gracious speech at the victory banquet. South Africa was the first real Cup winner, he said. "There were no true world champions in the 1987 and 1991 World Cups because South Africa were not there. We have proved our point," he said. In response, the New Zealand, French and English players walked out. Undeterred, Luyt then offended the tournament officials by attempting to present a gold watch to the same referee—"the most wonderful in the world"—who had controversially disallowed France's match-winning try against South Africa in the semi-finals.

"It was something I could have done without," the referee, Derek Bevan, said later. "It could be misconstrued."

After 1995, it was all downhill:

"… South Africans are all masochists. How else do you explain their continuing support for the Springboks?" Chris Roper, 2004.

Police in Perth suspect that expatriate South Africans may be behind a new type of mugging. The modus operandi has been consistent—tourists are gently knocked down and held to the ground while pieces of paper are stuck in their pockets. After the muggers' rapid disappearance, the pieces of paper are found to be tickets for the Springbok World Cup games.

"It was just as well it was the B teams out at Loftus yesterday—it was a B-grade match with the Boks most to blame for serving up a smorgasbord of mediocrity." Clinton van den Berg, of the *Sunday Times*, on the August 2006 match between the Springboks and the All Blacks.

Manne from hell

"If you're not a rugby player here in the Free State, then you're a sissy and you're out. It's one of the main ingredients of being a man, a man amongst men or whatever." Comment in the documentary *Voortrekker Ruck*.

Rugby has always been the ultimate test of South African masculinity. So it came as something of a surprise to discover that, according to one anonymous player who participated in Kamp Staaldraad, "Springbok rugby players spend more time naked in one another's company during a season than with their clothes on."

Apparently, Springboks shower together, walk around naked in the change rooms, and see each other naked in hotel rooms. "Every single [internal] Bok disciplinary hearing is held with everyone present stark-naked. That's part of tradition."

Now you know.

So, when Bryan Habana declared, "I'm confident that I'm not going to attract the gay community," after posing for the *Cosmopolitan* sexiest men calendar, perhaps he knew what he was talking about.[3]

---

[3] He justified this observation by adding that he had been dating his girlfriend for eleven months. This is the same woman who told *Huisgenoot* that she had vowed to stay a virgin until her wedding night. Yes, Bryan, after digesting that interesting little piece of information, no gay man would *dream* of attempting to flirt with you.

"The idea of tens of thousands of bull-throated fanatics, well-oiled on Klippies, bellowing 'Hee wee go Seth Efrik-errr' as the Boks stumble to yet another humiliating defeat is too horrible to contemplate." Krisjan Lemmer, commenting on attempts to replace *Shosholoza* as South African rugby's crowd anthem.

In 2002, the generously proportioned Pieter van Zyl (Krisjan Lemmer described him as "that fat fool") ran onto the field during a South Africa–Australia match and tackled the referee, Dave McHugh. Rian Oberholzer, MD of SA Rugby, said: "This assault perpetuates the image of the boorish, boerewors-eating, brandy-drinking supporter when in fact our supporters are highly intelligent with a keen understanding of the game."

"Being a Boer does not mean having to be a boor." Krisjan Lemmer, commenting on Pieter van Zyl's pitch invasion.

Many South African fans felt that McHugh 'had it coming'. "How would any of these 'fans' feel if the criminal law were changed to allow strangers to *donner* you every time they thought you had made a mistake?" Lemmer pointed out.

Lemmer also offered some suggestions for a South African version of the haka. This would be enough to scare any referee into line:

Picture this: the massed umbilici of Potchefstroom bumping and grinding, burping and farting to music, possibly syncopated by that most famous of all South African poets, Leon Schuster. Maybe singing something like *Hier kom die Boere*.

"The sight of this 'impi' advancing menacingly towards the opposing team—brandishing Castle Lager cans—should really strike the fear of God into the players and would obviously also focus the attention of the ref on the matter at hand."

Anthrax scare: Springbok rugby practice was delayed nearly two hours today after a player reported finding an unknown white powdery substance on the field. Head coach Straeuli immediately suspended practice while police were called to investigate. After a complete analysis, Scotland Yard forensic experts determined that the white substance unknown to players was the goal line. Practice was

resumed after special agents decided the team was unlikely to encounter the substance again.

Kamp Draadtrek

In 2003, players selected for the Springboks were driven to Thabazimbi, stripped and searched, dressed in rugby gear, then dumped in the bush where they were subjected to various forms of mental and physical torture-lite.

"In the absence of army discipline, this helped build character," said team manager Gideon Sam, who recommended the approach for school sides too. "I would have had no hesitation in taking my first team there if I had still been a headmaster."

The character-building methods included sitting in a tarpaulin-covered pit for five hours, being drenched in ice-cold water at regular intervals and then subjected to loudhailers blasting the national anthems of selected enemies. Later, exercises were conducted in the nude. "And we were all naked together in icy water late at night and early in the morning, where we had to inflate rugby balls," said one anonymous participant, who added that the camaraderie had been "excellent". "Yes, we were all naked together at times, but so what? The only chaps who were perhaps a bit shy initially were those with small willies."

Laugh It Off entered the fray, producing a Kamp Staaldraad T-shirt modelled on the *Survivor* logo and featuring the motto, 'Outwitted, Outplayed, Came Last'. The illustration of the silhouetted springbok jumping over the rugby ball included dangling genitalia.

"The *Sunday Times* called Corné Krige the 'butthead of the week'. They were kind." Mark Keohane, commenting after Krige released his autobiography, in which he explained his role in Kamp Staaldraad.

Then the parishioners of the NG Kerk Tamboerskloof held a Kamp Staaldraad cake bake competition. The winning cake, baked by Ida Jordaan, was a pillow-sized piece of confectionary topped with naked grappling rugby players modelled in sugar. The runner-up, Carien Pansegrouw, iced a naked bum garlanded with barbed wire.

"Six members of the congregation baked cakes and the winning cake was really pretty," said Dominee Hendrik Scott, who added, "The people in the congregation don't care about nonsense."

Months later, Steve Hofmeyr was hurt by the Blue Bulls' refusal to allow the music video of his skit on Kamp Staaldraad to be shown at Loftus during half time. The video, called *Maak die Bulle almal Bokke* featured shots of various male backsides.

"I understand the sensitivity surrounding Staaldraad. But, hey boys, where's the sense of humour?" said Steve, explaining that he had persuaded a group of Pretoria students to strip and roll in the mud with the help of beer and money. "And now I hear there's unhappiness with the words 'Kamp Draadtrek', which shows fleetingly on one guy's bum."

Kamp Staaldraad, Kamp Kaaldraad, Kamp Draadtrek, Kamp Staalwol ... who cares?

"If you ask me, South African humour needs a face lift."

ATTENTION ALL SUPERSPORT STAFF
Internal Bulletin Re: Future broadcasting times of
Western Stormers and Cats
Super 14 games
In line with our commitment to broadcast only the best
sporting action and to ensure that we are in fact the
CHANNEL OF CHAMPIONS,
until further notice, all Stormers and Cats Super 14 games will be broadcast on
the Cartoon Network.

Zinc-brained incompetents

Actually, if anyone needed a face lift, it was Martin Locke. Remember him? Martin was a fixture in the lives of that generation of South Africans who grew up with television. He always used to cover horseracing, along with Francois Wolfaardt, a man who, as luck would have it, bore an uncanny resemblance to a horse.

But unlike Riaan Cruywagen, both Francois and Martin eventually went away.

Ah, our sports commentators, those intellectual giants of the airwaves. You've got to love them. What would Wimbledon Finals have been during the 1980s without the mellifluous intonations of Bob Hewitt, speculating on the outcome of Amazonian battles between

Chrissie and Martina, or Trevor Quirk droning on about Clive Rice on soporific summer afternoons?

"Will someone in the SABC either make Dylan speak through several folded socks or bash him solidly on the head till his knackers fall properly into place?" Robert Kirby on sports reporter Dylan Rogers.

"Which, out of this bunch of zinc-brained incompetents, is the worst?" Robert Kirby pondered, reflecting on the nation's cricket commentators. Was it Trevor Quirk's "waxen gapings", Edwill van Aarde's "flapmouthing" or Martin Locke's "emaciated superlatives"? Perhaps it was Glenn Hicks, whose physical presence, noted Darrell Bristow-Bovey, would not have threatened Dolly the sheep. "If a mad geneticist had been commissioned to create a human being, with only the phrase "little twerp" as a descriptive brief, he couldn't have done better than Glenn Hicks."

"His ability to be inane in two languages makes him far superior to that guy Darren Scott." Naas Botha, according to Chris Roper.

Writing years later, Tom Eaton could find nothing kind to say about either Quirk or van Aarde, except that compared to the Australian commentators, they were actually not bad.

Quirk's pedantic waffle and Edwill van Aarde's curious inability to gauge how many runs would be scored off a shot—*"En dis ses! Nee, dit wil se, ah twee lopies"*— seem retrospectively cogent next to the nasal, plodding insights of Ian Chappel and his merry band of organ-grinders cracking out bleached platitudes.

Australian commentators, complained Eaton, are "warped, stuck records who have two speeds: jingoistic gong-banging and jingoistic nay-saying."

"As for Neil 'Banger' Johnson, the Zimbabwean says 'bang' more times than is heard in Soweto over a weekend." Letter to *The Citizen*, 2006.

"It has been suggested to Tsamaya," noted the *Sunday Times* soccer column on the subject of SABC TV soccer presenters, commentators and studio experts, "that sacks of potatoes would do a better job in front of the cameras and behind the microphones." *Sunday Times*, on SABC TV soccer presenters, commentators and studio experts.

Tom Eaton recorded, with appalled fascination, the performance of the SABC's studio team of Walter Mokena, Steve Khompela and David Kekana during and after the World Cup final in Germany. "Nothing even partially sentient," he observed, "could have withstood the lobotomizing chute of SABC Sport's scratching-will-just-make-it-worse studio this past weekend."

> Walter Mokoena ... knows football. And he never, ever shuts up. Walter talks and talks. If there is silence, Walter will fill it. If there is sound, Walter will howl in close harmony.[4]

After the Italian victory, viewers unlucky enough not to have DSTV were denied the sounds of jubilation. Instead,

> All we heard was Walter, Steve and David; the former puking words, the latter providing careful, precise and eyeball-shrivellingly dull analyses. Oh, where was the SABC blacklist now, one wondered? Please God, let Walter say something lukewarm about Zimbabwe, and let Snuki lunge for the Big Red Lever. Let silence descend, and let us watch the spectacle sans the pathological verbal muzak.

Liewe Hansie

"Fuck Hansie and all who sail with him." Robert Kirby.

So rugby had Louis Luyt, fans who took out refs, Kamp Staaldraad and Brian van Rooyen. Cricket had Hansie Cronjé.

---

[4] Eaton also devoted space to describing Walter's eyes, which suggested a "teasing, flirtatious sleaziness". Mokoena later demonstrated this aspect of his personality by planting a kiss on Carlos Alberto Parreira's cheek after an exclusive interview, thus earning himself the sobriquet 'Smooches'. "We know the charming Mokoena has kissed the girls and made them cry, but snogging the national coach was out of order," the *Sunday Times* commented.

Hansie Cronjé is the Princess Diana of South African cricket. There are those who believe that, if not the devil incarnate, he is on intimate terms with Satan; to others, he is a bright shining flame snuffed out before its time.

There are those who still refuse to believe that a born-again Christian national hero could possibly take bribes from Indian bookmakers. Sadly, after he was found guilty by the King Commission, not even eyebrow-tweezer manufacturers would consider an endorsement.

Even Robert Mugabe sympathized with Hansie. "I'm heartbroken by what the chap is going through. I never thought he would be lost to cricket so early in his career. He used to be very good but, as he said, Satan got the better of him."

Uncle Bob should know.

"Hansie Cronjé was an underhand shit, a venal conniver who brought the whole game of cricket into disrepute." Robert Kirby.

David Bullard wrote that Satan had contacted him to complain about being implicated in the Cronjé case. "Apparently, someone called Hansie Cronjé has blamed me for the fact he received unspecified amounts of money from Indian bookmakers.

"I've never met this Cronjé guy in my life and certainly never told him to throw cricket matches. The suggestion I am somehow to blame for Cronjé's crookery is bad for business. I'm losing respect down here."

"We said we were not interested and told him to get lost, but in harsher words." Jacques Kallis, on how he responded when Hansie Cronjé approached him to throw a Test match.

Satan complained about being dragged into "some squalid little sporting scrap" because Cronjé "can't wisely exercise the free choice he's been given."

The sports science department at Technikon Pretoria's sports science department took advantage of the case to offer its students the chance to study the ethics of the Cronjé case as part of their course. Professor Jacques Rossouw said they would be asked to discuss "Cronjé's significance as a role model and the effect his fall from grace had on cricket and his fans."

After Cronjé's death, the inevitable tasteless jokes did the rounds.

> Hansie Cronjé was buried and not cremated this week because no one was willing to throw the match.

Robert Kirby wasted no time in commenting. "If nothing else Hansie Cronjé's death has shown up the South African media for the bunch of seedy hypocrites they are," he told Reuters. "Yesterday they were screeching about the irreparable harm he'd done to South Africa, indeed world cricket; today you'd think a minor messiah had died."

After Shaun Pollock chose to dedicate a victory for South Africa against Pakistan to the memory of Hansie Cronjé, Krisjan Lemmer decided to switch allegiance to Australia. "At least the Aussies just do drugs," explained Lemmer.

> "The Hansie Was Framed, Darrel-Hair-is-Satan brigade are as lame and misinformed as they always were, and should not have a single one of their store-bought opinions endorsed in any way." Tom Eaton. That said, subsequent events have proved beyond reasonable doubt that Darrel Hair is indeed Satan. Presumably, his 2IC runs Hell while he is on the field.

Our national team, the Pansies

Only Tom Eaton could liken Graeme Smith's performance in Australia over the 2005/2006 Test series to Uma Thurman and Michelle Pfeiffer. Both of course starred in *Dangerous Liaisons*, in which "the fiendish Vicomte de Valmont has his way with both as only an eighteenth-century cad knows how".

> Ricky Ponting is no John Malkovich, and heaven knows Shane Warne is no Glenn Close, but nonetheless this week Smith emerged looking like a naive debutante, flattered and patronized by a devilish French noble, lured into believing that she was loved, only to wake up roughly deflowered and pathetically alone. Smith's declaration … seems to have been motivated by a sloppy romanticism.

"Suddenly we are the dunces again," lamented Eaton, "the choking Japies who bumble about with our thick necks and fragile tempers."

"Of course Smith's declaration delighted the Aussies. They sang the South African skipper's praises: bold and daring were two popular adjectives. Dof, more likely." Letter to *The Citizen*.

It all started when Graeme Smith accused the Australians of losing their edge following the Ashes defeat. Then Shane Warne, hearing that the South Africans would be employing a team psychologist, snorted, "They will need one after we've finished with them."

Smith described the Australians as the "bullies of world cricket", and said that touring Australia is a "mental and physical nightmare". Warne wrote that Smith was a "fool" in his newspaper column. "You can fry an egg on his [Smith's] face within two minutes."

The Australian crowds chanted racist slogans at the South African players, prompting a flood of speculation in the media as to whether they'd picked up bad words from South African expats over the years, or that expats were themselves involved.

"I feel sick every time I watch our cricket team. They should change their name from the Proteas to the Pansies because they play like a bunch of girls." Comment, *Mail & Guardian* Forum.

Then things got even worse.

"Get this John Blackman out," Shane Warne urged his teammates while Makhaya Ntini, still nursing a fragile knee, was batting during the 2005/2006 Test series against Australia. Ntini, annoyed by what he interpreted as a racist remark, said, "Less of the black please." It turned out that Warne was actually referring to the Australian television actor John Blackman, who had played a character called Dicky Knee.

It was a mistake that anyone could make. Our cricketers can hardly be expected to be in touch with the more arcane aspects of Australian popular culture. The expat whingers rushed off to their favourite online chatrooms to offer sage and considered opinion of how Ntini was overreacting, and overrated.

An Australian resident wrote to the South African papers:

South African cricket captain Graeme 'Warne is a wannabe captain' Smith is as big a bullshit artist as the late and not so great Hansie Cronjé.

"This Australian cricket side are the biggest cheats to have played the game. Everything that is bad in cricket was introduced by the Aussies," retorted a letter to *The Citizen*.

Six months later, Cricket South Africa CEO Gerald Majola said, "We just cannot get away from the Aussies as far as such racist incidents are concerned."

This was after the Dean Jones incident.

When Hashim Amla took a catch in the second Test against Sri Lanka, the Australian commentator said, "The terrorist has got another wicket." To the point, concise, the statement has a certain ring to it. It will certainly go on to be one of the classics of Australian cricket commentating. Perhaps not as memorable as "The batsman's Holding, the bowler's Willey" but a great effort nonetheless.

Naturally, Jones was fired immediately. This sort of thing tends to happen when your employer is based in the United Arab Emirates. "It was never meant to be heard on-air. I am extremely sorry if I offended anyone. It was the last thing I wanted to do," the newly unemployed Jones said later.

Rather disappointingly, he switched to politically correct mode, going on about how he had nothing but respect for the Muslim faith and that some of his best friends were Pakistanis.

As Darryl Cullinan was on his way to the wicket, Shane Warne told him he had been waiting two years for another chance to humiliate him. "Looks like you spent it eating," said Cullinan.

Shaun Pollock, bowling to Ricky Ponting, delivered a couple of balls past the outside edge. "It's red, round and weighs about five ounces," Pollock called out. As luck would have it, Ponting hammered the next ball out of the ground. "You know what it looks like," Ponting shouted to Pollock, "now go find it."

Allan Donald, bowling short to Allan Lamb, yells, "Lambie, if you want to drive, go hire a car." Allan Lamb drives the next ball for four and calls back, "Go park that fucker."

Glenn McGrath once asked Eddo Brandes, the Zimbabwean chicken farmer who has been described as 'portly', "Hey Eddo, why are you so fat?"

"Because every time I fuck your wife," says Eddo, "she gives me a chocolate biscuit."

Michael Vaughan: "queer" according to Graeme Smith. Graeme Smith: "odd and childish" according to Michael Vaughan. Or at least, Smith's statements are odd and childish, "the kind of thing you would say in the playground".

Slipping on a Bafana

Why is a teabag better than Pirates? A teabag stays in a cup much longer.

Where else but South African football would you find characters like Jabu 'Ngwana wa Tshwenya' ('Problem Child') Pule aka Mahlangu, Putco Mafani, Chad 'Pudding Belly' Harpur, Reuben 'Sleepy Wonder' Mahlalela, 'Calamity Wayne' Roberts, Andrew 'Jaws of Life' Rabutla, Lesley 'Slow Poison' Manyathela, Walter 'Time Bomb' Kutumela, Fabian 'Teletubby' McCarthy, Naughty Mokoena and Lovers Mohlala?

"It seemed the players from the Karoo were so excited at the prospect of a once-in-a-lifetime opportunity to spend a night at the Formula One hotel that they forgot about their game." Tsamaya, commenting on the 6–0 defeat by Santos of Beaufort West side Beau West City FC.

Pirates were nicknamed the 'Nappy People' instead of the 'Happy People' after coming down with a stomach bug in Cape Town. Then there was former Chiefs defender, Jacob Tshisevhe, who was prematurely declared dead by various websites and radio stations. One radio anchor, noted the *Sunday Times*, "while reading Tshisevhe's 'obituary', nearly fainted when he called in to confirm he was alive and well." South African football supporters, caring lot that they are, subsequently nicknamed Tshisevhe 'The Ghost'.

Kaiser Chiefs fans nicknamed Dynamos, a team they had beaten 4–1 and 4–0, '4x4s'. Naturally, later in the season, Dynamos held them to a 1–1 draw. At least it wasn't a 2x4.

"Benni, you are a *moegoe!*" The *Sunday Times* on Benni McCarthy, after he withdrew from the Nelson Mandela Challenge against Senegal.

To get the story behind the football story, read Tsamaya in the *Sunday Times*. You'll discover, for instance, that Chiefs wing Arthur Zwane's sported a "womanish" afro. "Someone please give him a microphone so he can belt out a Donna Summer song!" Mark 'Viva Soweto' McVeigh of Swallows "looked a dork doing those tsamayas and vula-valas in last weekend's match against Celtic" while "Sarah Baartman's well-documented big rear is no match for that of [former Bafana Bafana captain Mbulelo 'OJ'] Mabizela".

Sizwe Nzimande, the PSL's chief operating officer, "looks as though he's swallowed a cement mixer since he started working for the league". Rich Mkhondo of SAA, communication head of sponsors of the SAA Supa 8, was known as the "king of crimplene".

> "Sometimes they run away to Durban. Maybe they will go to Limpopo this time after what happened in Durban." Bloemfontein Celtic coach Paul Dolezar, talking big ahead of an Orlando Pirates game.

Krisjan Lemmer and the manne at the Dorsbult once speculated on reasons why the Kaiser Chiefs' clubhouse in Naturena was so close to the Johannesburg prison. Was it a form of corporate social responsibility? A way to demonstrate that progress had been made by their presence in a former whites-only suburb?

Apparently not. "But it appears the real reason is beginning to emerge slowly. The club's superstar, Jabu Pule, is out on a statutory abduction rap after he convinced an under-age girl to go partying with him without the girl's parents' consent." That was after Phumlani Mkhize shot himself in the foot, literally. Then the club's spokesman, Putco Mafani, was hauled up on wife-beating charges.

"Club boss Kaizer Motaung has always been ahead of his peers as a visionary," mused Lemmer, "so maybe the choice of a venue close to a prison was not a mistake after all."

> "In his heyday, he was known for his pace, but he now resembles a tranquilized hippo." Tsamaya on Jomo Cosmos player Helman Mkhalele.

When in doubt, threaten to sue, and when that doesn't work, start muttering darkly about conspiracies. This maxim applies to sport as much as it does to politics.

When assistant referee Tiny Chandermoney declared a Sundowns goal by Joel Masilela offside during the 1998 Rothmans Cup final against Kaiser Chiefs, he unleashed [a storm of controversy]. Replays showed that the goal was definitely onside. This was a problem, because Sundowns lost 2–1 and went home with R500,000 instead of R1.1 million. Husband and wife pair of Angelo and Natasia Tsichlas, leading officials at Sundowns, were soon casting aspersions with the enthusiasm of a Corfu fisherman.

> "Too many palookas have easily found jobs in charge of PSL clubs." Tsamaya, *Sunday Times*.

"With the greatest respect to journalists from the mainstream press," wrote the *Mail & Guardian*'s Andrew Muchineripi, "some of the talk-before-you-think 'rubbish' uttered by the pair should never have found its way into print." Angelo Tsichlas, for instance, suggested that Sundowns would take the matter to court—despite the fact the Rothmans Cup rules forbade legal action. Tsichlas then claimed that there was a "mastermind" controlling a "clique" of corrupt match officials: "He controls many referees and linesmen and should one fail to take instructions from him, one must forget about refereeing."

> "Tsamaya agreed with Motsepe when he said he wanted to get rid of the dead wood at the club. He's got enough to make a bonfire." *Sunday Times*.

Not to be outdone by her husband, the Iron Lady of South African football then accused outgoing PSL chief executive Trevor Phillips of deliberating sowing confusion in South African soccer in order to enhance England's chances of getting the 2006 World Cup.

"I am not going to dignify her statements by commenting further," said Phillips. Muchineripi suggested that the Tsichlases should rather investigate why "a team of expensively assembled stars" could miss so many penalty kicks. "Instead of shooting your mouths off," he suggested, "why not help your players to shoot straight."

> "Why do you write so much shit about me? I'll get you, you arseholes." Solomon 'Stix' Morewa, speaking in Afrikaans to a group of journalists badgering him during a 1997 commission of inquiry into soccer.

Bafoona Bafoona

Though it boasts more than enough characters with nicknames to go around, South

African soccer really is no better than rugby or cricket. They might not be saddled with the legacy of Kamp Staaldraad or Hansie Cronjé, but they have Safa and Bafana Bafana, and that seems hardly fair.

> "Who knows what heights Bafana Bafana might reach should its prodigal Bafanae return home? 3–0 against Malawi? 1–0 against Zambia? Hell, we're talking a goalless draw against Nigeria if we play our cards right." Tom Eaton.

What can we say about Bafana Bafana? Tom Eaton reflected that they did have world-class flair and vibrancy. This was rendered moot by their lack of any actual ability, but still, as the Monty Python people said, always look on the bright side of life. "Unfortunately," sighed Eaton, "there isn't a World Cup of sideways skipping, slapping knees and hopping over orange cones for us to win, so in the meantime one can only hope the South African Football Association will see the light and install Kaizer Chiefs as the national team."

> "Bafana Bafana did us proud at the World Cup—and will go further when André Arendse stops practising his goalkeeping in the shower with a bar of soap." Krisjan Lemmer.

Tsamaya was inspired to form their own team, the 'BuFumblers BuFlumbers'.

> First-choice players in our team would be Butterfingers Brian Baloyi and his tjommie, Chad Harpur, in goal. Shaky-as-a-leaf Papi Khomane and own-goal specialists Lesley Langa and Andrew 'Jaws of Life' Rabutla will marshal the defence. With David Radebe in his element leading the attack with twin striker Ishmael Maluleke, plus the rest of the Bush Bucks squad, fans can look forward to an afternoon of unstoppable laughter. The PSL's 'longest-serving coach', Jomo Sono, will be tasked with the job of instilling "fresh and new" ideas to the side, with the 'Clown Prince' Bruce Grobbelaar as his assistant.

When Krisjan Lemmer heard that a disaster management centre, able to predict natural disasters up to five days in advance, was to be built at Nelspruit, he thought this was a good thing. He did assume, however, that some fine-tuning would be necessary after the system was switched on, "so that monitors don't just read 'succession debate' and 'Bafana Bafana' twenty-four hours a day."

Bafana Bafana players often can't make national games because of nightclub fixtures.

Jacob Zuma turned down the Bafana Bafana coaching job because he had his reputation to protect.

Bafana Bafana have only three weaknesses: dribbling, passing and shooting.

Brazil are scared to play Bafana—they are worried they might wear out their strikers.

Bafana Bafana play with four defenders—two advocates and two attorneys.

"This satan of an instrument … Ban it before it makes us appear like a bunch of clowns in 2010." Jon Qwelane, on the subject of the vuvuzela.

Chapter 4

Pomp and ceremony:
men, women and everything in between

"There are only two growth areas left in South Africa. Politics and sex." Myles Lancet, writing in 1996.

"The old Dutchmen in power had very narrow minds," Lolly Jackson, Lamborghini enthusiast and chief executive of Teazers, told a British journalist in 2006. "When we got democracy, people realized this is what they want to do."

And what South Africans want to do, apparently, is pay lots of money for Ukrainian women to jiggle around naked in front of them.

How long ago it all seems, when the models in *Scope* wore stars on their nipples and the sex scenes were deleted from the Saturday night movie on TV1.

Yes, those late night soft porn movies on etv, the *poes-en-patats* of *Die Son*, the Teasehers ladies review bar (the ultimate revenge) billboard on Rivonia Road—it's all progress. Back then, women knew their place, in the kitchen or under men. Today they form music groups, call themselves Rokkeloos, and declare, "*Ek hou van melktert, breiwerk, skaapbraai en hard naai.*"[1]

"More brain, less boep. Get it?" Letter to *You* magazine.

No sex please, we're South African

In this, the land of Jacob Zuma, it's strange to think that there was a time when South

---

[1] This translates as, "I like milk tart, knitting, sheep braaing and sewing hard." Which sounds perfectly innocent, except of course for the fact that *naai* has a double meaning. The song, played on a late RSG show, was the subject of the following complaint to the BCCSA. "The lyrics of the songs that where (sic) played on this specific date on the mentioned time above was (sic) extremely fowl (sic). In my opinion this (sic) type of lyrics condones (sic) to free and open sex, especially to our youth."

Africans did not know terribly much about sex. "The wonderful thing about Calvinism is that it's kept sex a mystery," Lin Sampson wrote of those years. (Nobody, though, has yet offered a compelling explanation of why there are quite so many synonyms for a) genitalia and b) sexual intercourse in the Afrikaans language.)

"I didn't pomp my sister." Headline on a *Daily Voice* poster.

Back then, sex was—officially at any rate—a bad thing. In fact, the only good thing about sex was that it was necessary in order to produce more members of the *volk* and so shore up the future of a white South Africa. In 1967, the arrival of the contraceptive Pill caused dire predictions of the end of civilization, with calls to the government to restrict its access to both married and unmarried white women. Mr. J. J. F. du Toit, the chairman of the Federale Raad van Skakelkomitees, described it as immoral and sinful:

> It is all right as a means of helping to solve problems arising out of the population explosion being experienced in China and India among the black folks in many parts of Africa. But to people like ourselves, part of the bulwark of Western civilization, the use of the Pill is tantamount to racial suicide.

Despite their dim view of sex, the apartheid powers that be were obsessed with it. The thought of who might be sleeping with whom kept them up at night, and not always in a good way. Non-white with white, men with other men: these were the private acts that, apparently, could wreak public havoc. The years of the Immorality Act meant that the police could legitimately invade private homes in order to feel whether the bed was still warm and haul off suspects to a district surgeon to see whether sexual intercourse had taken place.

J. H. B. Reitz told the Senate in April 1950, "You know, it is in the nature of the native that when he can have intercourse with the European he prefers it." In 1962, Dr. A. Radford of the United Party considered the awkward problem of white South Africans who seemed to prefer having sex with non-Europeans. He felt it was a sociological problem. The "unfortunate man who has a predilection for colour in sex" should not be arrested by the police, but treated by a psychiatrist. White men who preferred to have sex with black women, he said, were often "dullards or recidivists".

"Women degraded." Headline in a January 1919 issue of the *Natal Witness*. The newspaper was warning about the evils of Bolshevism.

1974 represented something of a high point for South Africa: this was the year that the moderator of The NG Kerk, Dr. J. D. Vorster, tried to have the bikini banned as "scandalous". Sales of bikinis were particularly brisk that year.

The onslaught against fashion continued, with the 69th congress—you laugh, but that was not a misprint—of the Vrouefederasie near Naboomspruit in September 1976. This time, the target was denim jeans. The *Sunday Times* reported delegates complaining that "where there were no real moral or religious principles left, women should stand apart from the modern world of denim culture."

Mrs. M. Kritzinger of Nylstroom told the congress that denim clothing made all races look the same, making it easier for "outside indoctrination to take a hold on people ... I feel the original idea of wearing denim is an attack against the West," she said.

Another form of outside indoctrination—the F-word, Feminism—was something that happened in other countries, ones infected with other isms like Communism, Marxism and Liberalism. According to a 1978 brochure for the East London Technical College's Department of Secretarial Studies, getting to be a secretary was as much as the ambitious woman could hope for:

> The post of private secretary is the apex of feminine occupations. This is because she has the distinction and honour of working and moving in the select company of bosses.

"The pink war will be won when dads call their sons 'girlie' as a compliment." Jenny Ridyard, 2006.

Scary naked Indian women

Lest we congratulate ourselves on all the progress we have made over the past thirty years or so, it's worth reminding ourselves that *plus ça change, plus c'est la même chose* is not a French expression for something that the Vrouefederasie would not approve of. When Beau Brummell announced the opening of a new nudist resort named 'Kaal on the Vaal' in

June 2006, he brought back nostalgic memories of 1980s Warmbaths when he informed the media that it would be reserved for whites only.

"If you are black, coloured, Indian or anything like that, you can't come," he said, without any hint that he was making some kind of pun. The decision was strictly business, he said. A whites-only resort would be financially viable. "White people don't want black people ogling them."

Not even his Indian daughter-in-law would be allowed in. "She is not white. She can't walk around naked. She will scare my guests."

Now, since science has proven beyond any doubt whatsoever that we are all the same species, and that without clothes, everyone has pretty much the same kind of equipment, why exactly a naked Indian woman would 'scare' anyone is a matter for some speculation. What exactly are white people trying to hide from their fellow citizens?

THE GEOGRAPHY OF A WOMAN (source unknown)

Between 18 and 20, a woman is like Africa. Half-discovered, half-wild, naturally beautiful with fertile deltas.

Between 21 and 30, a woman is like America. Well developed and open to trade, especially for someone with cash.

Between 31 and 35, she is like India. Very hot, relaxed and convinced of her own beauty.

Between 36 and 40, a woman is like France. Gently aging but still a warm and desirable place to visit.

Between 41 and 50, she is like Yugoslavia. Lost the war, haunted by past mistakes. Massive reconstruction is now necessary.

Between 51 and 60, she is like Russia, Very wide and borders are un-patrolled. The frigid climate keeps people away.

Between 61 and 70, a woman is like Mongolia. A glorious and all-conquering past but alas, no future.

After 70, they become like Afghanistan. Everyone knows where it is, but no one wants to go there.

THE GEOGRAPHY OF A MAN

Between 15 and 90, a man is like Zimbabwe. Ruled by a dick.

Vive la différence

"Now you can't separate the loose chicks from the ugly chicks." David Kau, on the consolidation of Wits Tech and RAU.

Now that we are free to enjoy the forbidden fruit of democracy, things have changed. In May 1999, a rock concert was held in the grounds of the Voortrekker Monument. Barry Ronge interviewed the organizers on radio, and commented,

> I have always looked at that old stupid monument to the past, called the Voortrekker Monument and have decided that the only sensible thing to be done with it is to paint it pink and turn it into an enormous gay disco at which they can have drug-crazed raves. Now that would be exactly what it deserves.

While the world's commentators focused on the political changes taking place in the freshly christened New South Africa, the nation loosened its collective chastity belt. Johannesburg hosted gay pride parades. *Basic Instinct* appeared on cinema screens, *Hustler* appeared on the shelves of the CNA. Nando's ran its famous Tailgunner ad, in which a sweet old couple invite their very obviously gay neighbours for supper at their local peri-peri chicken outlet. "So, my children tell me you're a tailgunner," the old man says to one of his guests. "I was a military man myself."

The Jenna Jameson Raid. Name of a Johannesburg pub quiz team.

This was the decade of Viagra, a heady time when citizens could talk about erectile dysfunction outside the context of the construction of Pretoria shopping malls. "A solid erection is the middle-class miracle of our time," Aldine Kaplan observed at the time. She had doubts about the new climate of openness:

> Masturbation is a habit that supports an industry worth billions, and it releases all sorts of healthful endorphins, so perhaps it is only right that we should talk about it in the same breath as customer service and the rise in the repo rate.

By 2006, South Africans were gatvol of politicians, according to Ingo Capraro, the editor of Afrikaans tabloid *Die Son*:

> Goodbye to hypocrisy. Up yours, establishment. Fokofpolisiekar. Bring on *Die Son*. Our main approach is: local, sensational, tongue-in-cheek, fun. A bit of voyeurism, a bit of malicious pleasure—thank God it wasn't my penis that got cut off and braaied.

Even the right wing were getting bored with politics. In February 2005, members of the Boeremag trial entourage defected to the 'Advocate Barbie' trial in a neighbouring courtroom. "This is much more interesting," they explained.

Prior to the trial, successful lawyer Cezanne Visser had earned fame for having her boobs enlarged at the behest of her lover Dirk 'Diggler' Prinsloo. The pair was arrested for luring young girls to their residence and sexually assaulting them. A year later, Prinsloo went on holiday to Russia and, to what we can only assume was the immense surprise of the judge who had granted him permission to leave the country in the face of protests from the prosecution, announced that he was not coming back.

> "Tell the bitches to keep their panties on." Translation of a line of a Xhosa poem read by the South African liaison officer of the World Health Organization, during a press conference to launch World Aids Day in 1998. He promised never to read the poem again.

Of course, just as South Africans were free to enjoy congress with whomsoever took their fancy, along came—Mother Nature, God, the CIA, who knows—and hit us with HIV/

Aids. Who would have thought that using a cucumber to demonstrate how to fit a condom would become an act of patriotism? In 2006, the *Sunday Sun*, disturbed by the prospect of so many deaths from Aids-related illnesses, took upon themselves to quote soccer boss Irvin Khoza, and told their readers "Stop fucking around."

> "Do you realize how tired you would be if you were having all the sex you are accused of having?" Nomakula Roberts.

Even white South Africans, not usually known for their interest in the Sunday edition of *The Sowetan*, were moved to complain.

"Our page-one headline last week ruffled a few pubic hairs. Could we not have written 'Stop poking around' or 'Stop fornicating around', instead of using that horrible F-word that African-American comedians love associating with their mothers?" wrote Mzala, one of the newspaper's columnists. The *Sunday Sun* responded with an editorial arguing that 'f***ing around' was not the same as 'screwing around', thus introducing a new level of semantic propriety and sociopolitical enquiry to what until now had just been four- and five-letter words respectively.

> Trouble with his 4-5! The *Daily Sun* summarizes the tragic case of Limpopo resident Modiba Nkwana, whose wife had left him for a man with a bigger penis. Apparently willing to make sacrifices for the sake of fame, Nkwana told the *Daily Sun*, "I am even ashamed to approach other women, thinking they know about my small dick! I have not had sex for the past year!" Nkwana said his businesses, a driving school and a supermarket, were suffering. His wife, when questioned, said, "My husband disrespects me and insults me in front of everyone. That's all I am saying."

Satanic and boring

> "I wish I was straight." Openly gay entertainer Somizi Mhlongo, after caressing one of his (female) dancers' crotches at a *Sunday World* event.

One of the major benefits of democracy has been the emergence of the gay community from the hideous chrysalis of apartheid into the magnificent butterflies of freedom seen every year at the Mother City Queer Party. While it must be acknowledged that gay men are just as capable of being dull, unkempt and tone-deaf when it comes matters of taste as their straight counterparts, South Africa has become a much more stylish place since the first gay pride marches. Debbie from Cape Town, writing to *You* magazine, compares South African heterosexual men unfavourably with their homosexual counterparts:

> Metrosexual, ubersexual, intersexual, ultrasexual … Seems to me they're all undersexual and just jealous of homosexual men who not only have a group label but really know how to dress and how to treat women (sadly, stopping short of the final step).

As the designer André Croucamp remarked at a Rooms on View launch, "If a bomb had fallen on the Sandton Convention Centre on Thursday night, there wouldn't have been a moffie left in town."

> "How can I possibly dislike a sex to which Your Majesty belongs?" Cecil John Rhodes, on meeting Queen Victoria.

Also, if it weren't for the gay community, letter writers to the *Citizen* would be forced to restrict their moaning to crime and Graeme Smith. Here is a typical example, from Theo Volker of Springs:

> The horrific decline in moral standards since 1994 coupled with the general collapse of services at all levels of government has been aggravated by the latest Constitutional Court ruling in favour of gay and lesbian marriages. Rather than resorting to a meaningless name like Azania I would suggest something more descriptive of our secular lifestyle. Sodom and Gomorrah come to mind.

Writers of letters to other newspapers also enjoy expressing their opinions on this issue. In a dazzling display of startling originality, 'Just Wondering' of Pietermaritzburg wrote to the *Cape Argus* on the subject of gay marriage, wondering whether the Constitutional Court will "issue a ruling that the Bible should be rewritten to provide that Genesis 1 should henceforth read: "And God created Adam and Steve, and when they wanted to procreate they were not Abel."

> "Not that the Z3 did too badly for BMW. It was hugely popular among hairdressers, ballet choreographers and flower arrangers, particularly when BMW started to produce the car in pastel shades to match their eye shadow." David Bullard. BMW were not happy that Bullard positioned the Z3 as a 'gay' car.

On 17th February 2006, the *Daily Sun* letters page included two missives on the subject of the gay community. The first was titled 'Gays are Satanic', the second 'Gays are boring'. "Gays are destroying the human race. They are messengers of Satan on a mission to destroy humanity," opines Sam Lumamba. Godfrey Masindi, on the other hand, has a different take. "Just imagine, a man having an affair with another man. This is so unnatural and boring!"

You have to take your hat off to a group of people who manage to be both Satanic and boring.

> "Say no to a man marrying a man." Africa Muslim Party slogan.

It is not only the letter writers of South Africa who obsess about their gay compatriots. Politicians across the political spectrum do it too. The so-called Clown of Cape Town—otherwise known as the Premier of the Western Cape, Pieter Marais—accused the Mayor of Durban of being jealous of Cape Town's lovely, rich gay and lesbian tourists. Later Marais expressed his "shock" at the promotion of the city as gay-friendly. "Although the Constitution gives people the freedom to choose, I cannot support something against my beliefs," said Marais, renowned across the land as a man of principle and integrity and who, noted the Lesbian and Gay Equality Project, has "no principles, no convictions and no morality."

> "I just have to tell you that I am so gay it's not funny." Somizi Mhlongo again. Incidentally, he drives a Z4.

In 2006, Pan Africanist Congress (PAC) of Azania president, Motsoko Pheko, was

condemned by the Human Rights Commission for anti-gay comments. Pheko subsequently made what could be vaguely construed as an apology. Then, using truly infallible logic, he went on to explain that wasn't worried about losing votes because homosexuals can't reproduce anyway:

> Some people have said that we are going to lose votes of the homosexuals—fine, yes—indeed I think that they cannot be a population anyway as the population of homosexuals will disappear in no time—they can't bear—you can't have a man and a man having children, you can't have a woman and a woman having children.

"When you grow up as a moffie in a country ruled by Neanderthals," said Steven Cohen, "you soon learn there's nothing to fear but your fear." And Cohen made sure that even if South Africans were Neanderthals, he was going confront them with a moffie on metaphorical steroids scene.

From penis-printed dinner plates to tutus constructed out of crystal chandeliers, Cohen fascinated and horrified the country for much of the 1990s.[2] When he was announced as the winner of the 1998 FNB Vita Award, the audience contained "so many pursed lips you might have thought Cohen had stuck his trademark dildos up the bottoms of most people present," reported Brenda Atkinson. A judge at the 1999 awards resigned in protest at a performance that succeeded in combining the apparently incompatible elements of shoes with heels constructed out of gemsbok horn, ballet, *Fiddler on the Roof* and douching, and denounced Cohen as "pathogenic".

Over the years, Cohen showed up in astonishing ensembles at shopping malls, the Durban July, even Fort Klapperkop during a rightwing rally, where two beefy AWB types promptly escorted him from the grounds, performing the Nazi salute, shouting "Heil Hitler!" and swatting photographers out of the way.

Cohen also encountered strong criticism from other members of the gay community. "[S]ome of us have already become what we despise: judgmental moralists and finger-pointing accusers," he retorted. "And I've got nothing but scorn for you bitches."

---

[2] Perhaps his only—and distant—rival was the Wits student who had his penis pierced in front of an audience and later showed up at his graduation in a fetching green drag outfit topped with a large matching toilet-shaped headdress. After considerable consternation on the part of the ushers, he was allowed on stage to be capped by Justice Richard Goldstone.

"Boer stiffs moffie hooker." Headline in the *Daily Voice*, which reported the fascinating tale of "sexy Carmen, 23", a she-male prostitute "fuming after a larney client paid her with a *vrot* cheque". The client in question, a Wellington wine farmer, was apparently under the impression that she was a woman. After initially expressing disappointment, the appropriately named Andrew Pratt told Carmen, "OK, you bitch, let's try this thing since I already paid for it." Pratt dated the cheque 31/06/06 and "therein," observed the *Sunday Times*, "lay the rub."

Skande!

Jacob Zuma and Khwezi in the main bedroom, Piet Koornhof and Marcelle Adams canoodling in the pages of *Huisgenoot*; Narend Singh and the socialite bonking for the cameras in a Durban hotel room, Benni McCarthy and the schoolgirl in the bathroom, Brenda Fassie and assorted lovers all over the place: South Africa has produced a reliable supply of sex scandals suitable for page 3 of the *Sunday Times*.

One of the South Africa's earliest celebrities in the modern sense was Professor Chris Barnard. The darling of the world's media after the first ever successful heart transplant, he was soon providing more than just material of the more prosaic pioneering medical procedures variety. At the age of 46, he left his wife, Louwtjie, for a woman less than half his age. Remarkably enough, nineteen-year-old Johannesburg socialite Barbara Zoëllner was both beautiful and rich. His critics were simply jealous, Barnard maintained:

You know who resent me? The old professors who have an old wife they would like to get rid of, but can't. Those who would like to go out and swing a little, but can't.

In response, Louwtjie offered a few observations of her own. Her former husband, she said, had become a stranger to her. "Where once there was humility, now there is only arrogance, vanity and materialistic values. Therefore, the only emotion he manages to arouse in me these days is compassion."

Even today, her words resonate with the kind of deadly insight that all celebrities dread:

I feel sorry for Chris because he is desperately running from something that nobody, not even the brilliant, the famous or the wealthy, can evade. And that is growing old.

Impaled

Twenty years later, the affair between Jani Allan and Eugene Terre'Blanche produced what was until recently, the most famous instance of South African sexual intercourse. It certainly brought to light the most famous pair of underpants in South African history.

When Jani Allan interviewed the AWB leader in the dying days of the Old South Africa, she produced prose turgid enough to induce nausea and vomiting in a Mills & Boon editor. "Eugene Terre'Blanche doesn't walk into a room: he takes occupation of it," she gushed to incredulous readers of the *Sunday Times.* "To be honest, he's a hunk." His composure was "cool as a slice of melktert"; his voice alternated between "the loamy texture of a newly ploughed mielie field" and "a caress of worn corduroy".

> Right now I've got to remind myself to breathe. I'm impaled on the flames of his blowtorch blue eyes, you see.

Details of her fornication with ET might never have come to light had she not sued a London newspaper for alleging that they had had an affair.

Linda Shaw, her roommate, was called to testify. She reported that Jani described ET as "a great lay, but a little heavy". Later, when ET spent the night at the Sandton flat they shared, Shaw looked through the keyhole of Jani's bedroom door. Later she described what she saw to the court:

> I saw Jani's feet. Her knees were up. This large white bottom was on top of her … I didn't see the genitals. It was a large bottom. It was on top of Jani, rising up and down.

Later Kays Smit, an AWB official, was called out to Jani's flat in the middle of the night to remove ET, who was very drunk, from Jani's sofa. He was asked to describe what ET was wearing. A pair of underpants, he said. Asked to describe the state of ET's Y-fronts, he answered,

Green, and they had holes in them.

South Africans only started to forget about the underpants when ET fell off his horse in front of the television cameras. In public life, humiliating incidents are generally only erased from the public mind by even more humiliating incidents.

Good, with traces of evil

Perhaps Jacob Zuma should be paying attention to the case of ET. During the trial in which he was accused of raping a woman less than half his age (amazing, how the same details keep coming up), the South African public discovered, inter alia, that the showing of the knees was an invitation for sex; a Zulu man should not leave a woman in an aroused state; a shower immediately after sex helps prevents the spread of Aids; and the preferred term for vagina is *isibhaya sika bab'wakhe* or 'her father's kraal'.

Zuma's troubles focused the minds of his supporters on the problem of women. During the annual 16 Days of Activism in 2005, Friend of Jacob Zuma, Malusi Dlamini, encouraged South Africans to examine the Bible to remind themselves "how deceiving women can be".

> I can't stop to remember what happened in the garden of eden, what Delaila (sic) did to Solomon, how many men have fallen at the hands of women. This is no insult to women of South Africa but merely a reminder that even though they are good they have traces of evil in them. To me JZ is another figure in statistics of men who have been toppled by greedy deceiptful (sic) devious unscrupulous women.

"Somebody didn't get enough hugs from his mommy," remarked Krisjan Lemmer.

Euginia Yantcho of Bellevue East in Johannesburg was one of those fine, upstanding citizens who had earlier waved posters of Zuma's accuser and then burned them while singing "Burn the bitch". Waving a burning red G-string outside the Johannesburg High Court where Jacob Zuma's rape trial was underway, Yantcho offered her take on gender relations:

> A G-string takes away a woman's dignity. If a man sees a woman in a G-string, he

deserves to rape her … Women report rape too easily after they've enticed men with their bodies. Your body is a temple of God.

For good measure, she added that "our daughters are asking to be raped" when they wear G-strings.

"Thou shalt not covet thy neighbour's house, nor his ass, but his wife's ass is fair game." The tenth commandment of the Zuma-supporting National Union of Mineworkers' revised version, according to Zapiro.

More brain, less boep

The Reverend Motlalepula Chabaku says she has no desire to achieve equality to men. "Their standards are below what I stand for."

"I'd rather date a dassie." Letter to You magazine.

South African men," says Rosie Motene, "need to chill, and to listen to women, and to get over their homophobia and their backward ideas of how things are."

There are times when it seems challenging to find anything nice to say about South African men.[3] "If the only South African male capable of making a decent pass holds a rugby ball in his hands, most girls are going to find themselves caught between a rock and a hard on," muses Caroline Hurry. When Patricia de Lille was voted South Africa's sexiest politician, Chris Roper speculated that perhaps this was because "South African men like their women to be part-fishwife, part-nanny."

"Guys, lose the carefully unbuttoned shirts, just-so flipped cuffs, ever-so gelled hair and just find yourselves," advises Debbie from Cape Town. "We women so often have to do the finding for you because too many of you dorks don't know who you are."

"Men!" sighs Rebecca Magi, a female diamond digger quoted by Pat Hopkins. "They have no brains."

---

3 Ag man, that's not fair, you're thinking. Give the okes and the magents a break. If you require reassurance, turn to the glossary at the end of this chapter, you will see that there are many different rude words for women, and hardly any for men. So things do even out in the end.

"Today every girl has a gun, and the way to a man's heart is no longer through his stomach, but through the hole she can blast in his chest." Irit Noble.

South African men are not known for their refinement, either. "Good-looking women aren't leaving South Africa because of the violence," Mike Lipkin commented once. "They're leaving to find thinking men who do more than grunt."

"Local men have all the subtle romance of a randy bullfrog," sighed Nomavenda Mathiane, writing during the late 1980s. They can be entertaining, though. It is the labourers sitting on the back of bakkies, rather than the executive types, who entertain even "high class" women. They will call out "*Dudlu, nongenabaskidi uyangena emakethe*" (One does not need a basket to get to the market) or "*Nongena butcher uyayidla inyama*" (It is not only those who own butcheries that eat meat).

"I'm single and fairly attractive so I have no problem dating attractive women. But I'm obsessed with how clean their hair is, so much so I behave inappropriately by telling them they should wash it more often." Letter to Dr. Louise of *You* magazine.

In the wake of liberation, South African women have even higher standards. "It goes beyond the physical, it's that empty brain and the sheer crap they talk. When you shag an illiterate boy, you must insist they don't talk," *Mzansi Gals*' Misty Blade quoted her friend Thembi in 2006.

"If you lost some weight, it would be good for your wife because she'd be able to find your genitals." Sam Cowan to Jeremy Mansfield, on *The Rude Awakening*, Highveld Stereo.

Zebulon Dread likens the typical (white) South African sex act to a roll-on deodorant that clings to one "like an unwanted octopus". He imagines the plight of the unsatisfied woman in a short story published in his magazine *Hei Voetsek*:

She turned her head toward the snoring behemoth who lay content in the bosom of ignorance—so pathetically male—that it was hard for a good woman not to cry and question the Creator with a massive Why.

"Marriage! One man's slave all your life, slog away until you're in your grave," is the maudlin opinion of Hester in Athol Fugard's play *Hello and Goodbye*. Later she adds, "Happy families is fat men crawling onto frightened women."

"Girls should just marry horses," a little girl said to Marianne Thamm.

"Some do," Thamm told her.

"Swazi men are so open to polygamy, and I don't need that stress in my life." Princess Sikhanyiso, daughter of King Mswati III, explaining why she has no intention of marrying a fellow Swazi.

Abdul Milazi reflects on the problem of *ilobolo*. "You can't buy a Hugo Boss suit with a live cow. First you have to get the cow to the shop, and that's a mission in itself." Letter to *The Sowetan*.

"There is nothing in the world quite as gay as a wedding," Marianne Thamm has observed. That of Naas Botha to Karen Kruger in 1991 set new standards for kitsch Afrikaner nuptials. Fashion critics were unkind, one describing the wedding as resembling a Waterkloof dining-room table. Another observed that the extravagant collar framing the bride's head made her look like a frilled lizard.

Good Afrikaner weddings require lots of libation to get going. Yolandi Groenewald took care not to supply her guests with Klippies, based on the experiences of another couple, whose families ended up in a fistfight over the bride's chastity. "Looking back, I did not enjoy my wedding day at all. Today I would do it in Spain or anywhere else, but for sure not the stoere boere thing," wrote Manda Cronjé.

"Afrikaner weddings provide an equal chance of becoming the party of the year or the most grotesque event the guests have ever attended." Yolandi Groenewald.

After the *ilobolo* has been paid and the honeymoon is over, South African couples settle down to married life. Some of them, like the Motshekgas of Gauteng, do as nature intended.

She cooks, while he sits around—doing what? He doesn't say. Poor Mrs. Motshekga, who is Gauteng MEC for education. You'd think she has enough on her plate, metaphorically speaking but, says hubby, they have never quarrelled over domestic duties.

> When she gets home there is no debate about who should do what. She goes straight to the kitchen and cooks. One cannot teach this, it's a matter of common sense and practice, otherwise you would destabilize nature.

(Does this mean that Jamie Oliver is a deviant?) Feminism, says Motshekga, is a foreign concept which "can destroy rather than build society".

Similarly, psychologist Ketso Mabusela believes that cooking ability was conferred by supernatural powers. Because men and women were created differently by God, men shouldn't be forced to cook. "Our biological make-up defines our role ... Let not us women put men in the laboratory of cooking if they can't."

"If you read the Bible, it was Eve who made Adam eat the apple and in each and every one of us, there's an Eve—and no man wants to see that Eve coming out."

> "We both have two hands, we both can do dishes. If I do not want to do them, I don't, and I do not think a woman's body is specialized to do that. Why must I be the dishwasher?" Lisa Vetten, gender activist.

Later, the challenge of course is to stay married. "Joining the mass exodus southward to get away from Gauteng crime? Be warned—in Cape Town they'll steal your husband from under your nose," *Style* magazine breathlessly informed readers in a June 1997 issue.

"They start to hit on your husband with their body language, their clothes, their sexual innuendoes. The tops are tight and the skirts are fanny pelmets." 'Ellie', to Lynne Kloot. 'Ellie' advised the direct approach. "I just said, when she came at us boobs first in her clinging top and tutu skirt, 'Please move away, I'm hanging onto him by the ankles.'" A male guest at a dinner party got up from the table, taking his wife, and said, "Must dash. Don't have a dick long enough."

The Art of the South African Insult

"My husband left me and that shocked me into dieting." Herbex Slimmers ad.

Robert Kirby felt it was unfair that white males were stuck with one wife at a time, while African men could have several. For example, once a white male divorced a wife, he was required to pay her maintenance, paying for her upkeep without enjoying any of the benefits. "This," he concluded, "is lobola on the never-never."

Since the law shows no sign of Africanizing, when it all comes to a sticky end, you will have to do something. No need to be as drastic as Sandra Wilters, who with what may be described as an unerring sense of place, fatally stabbed her abusive husband, Hendrik, in the chest in front of the Klerksdorp MacRib in 2002.

If you need to call a lawyer, let it rather be Billy Gundelfinger, South Africa's duke of divorce. Estranged spouses are known to burst into tears upon hearing that the erstwhile love of their life has managed to hire him first. "*I'm* scared of me," he has said. In a variation of the adage about the cobbler's children, Gundelfinger himself has been happily married for nearly three decades.

"Now there was a marriage made in Grabouw." Entertainer Alvon Collison on his constantly bickering parents.

Perhaps no incident demonstrates how much attitudes have changed in South Africa than the response to an apparently innocent ad for South Africa's favourite family burger chain. In the ad, for a 'Burger for Men', a father makes an announcement that his young son has finally become a man: the boy has left his first towel on the bathroom floor. The store erupts in applause. All very tongue-in-cheek, a very mild satire on the way in which 'real' men actually behave.

Soon enough, the complaint lines were ringing. "This is shocking! Is this what makes a boy a man?" said one man. "All our friends we have spoken to, with young kids, agree that your advertisement is degrading and portrays improper values."

The boy that your advertisement portrays as the hero is exactly the little asshole I wouldn't want my daughter to marry one day, because he would be an inconsiderate selfish spoilt brat, and that not even through his own doing, but through his dad's wrong teaching.

"This is very degrading to the family-image that should be upheld," complained another erstwhile loyal customer. A third complainant—a 'Real Woman'—wondered whether the advertising agency's next idea for an ad would be a man raping a woman. "The advertisement left a very sour taste in my mouth," said yet another woman, presumably a real one. The advertisers, she added, should rather have shown the boy taking out the rubbish bin.

What can we learn from all of this? Firstly, that some South Africans have embraced the idea of gender equality, which is encouraging. Secondly, that a lot of South Africans don't possess anything resembling a sense of humour, which is mildly depressing. Thirdly, that most South Africans are very good at being Offended, which is not surprising at all.

"Men: stuck between a rock and a hard-on." Andrew Donaldson.

A South African Love Poem

Of Course I Love You Bokkie
I Only Smaak You Dik
You Cook And Clean And Iron My Shirts
And Look After Me Wen I'm Sick
So Your Bum Is Only Big Hey
But I Don't Mind A Bit Of Flab
It Means That When I'm Lekker Jags
There's Somethin There To Grab
So Your Belly Isn't Flat No More
I Tell You, I Don't Care
So Long As When I Druk You
I Can Get My Arms Round There
No Stukkie Who Is Your Age
Has Nice Round Perky Breasts
They Just Gave In To Gravity
But I Know You Did Yor Best
I'm Not Tuning Kak Now
I Never Tell You Lies
But I Think It's Lank Sexy

The Art of the South African Insult

That You've Got Dimples On Your Thighs
I Swear On My Ouma's Grave Now
The Moment That We Met
I Said To All My Chinas
"Now That's A Lekker Slet"
So No Matter Wot You Look Like
I'll Always Love You Dear
Now Shut Up While The Rugby's On
And Fetch Me Another Beer!

(courtesy gpsa.co.za)

Vocabulary

Word	Language of use	Meaning
Afghanistan	eKasi	A woman with a flat backside. *See Pakistan*
Cherry/Tjerrie	Tsotsitaal and others	Girl, girlfriend. A truly democratic word, it appears in most South African slang dialects
Chicken murder	Tsotsitaal	To have a romantic relationship with a much younger person
Doos	Afrikaans, Tsotsitaal	Female genitalia. The equivalent of 'box'
Drop	Tsotsitaal	A sexually transmitted disease
Fok	Afrikaans, Tsotsitaal	Fuck. Obviously
Givist	Tsotsitaal	A promiscuous woman (adaptation of English 'to give')
Hit and run	Tsotsitaal	One night stand
Hoerboer	Afrikaans	A pimp

Word	Language of use	Meaning
Hoermeid	Tsotsitaal, Afrikaans	A promiscuous woman. (There are lots of words for promiscuous women. But very few for men)
Gwang	Tsotsitaal	Female genitalia
Kont	Afrikaans	Female genitalia
Losgavie	Tsotsitaal	A loose woman
Melk-en-koekie-doekie	Afrikaans	Bikini
Melkweg	Afrikaans	Cleavage
Moffie	Afrikaans, Coloured slang	Homosexual. Originally 'dandy'. Also refers to an effeminate man
Moneymakers	Tsotsitaal	A young woman's buttocks
Mzansi Account	eKasi (entry level bank account)	A low-maintenance girlfriend. *See Talk 1000*
Naai	Afrikaans	To have sex; equivalent to fuck
Pajero with spare	eKasi	A woman (usually a girlfriend) with a child
Pakistan	eKasi	A well-endowed woman. *See Afghanistan*
Piel	Afrikaans	Penis
Plooipleister	Afrikaans	Make-up. Literally, 'wrinkle plaster'
Poes	Afrikaans	Female genitalia. Ruder than *doos*, slightly less rude than *kont*
Pomp (verb and noun)	Afrikaans	Sexual intercourse. Slightly less rude than *naai*
Poona	Tsotsitaal	Sexual intercourse

The Art of the South African Insult

Word	Language of use	Meaning
Skêr	Tsotsitaal	A woman who sleeps around
Slet	Afrikaans	Slut
Social worker	eKasi	A promiscuous woman
Strikkie griep	Afrikaans	HIV/Aids (literally, 'Ribbon Flu')
Suzuki	Tsotsitaal	A loose woman
Talk 1000	eKasi (the name of an expensive MTN cellphone contact)	A high-maintenance girlfriend. *See Mzansi Account*
Tril	Afrikaans, Tsotsitaal	Penis
Troosdoos	Afrikaans	A blow-up doll

Chapter 5

Democracy se voet:
politics

"I'm trying to understand what makes the ANC dooses more attractive than the DA dooses. Perhaps you support some dooses more than others?" Comment, *M&G* Forum.

"Democracy," Lourens Ackermann observes, "does not come from a sense of wondrousness at our fellow human beings. It comes from being pissed off with them." Pieter-Dirk Uys has a slightly different suggestion. "Democracy," he offers, "means that everybody gets the chance to have an ulcer."

In this, the land of the Xhosa Nostra, of conspiracies and smear campaigns—isn't iLuminati, after all, a Xhosa word? —politics is always entertaining. Remember the words of Mel Miller: "Cape Town has the best comedy in South Africa. Parliament." (Barry Ronge has a slightly different take on parliamentary democracy. "Being boring," he writes, "is not yet a crime. If it were, Parliament would be a prison.")

"Isn't local government just a big kindergarten, with toy-throwing and hands wedged into cookie-jars?" Krisjan Lemmer

"Those motherfuckers will burn." These are the words of Zameka Mangcu, an unemployed township resident. "If we see anybody we will burn them. It's time we got rid of these shit councillors who drive around in big cars that were bought using our money. *Bazonya!* [They'll shit]!"

Was this the height of the unrest during the Emergency years of the mid 1980s? The political turmoil prior to 1994? As it turns out, Mangcu is a resident of Khutsong, and she was speaking prior to the local government elections in March 2006.

Plus ça change

The more things change in South African politics, the more they stay the same. Take the following complaint, by Florence Phillips, to The *Times of London* in 1896:

> The education grievance has been so widely circulated that it is needless to mention it now; but what can be expected of a government composed of men barely able to write their own names?

Compare and contrast Phillips' remark to this one by David Bullard, commenting on the attitudes of Jacob Zuma's supporters, 110 years later:

> That's what happens when you hand democracy to people who can barely write their own names.

Sometimes politicians are unexpectedly right about things. Not often, granted, but it has been known to happen. Take Sam Kahn of the Communist Party of South Africa, who declared in 1950: "Communism will outlive the Nationalist (sic) Party. Democracy will be triumphant when members of the Government will be manuring the fields of history."

He turned out to be right, but probably not quite in the way he would have thought.

"The free world wants to feed South Africa to the Red Crocodile, to appease its hunger." P. W. Botha said of Communism. PW knew a thing or two about crocodiles, being, of course, one himself. PW also said (and it must be admitted that he was asking for trouble): "Who would rejoice if the Nationalist Party Government was toppled?"

"The whole bloody world will rejoice," retorted Donald Woods.

This was a time when the ridiculousness of apartheid bureaucracy became truly sublime. When race relations became known as plural relations, and the department of Bantu Administration was renamed Department of Plural Relations, a joke went around that Bushman rock art should be renamed 'rural plural murals'.

> "My dear friends, it's very clear: democracy is too good to share with just anyone."
> Evita Bezuidenhout, pre-1990.

Fred Khumalo recalls growing up in the 1970s, when Inkatha was becoming a powerful political movement, and residents of the townships were warned against the dangers of communist-sponsored (ANC) terrorism and terrorists. Disagreement with Inkatha, notes Khumalo, "was tantamount to denying your Zuluness." Terrorists, according to the radio, "killed people, ate their hearts and livers, and drank their blood." Fortunately, it was easy to spot terrorists. "They spoke about matters of government. They pretended to have book knowledge. They didn't comb their hair. They wore dungarees."

> "Voetsek Malan! Fuck off Malan! Fuck off! Fuck off!" Youths chanting during the 1976 riots, as recorded by Rian Malan (no relation to Magnus).

In the late 1970s when the Bantustan policies of the Nats were still steaming ahead, Chief Patrick Mphephu was quoted as saying he wanted independence for Venda. "Transkei did it. Ciskei did it. Bophutatswana did it. So why can't we did it?"

Naturally, Mphephu immediately became known as Prime Minister Did It Mphephu, and Venda became known as Did It Homeland.

> "I am not glad and I am not sorry about Mr. Biko ... He leaves me cold." Jimmy Kruger, Minister of Justice, 1977.

During the 1980s, the government became what Anton Harber described as a "sjambokracy". Winnie Mandela planned to liberate the country using matchboxes and necklaces and Max du Preez started *Vrye Weekblad*, which between 1988 and 1998 showed "a fat middle finger to the institutions of Afrikaner power".

"When P. W. Botha and Pik Botha invited me to join the Diplomatic Corpse, I realized that a great millstone had been reached," Evita Bezuidenhout trilled at the time. She also noted that there was a competition to raise money for the new National Party Home for Retired Ministers. "It's very easy—if you can guess Elize Botha's weight, you can win a Homeland."

New! improved recipe

> "Apartheid is just a pigment of the imagination!" Evita Bezuidenhout.

In February 1990, F. W. de Klerk announced that a new South Africa was now open for business. By August 1990, the Zulu residents of Soweto's single-sex hostels had coined a new word for the New South Africa. *Ayinamasando*, they called it; it has no wheels.

When de Klerk visited Soweto while campaigning in 1994, he was given a gift of a chicken, and an apple. Sy Makaringe interpreted these gifts to mean that residents of Soweto were telling de Klerk that the chickens had come home to roost, and that the National Party would become "chicken feed" during the elections. As for the apple presented by a fruit and vegetable trader, "An apple a day keeps a de Klerk away".

"Mr. Mandela and his party are searching for a new species of flora to finance its promises. It's called the money tree and banknotes grow on it to pay for the ANC's promises," F. W. de Klerk said prior to the 1994 elections. FW also said, "We are not a mouse: you will hear the roar of the NP lion when the results come out," but we try not to remind him of that.

"If you touch a right-winger before or after the election then we will *donder* you harder than we have ever *dondered* you." Eugene Terre'Blanche.

As 27th April rolled around and the world failed to grind to a halt, poncy British journalist Peregrine Worsthorne wrote, "Dawn of freedom, my foot. Black majority rule in South Africa should send a shudder around the world." (When you think about it, what could be a more appropriate surname for somebody writing about South Africa than 'wors' and 'thorn'?)

"No anthem, no flag, no choice, just bullshit." Graffiti prior to the 1994 elections.

After the elections, Evita Bezuidenhout said, "Now everyone is out of jail and in parliament, so what can you do?"

With the dismantling of apartheid, former homeland rulers had to find themselves new jobs. When it was rumoured that former Ciskei supreme Oupa Gqozo was considering starting a furniture manufacturing business, Sy Makaringe suggested that he might even be in competition with Joshua Doore. His slogan could be, "You've got an *oupa* in the furniture business".

The former Gazankulu Minister of Agriculture attempted to cultivate bananas. "As they say, you can take a homeland leader out of a banana republic, but you cannot take a banana republic out of him," commented Makaringe.

Makaringe also noted that the release of the R2 coin coincided with F. W. de Klerk's reforms, and so was nicknamed a De Klerk. After the coins were minted featuring Xhosa wording, Makaringe suggested they be renamed after Eastern Cape premier Raymond Mhlaba: "After all, the R2 coin is becoming more worthless by the day."

"RDP: Revenge of the Dark People." Evita Bezuidenhout.

Ndaweni Mahlangu, the premier of Mpumalanga, confirmed what everyone had expected when he declared, "Lying is nothing new. It is accepted anywhere in the world. I personally don't find it to be such a bad thing." In honour of Mahlangu's refreshing candour, the *Sunday Times* renamed his province Mamparalanga.

The rough and tumble of South African politics took on new overtones in 1998, when a brawl broke out in the National Assembly after the House adjourned. The action was covered in glorious technicolour by the Parliamentary CCTV system, and would certainly have been rated R18. ANC MP and chairman of the justice portfolio committee, Johnny de Lange, sent NP Eastern Cape leader Dr. Manie Schoeman straight to the floor after punching him in the jaw.

Apparently, de Lange had approached Land Affairs Minister Derek Hanekom and NP caucus chairman André Fourie, who were in the midst of a heated argument, when Schoeman punched him.

> And I heard Mr. Fourie shouting "*Ek sal vir jou opfok, fok weg hierso.*" Mr. Hanekom was saying similar words to him ... Just as I got there Mr. Schoeman came from my left side, and the next minute I felt something hit me on the jaw, and I instinctively retaliated ... and it was him who hit me, and he then sprawled on the ground and that was it.

It was then that Speaker of the House, Frene Ginwala, marched in and demanded that names be taken.

"I really believe that the ANC action this afternoon is a disgrace to democracy and to Parliament," said Schoeman, who claimed that NP MPs had been "physically confronted" by ANC MPs after the Assembly adjourned. Freedom Front chairman Dr. Pieter Mulder reported hearing ANC members shouting "*Moer die Boere*" during the upheaval.

De Lange apologized for what happened, but "unfortunately it was instinctive and I don't have anything to apologize [for] necessarily, except that I think these things ... shouldn't be happening in Parliament."

"He broke the teacup on the mayor's head when the mayor gave him information he did not like." Northern Cape ANC spokesperson Neville Mompati in 2006 after Kimberley mayor Patrick Lenyibi had a teacup broken over his head by someone who did not like what he had to say about tender procedures. Lenyibi required stitches.

In 1998, the notion of the Rainbow Nation, which had reached its zenith in 1995, finally fell out of favour. Thabo Mbeki had been talking about the African renaissance for two years already and Mandela and Tutu were criticized in the press for their promotion of the "nauseating", "nonsensical" and "superficial" concept of "rainbowism". South Africa's black chattering classes, Phylicia Oppelt noted with irritation, insisted that the media "should get off its collective backside and become pompom-waving cheerleaders for a president's heroic vision ... But praise poetry is not my forte, and paying homage to a politician is not part of my job description."

"NEPAD: Not Exactly Proposing Anything Different." Richard Owen, Harare.

In 1999, Max du Preez staked his claim in *The Star* to be both "an African and an Afrikaner". "Max, mind your own baas business," Lizeka Mda wrote back. Du Preez was hurt. "Five, six years into the 'New South Africa' I am forced back into the little box of the white Afrikaner," du Preez wrote, reflecting on his years of commitment to exposing "the falsehoods and evils of Afrikaner Christian nationalism."

I've never felt so white in my life. And still I don't want to go back to the bosom of my tribe or join the DP. I think I'm screwed.

"Hysterical materialist: Cosatu trade unionist." Hogarth

It was in 1999 that Thabo Mbeki became president, Jacob Zuma deputy president, and

The Art of the South African Insult

Manto Tshabalala-Msimang Minister of Health. The latter two are so entertaining that they almost get an entire chapter all to themselves (see *Political Vaseline*).

> "Did you read that we are going to vote by cell phone in the next election? 'Welcome to the 2004 elections. Your vote is our secret. To vote for the ANC press 5. To use your fake ID press 1. To vote again, press 2. To vote for your grandfather who fought in the struggle, press 3.'" David Kau, 2003.

South African voters were soon to discover that just because you voted for a particular party did not mean that the people you indirectly voted in had to stay with that particular party. If the trough on the other side was better filled, you were free to cross the floor. Inevitably, somebody came up with the term 'crosstitute'.

> "I am not a crosstitute." Badges worn by IFP members after the closure of the floorcrossing window in September 2005.

King of the Crosstitutes was undoubtedly Craig Morkel, son of the Charles Bronson of the Western Cape. Craig left the DA to found the Progressive Independent Movement. Which meant that a PIM member of parliament would be known as a PIMMP.

Hogarth of the *Sunday Times* anointed Morkel their Mampara of the Week. Pimp was entirely appropriate for Morkel, now that the man had "qualified his snout for a feed in the taxpayer trough". Morkel had crossed from the NP to the DA two years before. "Maybe," speculated Hogarth, "that's why they call him the two-year-guarantee MP."

Chris Roper reflects on the current political situation:

> More yawning. Do you care anymore? Do I care anymore? Every year it's the same old thing. Politician caught with fingers in till. Politician caught with body in Merc given as a bribe (the Merc given as a bribe, not his body. Ugh!). Politician caught with virgin-testing penis in woman. Politician caught eating babies. Ha, just kidding about the last one. Mind you, it's only a matter of time I suppose. Can you imagine that? An ANC voter eagerly holds up her baby for President Mbeki to kiss, and suddenly ... MUNCH! Finally, South Africa has its first black DA supporter.

"You can't use the same condom twice." Maxwell Nemadzhivanani, on leaving the Pan Africanist Congress for the ANC, saying he felt used by the PAC.

The National Party

"A motley band of Neanderthals." Kader Asmal.

"We in the National Party believe in the truth, that's why we only use it on special occasions." Evita Bezuidenhout.

"Putting the National Party in charge of the new opposition in South Africa is like putting King Herod in charge of a crèche." Tony Leon.

"The NP has become a party of kissing [black] girls and garden kaffirs." Eugene Terre'Blanche, during the 1994 election campaign.

"They've been on more roads to Damascus than the average Syrian truck driver." Tony Leon, on the NP during the run-up to the 1994 elections.

"Seven DP MPs make their National Party counterparts look like 80 feather dusters." Howard Barrell.

Black diseases

When apartheid was over, the Nats and the leftists discovered that they'd had something in common all along. They both hated liberals.

Verwoerd hated liberals and their repellent notion that racial purity was hardly something to aspire to. Vorster used 'liberal' and 'communist' as synonyms. Liberals were dismissed by the Nationalists as *kafferboeties* or *hanskhakis.*

Thami Mazwai, echoing their sentiments, dismissed white liberals as *bangbroeke.*

"Meddling old aunties who go around inciting Africans to break the pass laws." De Wet Nel, Minister of Bantu Administration, on the Black Sash.

Head of Azapo, Itumeleng Mosala, wrote in *The Sowetan* in 1993 that liberalism is a "powerful tool by means of which black people can be paralyzed into perpetual slavery and dependence." Liberalism "is a useful and highly valued weapon in the hands of white people. They love it, it works for them, and they threaten to kill anybody who threatens to disarm them of this weapon."

"Like all black diseases which emanate from white people, black liberalism is fatal." Black liberals, he added, are "political prostitutes."

Mosala also went on to argue that the deaths of Steve Biko and other activists is testimony to the lengths to which white people will go to defend liberalism. (Huh? If you'd called Vorster and Jimmy Kruger liberals they'd have had you bliksemed. But I digress, as they say.)

Even future deputy presidents despise liberals. Anglophone liberals are mostly "peace-time heroes ... who were only prepared to bleed ink through their pens at the height of the struggle," Phumzile Mlambo-Ngcuka said in 1996. "They think they are the most politically correct people to speak about the human rights of people whose languages and cultures they have never bothered to understand."

Liberals were wounded by all this criticism. Even Judge Dennis Davis, after being accused of being a racist by Barney Pityana, skulked around "like a whipped dog, snivelling about this being the final straw that might compel him to emigrate" in the words of William Saunderson-Meyer.

The PFP, the DP and the DA

"We know that the PFP is the cream of our society: thick, rich and full of clots." Evita Bezuidenhout.

"Its petulant appeal belongs to a party of spoiled brats, not visionary leaders." Kader Asmal.

"The DP these days is a party of raincoat politicians. They lurk in doorways and never miss an opportunity to flash their itchy liberal white morality at the passing public." Robert Kirby.

"They do not want to be top act, they reckon second-best or third-rate will do them just fine." Jon Qwelane.

"The DP is electorally anaemic; all it has to offer is its whiteness as a form of 'rainbow dressing'." Ronald Suresh Roberts, who himself was once described by Ken Owen as an "egregious carpetbagger".

"White opposition parties seem to be operating like computers which have been programmed to reject anything which contains the word 'transformation'." Thabo Mbeki, 1998.

"A Vote for Us is a Vote for a better Europe." Chris Roper.

Visible panty lines

The rather unfortunately named L. Cheong Pong of Kensington in Johannesburg is not a fan of the DA, accusing these "upmarket elitists" of "bankrupt, childish behaviour, undoubtedly learned on the knee of the many Nats they so eagerly absorbed, to maintain their obsession with hysterical anti-ANC mania."

Ever ready to pass comment on the childish activities of other political organizations, the DA occasionally makes a complete arse of its collective self. In order to highlight the problem of violence against women and children in 2005, some bright spark in the DA came up with the idea of stringing symbolic girls' and women's panties—20,000 of them—up on washing lines in one of the poorest areas of the Cape Flats. Chaos immediately erupted as the locals rushed for the free underwear on offer, ripping it down in full view of the TV cameras.

Krisjan Lemmer reflected on the impact of the visible panty lines on the DA's credibility:

The Deeyay is fond of pointing out the ruling party's penchant for conducting itself in a manner befitting a schoolyard; but this week's fiasco on the Cape Flats will make it difficult for the opposition to keep the higher moral ground. After all, how do you retain your adult aloofness when you've managed to organize the biggest panty raid in history?

Tom Eaton, following the 2006 local government election trail, describes DA supporters with "lockets containing photographs of De Villiers Graaf clutched to bosoms."

"In a moment that would have been hip to the max, if one hadn't been so busy finding somewhere to vomit," as Eaton describes one event, "stern [Dene] Smuts introduced sterner [Helen] Zille as her 'homegirl'." The audience didn't get the joke. Most "just assumed that a homegirl was something like a houseboy and marvelled that Zille should have worked herself up from Smuts' scullery to be a mayoral candidate."

At the same time, Chris Roper found the ANC's suggestion that the blackouts, on the eve of the elections were somehow caused by Tony Leon and his pals, faintly laughable. As if the DA, "those running Chihuahuas of capitalism," would do anything "to piss off their Holy Trinity of Big Business, Constantia Housewives, and Foreign Landowners."

"The DA represents everything I loathe about this country." Zingisa Mkhuma.

Cures irritating infections in seven days

The ANC Youth League, or ANCYL—which sounds like a fungal cream; if only it was—has failed in recent years to make its reason for being clear to the general public.

"Does anybody know what the ANC Youth League actually does?" David Kau often asks. "The ANC doesn't know what the ANC Youth League does. Their president is 35 years old!"

"The last thing real motoring journos want to hear is that a car has more airbags than the ANC Youth League." David Bullard.

So one can only assume that in this day and age, the purpose of the ANCYL is to provide light relief. For as far as sheer entertainment value goes, no political organization comes within spitting distance of the heights reached by the average ANCYL press release.

When the DA boycotted the 2005 Freedom Charter celebrations, the ANCYL released one of its characteristic rants so eagerly awaited by journalists weary of all work and no play. Nothing quite hits the spot like an ANCYL press release and this one did not disappoint.

"The most backward, racist, conservative, rightwing Democratic Alliance," charged our future leaders, had chosen instead to "have its own dinner party."

Like Ku Klux Klan of the eighteen (sic) century in America, the most racist bunch of people, DA philosophy of supreme race must be challenged and rejected by all people as fictitious, rightwing, ideological abomination and a dying breed of political dinosaur.

The statement concluded with the encouraging words, "South Africa Belongs to All those Who live in it, black and white."

On the occasion of ANCYL president Fikile Mbalula's impending 35th birthday, Krisjan Lemmer welcomed the man "to the gates of middle age", adding that he hoped that "in the meantime he enjoys his last year of riding political tricycles and throwing his toys out of the cot."

The following letter, from Glenn Steel of Vereeniging, appeared after a *Sunday Times* report on high levels of lead in the paint on children's toys:

How shocked I was after reading your report on the toxic toys. The symptoms of the poisoning include lethargy, reduced IQ, aggression, anaemia, hyperactivity or delayed puberty. Can somebody please remove ANC Youth League president Fikile Mbalula's toys, or is it too late?

Thus suggesting that, contrary to popular assumption, wit survives in the deepest Vaal Triangle.

"The ANCYL views Bester's resignation as a scapegoat masterminded by DA boss Tony Leon and his Mafia. Bester is just a porn (sic), which was deliberately sacrificed; the real king, Tony Leon, is still standing." ANCYL response to the resignation of the DA's Hennie Bester.

When Delmas experienced a typhoid outbreak, Mbalula wrote that if sewage leaking into a borehole in Delmas was "the sole cause" of the typhoid outbreak "then all efforts must be focused on remedying this malice". Krisjan Lemmer was flummoxed, and could "only assume this was a veiled allusion to the overwhelming evidence, caught on ANCYL Box Brownies", that it was Tony Leon and Douglas Gibson poeping down a well that caused the outbreak. The alternative is too loopy to comprehend. After all, even Vorster and PW never went as far as seeing demonic, moustache-twirling malice in a piece of poo.

In reflecting on the likelihood of ANCYL top brass one day running the country, it is worth noting that Brett Kebble gave them money (yes, he also gave money to the DA, but not so much) and that they are JZee's biggest fans. This shows that, if nothing else, they are fine judges of character. Their representatives make sensible public statements like: "You must hit Pikoli, Pityana, Ndebele and Ngcuka very hard until their owner and handler comes out. All the witches who have plotted against Zuma will sink when we get to Durban for the corruption trial".

Sindiso Malaku, reflecting on the shenanigans outside the courtroom wrote, "The ANCYL president fat-head, with his appendages, are often heard outside the courtroom magniloquently running their mouths with ear-splitting overtones to anyone who cares to listen. In fact, this bunch of misguided self-ordained messiahs blamed everyone but Jacob Zuma for the quandary in which he finds himself."

"Fikile Beebopaloola." Krisjan Lemmer's rendition of the ANCYL president's name.

Political mosquitoes

The Congress of South African Students, Cosas, have not quite reached the glorious standards of the ANCYL, but the members of the self-described "gallant student movement" do their best. After expelling its president, deputy president, secretary-general and treasurer-general at the close of 2005, the acting leadership of Cosas issued a statement to clarify matters. The disgraced foursome had apparently "behaved in a manner that is not different from those animals kept in the Johannesburg Zoo to entertain when are in holidays (sic)". Furthermore, Cosas noted, the movement "has a rich history in this country therefore it cannot allow confused molecules highly excited of adolescent stage not knowing were to practice such behaviour (sic)."

Perhaps their recent exams were on the minds of our diligent student leaders, though it appears, judging by the following statement, that the lecture on tropical diseases was not fully understood:

> Cosas remains a breeding school of leaders for the country as a whole hence the acts of corruption cannot find a home of justification in Cosas and the will be no home for political prostitutes who cannot even use political condoms to protect themselves from getting political malaria that is very dangerous and having potential to turn one into a political mosquito (sic).

"Our interventions in the education system must not be a knee-jack (sic) reaction to achieve particular outcomes at a particular time."

Cosas only ever seem to get in the news when they make public pronouncements more obviously dimwitted than their usual brand of waffle. After Archbishop Emeritus Desmond Tutu called on Jacob Zuma to renounce any claim to the presidency, they dismissed him as "a scandalous man" and questioned his own sexual history. Even Thabo Mbeki emerged to defend Tutu, asking "How was it possible that these children became so emboldened that they could easily dismiss the views of their grandfather ...?"

The IFP

"Indignant, Filibustering, Problematic." Alternative interpretation of the initials IFP, as reported by Sy Makaringe.

"The devil was living with us." Former Thokoza self-defence unit commander Patrick Mqibi, while applying to the TRC for amnesty for killing IFP members.

"I've had a case of the Buthelezi blues or is it just pre-Natal depression?" Anonymous, graffiti.

"Help your local branch of the ANC/IFP on April 27. Beat yourself up." Anonymous, graffiti.

ANC sez Mango U R 3RD R8 >:-(

ANC sez DA R skrwd :-)
Tom Eaton speculates on the ANC's new SMS news service (R1 per SMS for pearls of ANC wisdom and cheap at the price).

Right wingnuts

"AWB voetsek! We cannot survive on pap en boereforce." Anonymous, 1994.

"A British-Jewish invention designed to weaken Afrikanerdom" is how the esteemed Eugene Terre'Blanche described electoral politics, after losing as an HNP candidate in the 1971 elections. Later events would suggest that actually, Eugene himself was an invention designed to weaken Afrikanerdom, and could well have been cloned by Soviet scientists with the specific aim of bringing down the false consciousness of Boer nationalism.

Decades later, after the rightwingers had apparently consoled themselves with a little piece of Utopia they called Orania, South Africans were then informed of a plot by the so-called Boeremag to take control of the country by, among other strategic initiatives, placing mielies alongside major routes to lure local blacks north to Zimbabwe.

"I want to ask these Boeremag people one question," said John Vlismas. "There's like 150 of them. And they want to take over the country—AGAIN. It didn't work the first time."

"Four suicide bombers messed up at exactly the same time in London—must be the Boeremag branch of Al Qaeda." John Vlismas.

Under the heading 'Back from the dead', Hogarth reported on the miraculous reappearance of the HNP in July 2006, shortly after the handover of the World Cup from Germany to South Africa:

Just when you thought all the verkrampte, old octogenarians of the Herstigtige Nasionale Party had shuffled off the ox wagon; they produced one last kick in the form of a letter to the president of Fifa, begging him to save the international community from the perils of visiting South Africa for the 2010 World Cup.

Naturally, observed Hogarth, this concern for football fans of the world was "sudden and totally sincere". He was a little bemused, however, by the HNP's assertion that it is "the most powerful nationalist movement in South Africa and is probably also the strongest in Africa".

The HNP website "sports powder-horns, the Vierkleur, and riveting paranoia about the black Jewish communist lesbian crack-whores who run the world." Krisjan Lemmer.

Dan Roodt, voice of the disaffected middle-aged Afrikaner, did not react well to Adriaan Vlok's washing of Frank Chikane's feet. He called it "pseudo-religious feet-washing histrionics" and sniffed, "I need a pedicure myself and if he is in the business of attending to people's feet free, I would not mind being next in line."

No one must underestimate the intense anger felt by the vast majority of Afrikaners at the loss of their universities, schools, theatres and other institutions, as well as their second-class status in this hell-hole of a country.

Poor Dan Roodt. What a hard life it must be, leading your people from exile within the gilded ramparts of Dainfern, twirling around in your designer French suits for the press, and still getting to spout the kind of ethno-nationalist crap that led South Africa down the political and ideological cul-de-sac that was apartheid.

"Dan Roodt—a pluperfect arsehole. With reference to both definitions of 'pluperfect'. An exemplary, superlative arsehole and one that lives in the past, whose notable achievements began and ended before the present." Paul Berkowitz.

The ANC

"Asking an ANC councillor not to be corrupt is like asking a crocodile to become a vegetarian." Tony Leon.

"The chocolate layer covering the hard niggerball." Fanus Schoeman, politician, talking about the ANC's government policy.

"Dealing with rats is easy. I have had to deal with the ANC for the last ten years, so I am not scared of rats." DA mayoral candidate Mike Moriarty, after being warned about rats when he spent a night on the floor of a shack in Freedom Park.

"We will know when the ANC win the Western Cape because the noon day gun will go off at 1.30pm for a few weeks before being stolen." David Bullard.

"If I pay I will be helping the city of Jo'burg and the ANC government to sustain a capitalist agenda." Former ANC Councillor Trevor Ngwane, explaining why he has not paid rates and taxes for the past five years.

"You only have to drive around this city and smell the overflowing sewers, see the rivers choked with shit to see that the ANC's way of running municipalities was more than successful." Robert Kirby.

"Attacking the African National Congress on crime is like shooting fish in a barrel." Tony Leon.

"The ANC's convulsions are clumsy gear-changes, not the wheels falling off." Rory Carroll.

"South Africa is the capital of hypocrisy, with the ANC as its high church." Christopher Hope.

"What's that got to do with the price of mealie meal?" SABC board member Thami Mazwai, commenting on allegations that head of news Snuki Zikalala is biased in favour of the ANC.

Shopping and voting

"If sin is as old as humankind, so too corruption is as old as government." Thabo Mbeki.

"We are not going to live as fat cats," Nelson Mandela said in 1994. Ah, the paving on the road to hell and all that. Naturally, following Mandela's pronouncement, politicians and public servants rushed to board the gravy train.[1] Eleven years later, Jon Qwelane remarked acidly: "It is ... my constitutional right to refuse to trot along to the voting stations to help line a queue of pigs at the feeding troughs to wallow happily in the muck they make of our taxes."

"Politics is for rich fools who want to rob ordinary people." Mr. Mcoyi, Mpumalanga township's biggest tycoon, quoted by Fred Khumalo.

Thabo Mbeki was right: corruption really is as old as government. In fact, South Africa's first corruption scandal dates back to 1700. This is when Governor Adriaan van der Stel was granted the estate of Vergelegen and set about establishing himself as the settlement's biggest farmer—despite the fact that all VOC officials were technically forbidden to do so. Van der Stel's cronies followed suit, and dominated produce markets at the expense of the free burghers. Van der Stel also used his position as governor to manipulate market regulation in order to benefit both his friends and himself. Opposition to van der Stel grew until the VOC was forced to recall him.

Three hundred years later, the spirit of Adriaan van der Stel lives on. Eschel Roodie, Allan Boesak, Tony Yengeni: all are his spiritual heirs. In fact, if Adriaan were around today, he'd already have formed a consortium involving the ANC Women's League and launched the ad campaign to market the golf estate to be built on land he'd tendered for at a very special price.

---

[1] This was not the first time the concept of the 'gravy train' had been used to criticize South African politicians. Bob Connolly, the cartoonist for the *Rand Daily Mail*, used the 'gravy train' to parody Nationalist profligacy during the 1950s. Prior to the 1981 elections, Connolly also mocked "fat cat Nats". It seems that corruption is like fashion: even if it looks new, chances are it's been done before.

"I'd rather shop than vote for someone who's going to use my tax money to go overseas." BCom student Thembi Nkosi, interviewed on election day, 2006.

Robert Kirby imagines the venal civil servant filled with desire for a "tasteful new Joshua Doore combination queen-size trampoline-bed, kitchen dresser and condom storage cubby-hole in matching 'Dying Bushveld Flame-Finish'."

If it's not enough that politicians use our tax money on fast cars and ugly furniture, they then have to spend it on advertisements telling us how wonderful they are for wasting it. "[E]very other day we are exposed to twaddle," complains Ramotana Mabote, such as:

Hi, my name is XXX, the MEC of Laziness and Cheap Publicity in this province. Over the years we have produced more than 100 mediocre adverts that have driven you up the wall. And you ain't seen nothing yet—worse is yet to come.

"It doesn't matter if an official has a voice that should be used only to scare children. If he/she is willing to pay top dollar to hear his or her voice on the advertisement, just use it." In the end—and this is the kicker—the consumer "is exposed to substandard, fatally boring advertisements—and they still have to pay for it."

"Instead we've been depicted as pigs at a trough. That is shocking and disgusting." ANC kingpin Smuts Ngonyama, complaining at the lack of appreciation of the R6.5bn Telkom deal he helped broker for the politically connected Elephant consortium in November 2004.

Given the typical profligacy of our politicians, it is encouraging when they display concern for taxpayers' money. Take, for example, general secretary of the ANC Women's League, Bathabile Dlamini, who told the *Mail & Guardian* that she was overseas and "did not want to incur unnecessary telephone costs" when asked to clarify the role of a Women's League-owned company which had been involved in a bid for a radio licence.

"Our sleepy fat cats don't come to the party because they're always going to them." *Sunday World*, criticizing the fondness of politicians for hosting lavish parties at taxpayers' expense.

"Our society is sick and government, it appears, is infected with a severe case of foot-IN-mouth disease," complained Charles Ash of Bruin-ou, the website for coloured South Africans:

> The symptoms of foot-IN-mouth disease can be seen every time a high-ranking government official opens his mouth on TV and lets the drivel flow.

"Our perfunctory acceptance of mediocre standards and results permeates all levels of our society, from our national teams' consistently uninspired performance on the sports field; to the lacklustre, delayed delivery of government services."

> "Welcome to the Banana Republic of Azania." Cornwell Ndlovu, one of our great writers of letters to the editor.

We will give the last word to Jon Qwelane, bête noir of DA whinger types everywhere. There are times when, if you did not read Qwelane's byline, you'd be convinced you were reading an essay by Douglas Gibson. "I am full up to my neck," Qwelane writes, "with the lame and romanticized notion of 'our young democracy'; for heaven's sake, at eleven years old a child is no longer a baby—he or she can be pretty much relied upon to do quite a lot of things on his own, with little or no supervision. But we, conveniently, choose to remain a baby democracy in perpetuity."

> "Did you know? There has not been a milestone of ten years of democracy in the last two years." Satirical Chappies label, *Laugh It Off*, 2004.

> "Democracy *se voet*." SMS to the *Cape Argus*, 2006.

Chapter 6

Political Vaseline:
politicians

"People in positions of power want to exercise control over others. We regain control, maybe just for a bit, by laughing at them." Chris du Plessis.

As many of us may recall from high-school biology, the typical politician represents a fascinating evolutionary tangent which branched off just before the evolution of the *phylum chordata* (backboned animals), and long before the evolution of the frontal lobes of the brain, where higher order feelings such as remorse and honour are situated.

(Religious fundamentalists have two strategies by which they account for the presence of politicians in our midst. The first is the assertion that juvenile dinosaurs marched two by two onto Noah's Ark. There is a museum in Arkansas that includes a dierama showing little skin-wearing urchins gambolling with a dinosaur. The second involves going back to the tried and tested method of blaming it on Satan.)

Other species closely related to politicians include televangelists, network marketers, 419 scam artists, real estate agents and second-hand car salesmen.

"He might have spat on the ground and said, '*Vok maar julle is stupid*' or something like that." Afrikaans rock musician Valiant Swart, speculating on what Paul Kruger would have thought of the New South Africa.

Early examples of *Homo politicus subsp South Africanus*: The pig-faced Verwoerd. Granite-jawed Strijdom. Four-eyes Malan. Then there was PW, with the googly eyes, the fantastically rubber lips, the Homberg hats, the monumental wife. Paging through photographs of pre-1990 Nat get-togethers, Robert Kirby reflected that South Africa must have the most physically repulsive set of politicians in the world.

They were a grim, humourless bunch. In May 1972, Parliament spent half an hour debating a cartoon on the front page of the *Wits Student*. It depicted a student bending over a toilet (lid up) with the caption, 'Ah, the Prime Minister, I presume', drawn by none other than the son of Rhodesian Prime Minister Ian Smith!

So it is that even a cursory glance over history reveals that South Africa has always been ruled, by and large, by arseholes, and there is little doubt that this will continue into the future. We should not feel ashamed of this, for every country is ruled by arseholes; some of them are just bigger than others.

> "Politicians are like monkeys. The higher they climb the pole of ambition, the more of their arses we can see. And after ten years of democratic government, I just have to look up and the inspirations are breathtaking." Pieter-Dirk Uys, February 2005.

At the time of the rat-tailed maggot scare, Zapiro illustrated rat-tailed maggots that had been sighted countrywide. These included *Zumas corruptus*, *Zimbabweus despoticus* and *Humungus Kebblescammus posthumus*. He advised anyone who spotted one of these nasty creatures to report to the health department, headed by one *Mantus vegetablis*.

> "We take care of everyone. You can be a hijacking, gay, lesbian, dwarf mime artist with a lisp and a wheelchair. Here, you don't get funny looks, you get a job in Parliament." John Vlismas.

"Groete Oom Krisjan," Neef Jan wrote to Krisjan Lemmer in the *Mail & Guardian* in April 2006, "I am very, very disappointed in President Thabo Mbeki. For a man who is known (not to say famed) for his use of the Internet, how could he miss this amazing software package: www.stopzilla.com?"

> This stuff is the answer to the African National Congress's prayers. Apart from the obvious function (taking care of Helen) it has an integrated spyware killer (there goes Billy) and an integrated cookie killer (there goes Patricia!) Even better, it deletes history! And it kills hijackers, as well as back-door Trojans (who can they mean?)

"I think that the prez should be informed at once, as a matter of national security."

"The trouble with political jokes is that they usually get elected." Pieter-Dirk Uys.

"You can tell when politicians lie: their lips move." Andy Capostagno.

"Every grey shoe has a black soul." The *Sunday Times*' political agony aunt, Sis Beatrice.

"The chap who sold me a used car also smiled like that." *Vrye Weekblad*, on F. W. de Klerk, 1989.

FW "kicked off with a drooled recital of some of his gaudier platitudes. Shiny with use, the same old half-truths and evasions poured out of him." Robert Kirby.

Tony Yengeni[1]

"How big is Tony Yengeni's jail cell? Apparently, it's 4x4." Anonymous.

"[Ngcuka] continues today to be an agent in the hands of the most backward reactionary right-wing political forces in the country." Tony Yengeni, repeating claims that former national prosecutions chief Bulelani Ngcuka was an apartheid spy.

"They are desperate words from a desperate man." Ngcuka's spokesperson Sipho Ngwema, reacting to Yengeni. February 2005.

"I wish Mr. Yengeni the best for his time in jail and sincerely hope that he comes out fully rehabilitated." Patricia de Lille.

---

[1] Tony Yengeni is one of those rare politicians who has had a vehicle named after him, rather than the other way round. In the wake of the arms deal discount scandal, Mercedes-Benz MLs became known as 'Yengenis'.

"What has happened to me is a great injustice, it is an unfortunate travesty of justice ... you would think that I broke into Parliament and stole the safe ..." Tony Yengeni explains that if you want to become a criminal in South Africa, make sure you enter Parliament through the front door rather than the back.

Patricia de Lille

"All that that does is to show two things. The first is that the honourable de Lille has no idea what she is taking about. And the second is that she's a useful idiot in the hands of those who failed in their bid to secure the contracts." Trevor Manuel answering questions in June 2005 by Independent Democrats' leader Patricia de Lille on her claims that the government spent more than the going rate on military equipment.

"Patricia's only skills lie in harping on about the emotive issues of the day, and dressing up like she should have dressed down." Chris Roper.

"Patricia de Liar." *The Citizen*, after the ID supported the ANC during voting for the Cape Town mayor.

A lot of mlambo-jumbo

"There's not much else to do in Abu Dhabi, though. I tried swimming, and the seawater was so warm I came out to cool off. I also tried golf, and was enveloped by a sandstorm. But people who say it's not worth paying R700,000 to go there are just talking a lot of mlambo-jumbo." John Scott, *Cape Times*.

Just what is it with our female politicians and planes? If they're not fraudulently exchanging Parliamentary travel vouchers for overseas shopping trips, they're abusing other airline passengers (as in the case of both Manto Tshabalala-Msimang and Lulu Xingwana, deputy minister of agriculture and a veritable cow among the chinas). Then Deputy President Phumzile Mlambo-Ngquka flew off to Abu Dhabi for a lovely holiday with family and friends in a Defence Force jet, bill footed by the taxpayer.

When details of the trip emerged in the pages of *Beeld*, the Deputy President changed her story more often than Dan Brown. It was a holiday, she said. No, it was business. No, actually it was business and pleasure. She'd gone to the UAE because they're in the midst of a construction boom and she wanted to look at their cranes.

> "The way I have messed things up this week, I really don't want to say anymore. There's really true meaning to the statement that everything you say will be used against you." An uncharacteristically frank Deputy President Phumzile Mlambo-Ngquka, on the excitement following revelations of her trip to the UAE.

Soon enough, the *Sunday Times*' Hogarth column was publishing pictures of cranes for the Deputy's edification and David Bullard coined the term 'aircraftiness' to indicate "using cunning and deceit to convince critics that you were crane-spotting and not just taking your mates on a free junket".

> "She is clearly a banana republicanist." Letter to *The Citizen*.

> "Mr. Aziz Pahad, who's always good for a bleak giggle." Robert Kirby.

> "Head ops sap." Anagram of 'Essop Pahad', as worked out by Hogarth, *Sunday Times*.

> "Essop's Fables." Martin Williams's take on Essop Pahad's refusal to answer questions about his involvement in the arms deal.

> "A damp squid." Inkatha Freedom Party press release, referring to the defection from the party of one Johannes Miles. Krisjan Lemmer wondered whether Miles had left to search for the 'Lost Tribe of the Calamari'.

Bolt from the blue

> "A token white lie." Robert Kirby, assessing Alec Erwin's denial that he had ever mentioned the S-word.

Thank God—oh wait, communists don't believe in God, so make that "Thank the forces of dialectical materialism"—for Alec Erwin. For our Minister of Minerals and Energy is proof to all those Affirmative Action naysayers that white men can also be useless.

Erwin's moment of glory arrived just prior to the March 2006 local government elections. The Western Cape was set to be closely contested between the DA and the ANC. The area had been beset by rolling electricity blackouts for months. Then it emerged that somebody—somehow—had left a bolt in one of Koeberg's generators, forcing a shutdown. Alec suggested in a press conference on the eve of the elections that the bolt did not end up in the generator on its own:

> This is in fact, not an accident. Any interference with an electricity installation is an exceptionally serious crime. It is sabotage.

Robert Kirby noted the inference of sabotage "turned out to be a magnanimous public acknowledgement that he is not satisfied with merely being in the Cabinet, he wants to be its designated ninny as well." Later, Alec backtracked, denied the use of the S-word and came up with a new term: 'human instrumentality'. The bolt in the generator was, he said, the result of "human instrumentality".

The term 'human instrumentality', Kirby pointed out, is meaningless: did the supposed saboteur drop the bolt into the generator while playing a banjo? The *Sunday Times* used the opportunity to add a new word to the dictionary. SHAMOTAGE referred to "a false allegation of sabotage made for short-term political gain".

> "*SIES*! We all saw you and heard you say 'sabotage' you lying, conniving Mr. Minister!" Charles Ash, Bruin-ou.com.

Later Erwin also stated that it was difficult to assess the impact of the Cape's rolling blackouts because the blackouts were not a "national problem". Krisjan Lemmer wondered whether this was perhaps because Erwin's department was not entirely up to date with latest geopolitical developments:

> Clearly, the maps down at the Public Enterprises ministry are still the old ones that label the Western Cape as the 'Rogue Secessionist Reactionary Papsak State',

issued in Pretoria while the Deeyay ran the province. But hell, Alec, the anschluss happened years ago. Rumour has it they're even using real money in the Visdorp, and no longer trade in wampum and hides. Or least they did until the power went off and the ATMs stopped working. But you wouldn't know anything about that, would you?

When a preliminary report Nuclear Energy Regulator (NER) had shown that negligence, and not sabotage, was to blame for the power cuts suffered by the Western Cape, the DA demanded that Parliament censure Erwin "for this gross lack of discretion". Erwin had shown "no remorse for employing this cheap and grossly reckless electioneering tactic".

The ANC appropriated one of the DA's favourite sayings when MP Yunus Carrim said, "We can't get stuck in the past, we need to move on" after they wouldn't stop harping on about Alec Erwin and the bolt. Zapiro announced that the loose bolt had been tightened, showing Alec Erwin's lips firmly screwed together. Ah, if only it were true.

Pik Botha

"A black-belt bullshitter." Jani Allan.

"You were the Errol Flynn of South African politics, but now that moustache looks like a dead mouse, Pik." Evita Bezuidenhout.

"Pik worked in National Party politics for forty years; of course he has a sense of humour." Evita Bezuidenhout.

"Mr. Pik Botha, the former Minister of Mineral Affairs, comes across as a very boring and monotonous politician." Sy Makaringe.

P. W. Botha

"Banality incarnate." David Beresford on P. W. Botha.

"An irascible bully." Helen Suzman. P. W. Botha once called her a "vicious little cat".

"Die Groot Krokodil."

"The Pangaman."

Winnie

"Mugger of the Nation." Headline in *The Sowetan*, 1993.

"Winnie's in the Pooh." Graffiti, late 1980s.

"Mrs. Mandela puts rubber around people while I put it inside them." Former Miss South Africa Michelle Bruce, promoting a new range of condoms.

"She has all the guile and cunning of a tape worm and the stubborn luck one usually associates with a bilharzia fluke." *Sunday Independent*.

"It comes in a two-litre can and it's guaranteed to set your husband alight." Conrad Koch suggests a Winnie Mandela celebrity perfume: *Diesel*.

"Together, hand in hand with our sticks and matchboxes, with our necklaces, we shall liberate this country," Winnie Mandela famously declared in the 1980s.

This is why, once upon a time, white South Africans were very, very scared of Winnie Mandela. Even Eugene de Kok and his pals at Vlakplaas were scared of her. "You could have thrown her from a height of 30,000 feet from an aeroplane and nothing would have happened to her," Prime Evil told the TRC. After all, this was a woman who smoked Stompie. It seemed that nothing—neither murder charges, nor corruption scandals—could bring her down. Zapiro once depicted a post-nuclear-holocaust world in which nothing was left except for cockroaches—and Winnie.

Madiba died and went to Heaven. St. Peter was giving him a tour of Heaven when he noticed that there were dozens of clocks on the wall. Each clock displayed a different time of day. When he asked St. Peter about the clocks, he replied, "We have a clock for each person on Earth and every time they tell a lie the hands move. The clock ticks off one second each time a lie is told." Special attention was given to two clocks. The clock belonging to Mother Teresa has never moved, indicating that she never told a lie. The clock for Princess Diana has only moved twice. She only told two lies in her life. Madiba asked, "Where is Winnie's clock?" St. Peter replied, "Jesus has it in His office ... He is using it as a ceiling fan."

Now, even scarier politicians have come along.

"We thought Mandela was higher grade, but he has become standard grade." A Venda student teacher, commenting on the appointment of Thabo Mbeki as deputy president at the expense of Cyril Ramaphosa.

"The Sari with the Whinge on top." Robert Kirby on Frene Ginwala.

"A purse-lipped, pinched-anus, old fart." Harold Strachan on Kader Asmal.

"Tame sock puppet and court Jew." Ronnie Kasrils, according to a comment on the *Mail & Guardian* Forum.

The revenge of Dr. No

"It is an insult to every South African citizen that Manto Tshabalala-Msimang is still a member of the cabinet." Max du Preez.

Manto, writes *The Star*'s Peter Fabricius, "does such a wonderful job of caricaturing herself that it seems superfluous to do more than simply report her words and actions."

So, without further ado, here are Manto, aka Minister of African Potatoes, aka Dr. No's words and actions.

Like Winnie, Manto is fond of hats. "Yes, I like hats," said Manto at the 2005 opening of Parliament. "They just pep you up a little bit."

"Is that an official prescription?" wondered Krisjan Lemmer. "Should we be adding hats to our garlic and African potatoes? And did she wear a hat because she needs pepping up? *Ag siestog.*"

At the opening of Parliament in 2006, Manto again showed a penchant for peppy headgear, turning up in a tall black number that invited comparisons to the work of Doctor Seuss. Interestingly, the hat bore a curious resemblance to one that Zapiro had illustrated when depicting the Minister as the Mad Hatter. Say what you like about Dr. No, but any woman who can take fashion advice from a cartoonist has balls of steel wool.

> "Our Health Minister Manto Msimang—that's Zulu for mass genocide. What's her name? Ah, Dr. Dolittle. And a walking picture of health. The only way you can photograph her these days is by satellite." Mark Banks.

"I hope you have come in such big numbers not just to focus on one ailment," Manto said at the opening of a recent national Aids conference, "but to focus on all of them, because many other people are dying of other diseases in this country."

"Jirre vroumens … Maybe she thought she was at the National Other Diseases Conference," Lemmer snorted. "Or maybe she just needed her bolts tightened."

> "On the defensive or dripping charm, Manto Tshabalala-Msimang, the health minister, couldn't sell sweets to a child." Maureen Isaacson.

In April 2004, Manto chose the occasion of a gala dinner involving the United Nations and top diplomats to launch an extraordinary racist attack on the TAC. She told the assembled VIPs that the black protestors demanding ARVs "come with two buses and go to the two commissions where they wait for the white man to tell them what to do … Our Africans say: 'Let us wait for the white man to deploy us … to say to us … you must go toyi-toyi here.'"

Considerable excitement was added to the evening when it turned out that the object of her attack, Mark Heywood, was sitting among the guests. "You are lying, minister," he shouted out. She wasn't expecting that one. After a short, supremely uncomfortable silence, she thanked him for speaking up, saying she was happy she did not have to mention him by name. "You are a liar," he shouted as she carried on speaking.

"Did you know? Only poor gay drug users who do not eat African potatoes get Aids." Satirical Chappies label, *Laugh It Off*.

A fast-moving truck

"We have a saying in my country. If a truck is standing still, dogs will go under it and pee. If the truck is moving, dogs will bark." Manto rather bizarrely, if not entirely inaccurately, likening herself to a truck, for the benefit of a Canadian journalist, 2006.

South Africa's 'salad stand' at the International HIV/Aids conference in Toronto in 2006 garnered a great deal of attention. Baskets of garlic, lemon, beetroot and African potato alongside two bottles of anti-retrovirals hastily produced after their absence was noted.

"It's despicable that you [members of the Khomanani communications campaign] bow to the minister's wishes and put the exhibit together in such a way." Dr. Harry Moultrie of the paediatric Aids clinic at Chris Hani Baragwanath hospital said to the organizers of the exhibit.

The TAC protested by vandalizing the stall and chanting "Fire Manto now!" Some of them lay on the ground to symbolize the dead. "How many lemons are you going to eat when your CD4 count drops below 200?" shouted one woman.

South Africa's Aids response, they said, was "the worst response in the world to the epidemic and not the most comprehensive."

"I'm so embarrassed." Dr. Lucas Ntyintyane, on Manto's performance at Toronto. He challenged President Mbeki to employ him as minister of health in her stead.

"I, for one, am not proud to be a citizen of a country that is the laughing stock of the world." Cheryl Gous, letter to the *Sunday Times*.

The UN special envoy on Aids, Stephen Lewis, added that South Africa "is the only country in Africa whose government continues to propound theories more worthy of a lunatic fringe than of a concerned and compassionate state."

"Lewis is not Africa's messiah," was Manto's response.

Later Manto said she didn't mind being called 'Dr Beetroot'. "We haven't shocked the world, we have told the truth," she said. Dov Fedler drew a cartoon of Manto taking a patient's temperature with a carrot and saying, "I need a second opinion on this. Get me my greengrocer."

Manto said on returning from Toronto, "When a person says he or she is feeling better, I must say no, I don't think you are feeling better. I must go and do science on you?"

'Do' science. Is this like 'doing' crime? In Manto's view, apparently yes.

"Ambassador Tshabalala-Msimang is walking around the world with the proverbial 'Kick me' sign on her back. Somebody ought to tell her." Peter Fabricius.

"She is definitely not Mrs. Beetroot, she's a lemon." Letter to *The Citizen*.

"Rajbansi has Aids man." Rajbansi non-supporter.

"If he has Aids, he got it from you." Rajbansi supporter. As related by John Scott.

"Fat pig ... ugly bastard." Controversial DJ Nigel Pierce on then Cape Town mayor Pieter Marais.

Tony Leon

"The Napoleon of the Koi-farming set." Tom Eaton.

"The great white wail." Zapiro, who depicted Thabo Mbeki as Captain Ahab.

"Chihuahua." Various ANC politicians.

"Don't be absurd! Tony Leon is a midget next to Oliver Tambo." Pallo Jordan responding to the argument that the DA-controlled Cape Town municipality could theoretically rename Cape Town International after the DA leader.

"Tony Leon hasn't complained about Phumzile Mlambo-Ngcuka once because he can't say her name." Conrad Koch and David Kau.

DA MP and spin-doctor-in-chief, Ryan Coetzee aka Mr. Defy, labelled ANC MP Ben Turok a "clown" after Turok mocked Tony Leon for having his mugshot all over the DA's manifesto.

Deputy Speaker Gwen Mahlangu objected. "There are no clowns in the house," she said.

"Hello, Mickey, this is Goofy come to visit you." Nelson Mandela, paying Tony Leon, who was recovering from bypass surgery, a surprise visit. Mandela had called the NP and the DP 'Mickey Mouse' parties. Tony Leon replied that "the ANC sure has some Goofy policies."

Krisjan Lemmer commented on Tony Leon's body language as he spoke to the SABC at the opening of Parliament in 2005:

The leader of the Deeyay, the officious opposition, quickly set up a hypnotic swaying motion from left to right, as if in urgent need of a bathroom. The manne suggested he might be presenting his party's policy vacillations in a kind of interpretive dance, but Lemmer reckons he was simply acting out the role of the opposition as defined by the government: hanging by the neck, twisting in the breeze.

"I am told that there are a few persistent letter-writers in the newspapers who consider me too tough, too abrasive, too confrontational and even too arrogant. And that's just when I'm agreeing with the government." Tony Leon.

The SACP

"Cronin the Barbarian." Krisjan Lemmer's suggestion of a nickname for die-hard communist Jeremy Cronin.

"*Honky Socialist* by Jeremy Cronin." Hogarth's suggestion for a riposte to Chika Onyeani's book *Capitalist Nigger*.

"These days I just have to look at Jeremy Cronin and I feel tired." Black comrade businessman, to the *Financial Mail*.

"The Whinge-Warrior." *Mail & Guardian* editorial on Charles Nqakula.

"Minister of Sanctimony and Stupidity." Chris Roper, on Charles Nqakula.

"Perhaps we should borrow his own words and tell him: he can whinge about the president, or he can leave the ANC government." Tony Leon, commenting on the fact that Charles Nqakula is the chairperson of the SACP, which was highly critical of Mbeki. Leon also said that Nqakula deserved to be fired.

"No buffet table, no Ngconde Balfour." Kaya FM DJ, as reported by Krisjan Lemmer, *Mail & Guardian*.

Thabo Mbeki

"It is difficult to think of a single other democratic nation in which the head of state descends, with such dogged regularity, into public attacks on individual citizens. It is a form of intellectual or rhetorical 'necklacing'." Tony Leon on Mbeki, December 2004.

"If Thabo Mbeki had to do a song about AIDS, it would be instrumental." Tshepo Mogale.

"On one of his occasional visits to the country, Mbeki said that poverty causes AIDS. Ja, Thabo. Freddie Mercury fucked poor people." Mel Miller.

Robert Kirby described a John Battersby profile of Thabo Mbeki in the *Sunday Independent* as flattering to the point that he could only be described as "Mbeki's personal wet-wipe". Kirby expressed admiration for Battersby's "proctal navigation techniques". "Where do you start in analyzing a piece of colonic speleology as penetrating as the Battersby tongue?"

More succinctly, if perhaps less flamboyantly, Ashwin Desai described Professor Malegapuru Makgoba's likening of the significance of a Thabo Mbeki speech to Einstein's special theory of relativity as an act of *gatkruiping*. Clearly, the gravitational pull of political power bends all those who choose not to hide their particular light under a bushel.

> "You see how nice it is being president. When you are president, you get served water by premiers. If I asked him to polish my shoes, he would immediately get on his knees and do as told." Thabo Mbeki, joking after being given a glass of water by Mbhazima Shilowa at a Women's Day rally.

If anyone knows how easy it is to be misunderstood when you crack a joke, it's the President. In 2004, Thabo Mbeki told the crowd at an election rally that he would beat his sister if she told him she was in love with African Christian Democratic Party leader Kenneth Meshoe. A more sympathetic response might have been to have the poor woman committed, but nonetheless, the media and the opposition got hold of the remark and turned a tiny little molehill into Table Mountain.

"In making his threat—be it seriously or in jest—the president has made it clear that he has no regard for the rights of women," said Democratic Alliance national chairman Joe Seremane.

> "The Mbeki administration has this quaint need to accommodate and succour overbearing political turkeys … Perhaps that's how Thabo Mbeki wants to be remembered, as the man who both selected and nurtured some truly abject incompetents." Robert Kirby.

The ANC rushed to the President's defence. "He was speaking in the vernacular, jokingly with the crowd, and his intention was absolutely not to be denigrating of women or people's political choices," said ANC North West spokesman Elliott Mayisela. "He was joking."

"You have to be insane to think he was serious," said Smuts Ngonyama, the man who—perhaps apart from Putco Mafane or Whitey Jacobs is the most unfortunately christened figure in South African public life.

As usual, Evita Bezuidenhout had the last word. "Ja, skatties," she sighed, "as always when the electoral mouth opens, the electoral feet go in."

"Is President Thabo Mbeki entrusting the writing of his website letters to one of the many moronic members of the ANC Youth League, or is he simply 'losing it' as the Zuma scandal blares forth at him like a thousand vuvuzelas?" Robey Crament, letter to *The Citizen*.

"I love Zuma because I can see the incredible leader that he is. I see Africa's solution in this great man. Mbeki should back off with his coconut ideas and let real Africans lead Africa." Mthandeni ka Dumisani Langa.

"He is a dictator and a despot who thinks he is a small god who knows everything." Anonymous, Friends of Jacob Zuma Forum.

A four-latter word

"In the space of a year African National Congress (ANC) deputy president Jacob Zuma has gone from being the country's number two citizen to being its number one national joke." Karima Brown.

"What reputation? He has done everything that needs to be done to damage his own reputation." An unrepentant Zapiro, responding to the news that he was being slapped with a R15-million defamation lawsuit by Jacob Zuma.

"Say what you like about Zuma, but at least he was a four-letter word." Chris Roper makes a valid point.

Another four-letter word, Cosatu Secretary General Zwelinzima Vavi, predicted in early 2005 that preventing Jacob Zuma from reaching the summit of political power in South Africa would be like "trying to fight against the big wave of the tsunami". When an earthquake off the northern Californian coast failed to trigger a much-feared wave, Krisjan Lemmer suggested that a new term be coined for tsunamis that failed to materialize. All future "oceanic non-events" should simply be referred to as "vavis".

Lemmer just hopes that if Schabir Shaik's unregistered charity does become top dog, he won't similarly kill 300,000 people and lay the entire region to waste.

History would prove that the *Sunday Times* decision to award Zuma the title of '2004 Mampara of the Year' was somewhat premature. That year, the most embarrassing revelation would involve the fact that Zuma wore cheap suits. Who, back then, could have imagined short skirts, knees, anti-Aids showers and baby oil, from the leader of the Moral Regeneration Movement no less?

"Until recently, relieved of his Cabinet level position, he was, of course, a founder member of the exclusive National Association of Party Political Yes-Persons (Nappy)." Robert Kirby.

"Was it a case of subpoena envy?" Reader's response to *Sunday Times* columnist Hogarth's inexplicable exclusion from Jacob Zuma's otherwise wide-ranging defamation lawsuit.

"Some of them can barely muster enough brain power to keep their vital organs functioning." David Bullard on Zuma supporters.

"Zuma shouldn't be worried. If you've seen what he was married to … being a prison bitch isn't so bad." Chris Forrest. This joke did not go down well at all with a Sandton audience, and Forrest was booed.

Schabir Shaik, the Scorpions, Zuma going to live in a house called Idle Winds next to the zoo. There's a conspiracy in South Africa, and it's being run by stand-up comedians with a weakness for lame puns. Idle Winds, Robert Kirby was quick to note, is an anagram of 'I swindled'. "Jacob Zuma's home is called Idle Winds because he's a lazy fart," said John Vlismas.

Chris Forrest described staying at a log cabin on the Wild Coast with 47 scorpions and two snakes. "I thought, fuck, this could be the Schabir Shaik trial."

Schabir himself was not amused by all of these names. "In the new South Africa, it's the 'Scorpions', and you're supposed to shiver and shake (again)," he said. "Change it to pigeons, instead," he added. That won't help Schabir: they'll just shit all over you.

"I won't say anything about Jacob Zuma unless I think it's fucking funny." David Kau.

Zuma "is clearly not a leader of this decade, centenary, millennium or even this holiday weekend." *Sunday Independent* editorial.

During his rape trial, Zuma told the incredulous court that he showered after sex to reduce the chance of catching HIV. They say cleanliness is next to godliness, and the scrupulously hygienic JZ, who has compared himself to the better known JC, certainly endorses that insight.

M. F. Muhamed wondered who would hold the patent rights to Jacob Zuma's revolutionary HIV/Aids prevention measure—the man himself, or the high court.

"He must leave or form his own party—the Shower Party." Letter to *Drum* magazine.

"People like you have stained the face of Africa for too long now. Please go away." Poster to the Friends of Jacob Zuma Forum.

"Bliksem! There goes the neighbourhood." P. W. Botha, reading Jacob Zuma's comment that he had been banished to the political wilderness, in a cartoon by Dov Fedler.

Trevor Manuel

"If you think of Trevor Manuel as the future minister of finance you can understand why the Egyptians worshipped cockroaches." Robin Carlisle, politician. (Where are you now, Robin Carlisle? Do you ever feel embarrassed about having made this statement? Are you mocked in the streets? If you are not, you should be.)

"All in all, this Oliver was more Twist than Jamie." Investec portfolio manager Michael Power, after one of Manuel's budget speeches.

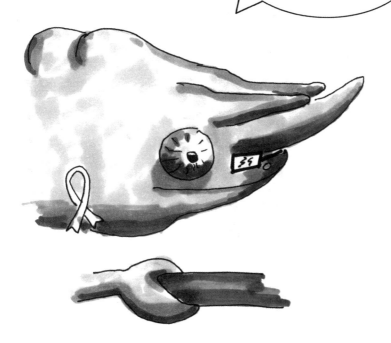

Cassie Aucamp

"Not that there is much to steal." Freedom Front Plus leader Pieter Mulder on whether his party had stolen votes from National Action leader Cassie Aucamp.

There's a stoepkakker under my Zulu

"A ventriloquist is someone who speaks without moving his lips. Like Mangosuthu Buthelezi." Conrad Koch.

"The prince-formerly-known-as-Gatsha." Krisjan Lemmer, *Mail & Guardian*.

Mangosuthu Buthelezi is quite possibly the only South Africna politician who appears in the Guiness Book of Records, for the longest ever political speech (400 pages, five days). In what one assumes is an unrelated incident in June 2005, he discovered a turd under his seat in the National Assembly. "I don't know what to make of it," he said at the time. "I'm just astounded that it should come to this in this holiest of holies." The source of what was assumed to be a succinct comment on Buthelezi's oratory turned out to be a police sniffer dog, rather than a political opponent.

But why would a highly trained sniffer dog decided to take a quick dump while performing his duties? Tom Eaton was perplexed:

After all, these are not cynical, incontinent dachshunds idling away their autumn years between the settee and the beef stroganoff. They're called things like Ajax and Mussolini, and have the willpower of Buddhist warrior-monks.

"These dogs don't just squat when the urge arrives: they fill out a form in triplicate and provide a notarized inventory of their stomachs."

"The leader of Piesangland." Krisjan Lemmer again.

"Chief Buthelezi defends his turf with his traditional weapons of ire and brimstone." *The Star.*

"Hogarth fears that the IFP may soon find itself with two centres of powerlessness." The *Sunday Times*, after Ziba Jiyane openly called Buthelezi a dictator.

"There were 11,600 people. Madiba looked at them and said, 'Who the fuck is that? Was he in the struggle?'" David Kau on Mandela's 85th birthday party.

Allan Boesak

"To use the Nats and the lieutenants of the tetchy chief from Ulundi as moral standards is to admit to being morally unambitious." Mondli Makhanya, after Allan Boesak, Tony Yengeni and Winnie's defenders complained that the Nats and the IFP got away with it.

"A looter continua!" *Noseweek* on Allan Boesak.

"The ANC's pet funds-hustler." Robert Kirby on Allan Boesak.

Kortbroek

"The country's favourite one-size-fits-all politician." Robert Kirby.

"Rather than allow the trough to move out of snout range, South Africa's most infamous political prostitute, Marthinus (Kortbroek) van Schalkwyk, has finally decided to join the ANC." David Bullard

Robert Kirby is a vinegary old git. He has his soft spots, though. He is fond of PVR and flyfishing; he has never met a trout he didn't like, with the possible exception of Frene Ginwala.

He is not fond of politicians as a rule, but even so, Marthinus van Schalkwyk comes in for short shrift.

"I've always believed Kortbroek missed his true vocation," Kirby writes. "He would have been far better employed in some worthy public duty, like running the customer care department at the morgue. Keeping corpses cheerful is a most admirable pursuit and, if his career so far is anything to go by, he'd do it with style."

This is also because everything around and about Kortbroek seems to be, well ... dead. His political ideas have always been in a state of advanced decomposition, or just frozen solid. The New National Party that he headed with such gusto was little more than a body bag for terminalized apartheid. Kortbroek had to play mortician to this noisome stiff, lurch it around in a wheelbarrow for months trying to find some hole in the ground willing to accept it.

"Eventually, in a fit of ecstatic compassion, it was the ANC who came to the rescue, embalming the NNP and all its rotting trespass in democratic perpetuity."

"An upward blip on a downward trend." Tony Leon.

"Peter Mokaba. The man who came up with the slogan 'One Settler, One Bullet'. They made him Minister of Tourism. That's like making Hitler Chief Rabbi of Jerusalem." Mel Miller.

"Real life is not satire," Smuts Ngonyama. (On that point, when is Smuts going to change his first name to Tambo?)

"Hypocrisy is the Vaseline of political intercourse." Pieter-Dirk Uys.

Chapter 7

Freedom of expression se moer: religion

"When I see non-Muslims get scared of an old man with a long beard in traditional dress, I think to myself: Do they realize that this is the equivalent of being terrified by a nun?" Riaad Moosa.

Religion has always been a part of South African life. On paper, we are a very religious lot. Marketing surveys are always revealing that going to church (or temple, or mosque) is one of our favourite leisure activities. "Church is an important factor in the life of a good Afrikaner family," reflects Yolandi Groenewald. "Like the Voortrekker Monument, it is a hulking part of your past, something you try to escape in the present, but know you won't be able to shed in the future."

Mess with religion at your peril. As Ferdi Hartzenburg, verkramp politician most famous for being inadvertently referred to, by a TV newsreader, as "Ferdi Farts'nburp", once declared, "God is our most powerful weapon, our spiritual atomic bomb." Take this view, for instance, from 'Born Again' from the Western Cape, to *You* magazine:

When God steps in to destroy Cape Town (as He told me He intended doing) we'll sit with an even bigger mess. I asked God when this will happen and he gave me Habakkuk chapter 2 verses 1-3.
The destruction will be caused by flooding from the sea. According to another Christian the flooding will be caused by an earthquake. Turn to God today and repent of your sins before it's too late.

And, on the other end of the spectrum, there is africans.co.za contributor Pinvictor, who writes, "For a so-called liberal, rainbow nation, I feel we afford far too much credit to superstitious idiots. I don't want to sound like a Nazi, and I'm all for tolerance of people's beliefs, but worshipping a god is so ancient-times, and in my mind it conjures up scenes from *The Mummy*, or *Indiana Jones*, and, as those films show us, the best way to reason with a zealot is through the medium of fatal gunshot wounds."

> "We don't listen to the Ten Commandments and we don't have to listen when Christians tell us that adultery is wrong." NUM leader Senzeni Zokwana, defending Jacob Zuma.

Nonetheless, advertising creatives continue to wade in where others fear to tread. During 2004, radio listeners heard a little girl saying her bedtime prayers in an advert for an insurance company. "To Jesus," piped the child,

> and Mohammed, and Buddha, and the Mother Mary, can I please, please have a bicycle for my birthday.

Then a perky male voice-over declares,

> For those who leave nothing to chance, XYZ Insurance ...

Sure enough, the complaints soon rolled in to the Advertising Standards Authority, most of them from self-professed Christians. (Oddly enough, no Hindus complained on the grounds that they had been left out.) In a truly miraculous turn of events, the ASA dismissed the complaints.

> "Why do people write 'Fuck the pope' on walls? Because it's easier than writing 'Fuck the moderator of the synod of the Dutch Reformed Church'." Old joke, repeated by Krisjan Lemmer.

Prompted to my revenge by heaven and hell

If you want an informed opinion on the wisdom of messing with religion, just ask the land of the Ugly Duckling.

The great cartoon débâcle of 2006 saw South African Muslims marching in the streets to demand, among other things, a boycott of Danish products. "Freedom of expression se moer," declared the placards in the Cape Town protests, which were certainly more entertaining that the "Butcher those who mock Islam" posters seen elsewhere in the world.

One wonders how many little Yusufs and Youmnas across the country were in tears after Daddy confiscated all their Lego.

There were death threats, as is to be expected. The only editor brave enough to reprint one of the cartoons; the *Mail & Guardian*'s Ferial Haffajee, was accused of having betrayed her religion; one prominent member of the Muslim community sent a chain SMS asking that the faithful pray that Haffajee burn in hell, a neat demonstration of how modern technology and medieval attitudes can complement one another.

> "When you enter the UK they do a 'random security check'—which they should call a 'Muslim security check' ... What, did they think I was part of the comedic wing of al-Qaeda? Later, we kill all you infidels. First, we tell you jokes." Riaad Moosa.

Meanwhile, the court-ordered pre-emptive banning of any reproduction of the cartoons raised profound questions about the implications for the Constitution—all in all, an average day in the newish South Africa.

It was moot, reflected Khadija Magardie, "whether a faith counting more than one billion followers across the globe could be shaken to its very foundations by the poisoned pens emanating from a country best known for butter and Lego."

The Danes were quite sniffy about it all, insisting that a boycott by South Africa would have no impact whatsoever. Some of us expressed a silent prayer of hope that we would never again be exposed to another stupid Lurpak TV ad featuring another stupid spoilt Danish cow (there is no need to clarify that statement because there are of course no Danish women that South Africans have ever heard of).

South Africans should not have been surprised by any of this. Any nation stupid enough to give money to Allan Boesak is capable of anything.

Fear Factor

After the Muhammed cartoon débâcle, Zapiro drew a cartoon of South African *Fear Factor* contestants being instructed to do crazy things. "Bath with snakes!" yells the host. "Okay!"

they cheer. "Draw Muhammed!" says the host. "Are you crazy?" shriek the contestants.

Yes, there are some things no sane person would do.

It's tough being a Muslim, Riaad Moosa reflects. "The other day I looked in the mirror and even *I* got suspicious." Perhaps part of the problem is letters from fun guys like Ishaad Mohammed, who writes letters like this to *The Citizen*:

> In my opinion a moderate Muslim is not a Muslim, but a mere puppet of the West.

And it's not just the Muslims. These days you're not even allowed to insult Scientologists.

Kieno Kammies and Gareth Cliff were the subject of a complaint after telling Tom Cruise and Katie Holmes jokes on air. Kammies said that Scientology was for rich people with nothing better to do, forcing the complainant to switch from 5FM to Jacaranda. The Scientologists were outraged, comparing the jokes to the mockery of Islam, Christianity and Judiaism combined. If Cliff had "publicly and mockingly declared himself to be Allah," fulminated the complainant

> and then quoted a principle of Islam which originated from Jesus in the Bible of Christianity, or perhaps declared himself to be Jesus and then mockingly quoted a Jewish Orthodox principle, I have absolutely no doubt that some outrageous protest or possibly even legal action would follow.

It is oddly comforting to realize that aggrieved self-righteousness is not the sole preserve of the traditional religions, but extends to the more recent ones as well. "This is highly offensive and totally unacceptable," wrote the aggrieved Operating Thetan. "In my opinion [Cliff] should have to make good with a public apology and then go and look for another profession."

> The Church of Scientology presently enjoys the highest respect all around the world and the founder, Mr. L. Ron Hubbard is a renowned humanitarian who has been awarded the highest accolades for his contributions to mankind in dozens of fields of endeavour, by governments and social orders across the globe.

At least most South Africans would agree that Gareth Cliff should find another profession.

"I always thought Mother Teresa was a ghastly old woman." Lin Sampson.

Some listeners presumably feel the same way about *The Rude Awakening* team on Highveld Stereo, who, in the spirit of nation-building, enjoy telling jokes about "fucking Jews" and Bangladeshis with ham on their heads (What do you call a Bangladeshi with two pieces of ham on his head? Mohammed). One Yom Kippur, the holiest day on the Jewish calendar and a day of fasting, *The Rude Awakening* team thought it would be a good idea to make prank calls to the numbers of obviously Jewish surnames in the phone book. "A phone call was made to a Mr. Cohen where the caller made chewing sounds and said how delicious his burger was," noted one letter to the Broadcasting Complaints Commission. "Mr. Cohen, without using any foul language, asked the caller if he had nothing better to do with his time, and put the phone down. *The Rude Awakening* team thought that this was hilarious and packed up laughing."

The complainant vowed never to listen to 94.7 again.

Then there is Jani Allan, who has always had a weakness for blue-eyed, rightwing nutcases. In 1999, she interviewed an American white supremacist, who stated, among other opinions, "The United Nations is totally controlled as I said by that litter-box in the Middle East, Israel ... I ain't got no time to hate them. ... Do I support the Holocaust, no I don't ... if you're practising Judaism I know exactly what that filthy thing says, it says we should have sex with three-year-old children and it will be alright ..." He also referred to the Anglo-Saxons as "stupid animals since they do not recognize their enemy and even spend their lives and fortune to help their enemy."

The Madonna of the Holey Green Y-fronts has moved to America, where we hope she stays.

If you had one question for Jesus what would it be?
When is he coming back? I mean, send me an SMS or something.
What would you want from him if he came back?
I'd ask him to teach me to walk on water 'cause I can't swim. David Kau (a Catholic who admits to going to church occasionally).

Helen Suzman was once asked what she thought of the Kappie Komando. "Oh well, they really belong in the days of witch-burning."

The ladies of the Kappie Komando were indignant. Their leader wrote to Mrs. Suzman to complain. The main thrust of her argument involved the fact that her ancestors had conquered mountains in order to take the Bible to the savages on the other side:

> And what were your ancestors doing at that time, Mrs. Suzman?
> Die uwe Marie van Zyl.

So Helen Suzman wrote back:

> Dear Mrs. van Zyl,
> My ancestors were busy writing the Bible.
> Yours faithfully,
> Helen Suzman.

Happy Clappies

When it comes to worrying about who is offending whom, nobody worries too much about the Anglicans. Justin Cartwright once remarked,

> The Anglican Church is so multiculturally sensitive that you could probably throw a maiden to crocodiles in front of the Synod without too much tut-tutting.

Cartwright was a little kinder about Archbishop Tutu, commenting, "There is nothing of that mincing apologia which one has come to expect of Church of England clerics."

Anglicans in turn are awkward around Happy Clappies. All that talk around the braai about being Born Again and Saved: it just isn't *done*. "Like many another buttoned-up Anglican," writes Michele Magwood,

> I am chary of evangelism with its stadiums and karaoke screens, pastors with toupees and sunbed tans and collection plates the size of Pikitup dustbins. That flailing, polish-the-ceiling wave sets my teeth on edge, as does the grotesque

parade of the infirm lurching around the stage. It all seems less like a church than one of Dante's nine circles of hell.

Despite the misgivings of cardigan-wearing biddies, many South Africans appreciate the fact that when you're Born Again, you get to be rich without feeling guilty, because wealth is evidence of the Lord's beneficence. Whole herds of camels pass through the eye of the needle. Conrad Koch has a little prayer he is fond of singing in honour of Rhema:

Jesus loves me
This I know
I have an invoice
That tells me so.

Even God listens to my show

If God listens to prayers, then he can certainly tune His dial to our local DJs every now and then.[1]

While behind the mike at Tuks campus radio, Gareth Cliff once prayed on air for a fellow DJ to get cancer because the guy was stealing his material. When the rival did indeed get cancer, Cliff went on air and told his listeners, "See, even God listens to my show."

Some years later, Gareth Cliff was suspended by 5FM, for broadcasting an 'interview' with Jesus, to coincide with the forthcoming Mel Gibson film, *The Passion of the Christ*.

"Well, we didn't get to interview Charlize Theron," said Cliff. "I went out and found the biggest star I could in showbiz for the Drive Show today: Jesus. That's right. He's just in time to promote his new movie, *The Passion of the Christ*, which is coming here soon. We are going to interview Jesus, the star and pal of Mel Gibson."

Jesus speaks with a Yiddish accent. "A film in Aramaic which is selling more tickets than *Lord of the Rings* on opening night, what do you call that?"

"I call that a miracle," says Cliff. He added that he had heard that special snacks were served at the movie. "Vel, one small bag of popcorn. It is enough to feed a crowd."

---

[1] Nobody has explored the possibility that the PA system in Purgatory is tuned to South African radio, which would explain a great deal.

Cliff also asks Jesus why he wasn't at the Oscars.

"I was terrified I would bump into more Jews. Mel Gibson warned me about them."

At the end of the interview, Jesus thanks Cliff. "It is a pleasure," says the putative son of God, "to be on such a great radio station with so many lovely listeners—except for that one man in Parkmore in Johannesburg. I can see what you are doing when the curtains are closed. Stop it, it is filthy!"

Cliff was temporarily taken off air for this interview, after complaints flooded in.

> "The Bible clearly states: 'If you fail to observe the Sabbath I [God] will drive you from your land'." Agriculture Union TAU-SA in response to reports that Absa was to open certain branches on a Sunday. Azapo might be interested to hear about this.

If Muslims could send a chain SMSs urging the faithful to pray for Ferial Haffajee to burn in hell, then Christians could use mobile technology to boycott Nando's.

When an advert depicting the Last Supper with the line 'Jesus has had his chips', members of the public quite naturally assumed that this was an ad for Nando's. Hell, so the reasoning went, if they could walk a blind lady into a pole, they could dis the Lord.

> "Let's leave it to the Christians to be intolerant, humourless and oppressive."
> Steven Cohen.

The faithful swung into action, sending out SMSs and emails urging fellow Christians to boycott their favourite peri-peri chicken.

As it turned out, a company manufacturing 'faith chips', designed to save the souls of gamblers, was behind the campaign. Nando's, realizing that they had something of a problem, met with Anglican Archbishop Njongonkulu Ndungane, general secretary of the South African Council of Churches (SACC) Molefe Tsele and a senior representative of the Nederduitse Gereformeerde Kerk, Ben du Toit. Following the meeting, the SACC released a statement exonerating Nando's of any responsibility for the campaign.

"It is part of our moral responsibility as Christians to establish the truth of information we receive before thoughtlessly passing it on," said du Toit.

F****verkramptes

Another casualty of the power of SMS and email was the Afrikaans rock band that goes by the euphonious moniker of Fokofpolisiekar. After a show in the thrumming cultural hub of Witbank, the band sat drinking with some of their fans. During an argument over Christianity, one of them—by then in a state of considerable inebriation—wrote "Fok God" on a teenage fan's wallet.

Quite what the impressionable young *seuntjie* was doing drinking with a bunch of rebellious rockers with a rude name is not clear. Whatever the circumstances, the boy told his mother, who started an email petition, which resulted in the dominees of Oudtshoorn demanding that Fokofpolisiekar be uninvited from performing at the Klein Karoo Nasionale Kunstefees. That, or they would withdraw their church halls as performance venues.

Or, as the irrepressible Pinvictor put it,

> The crying little nancy-boy told his mother and, being a blinkered, brainwashed cow from the NG Kerk, she started an email petition urging fellow Christians to boycott the band ...
>
> By causing such a fuss amongst conservative squares in ostensibly their own community, Fokofpolisiekar are keeping it real, by rebelling, and showing the lame-assed cliquey Cape Town music scene that rock 'n' roll still has power ...

Note how Pinvictor manages to insult both Capetonians and the religious in the same paragraph, no mean feat.

Better the Devil you know

> "The press seeks sensation and is the mouthpiece of the devil himself." Disgraced Barclays Bank manager and Isle of Man pastor Pieter van Rooyen, in an email to *The Star.*

In South Africa, you can't have God without getting the Devil thrown in as a package deal. Ask Hansie Cronjé. At the time of the match-fixing scandal, Robert Mugabe nodded sagely, remarking, "My brother, this Satan, we all have to watch out for him."

Uncle Bob, of course, knows all about the Devil. In fact, quite a few people seem convinced that, if Bob is not actually Satan, he is doing the dark prince's work on earth.

More recently, the ANC Youth League described Jacob Zuma's rape accuser as "Lucifer", proving at the very least that the Devil is always there when you need him. On the subject of Zuma, it should be pointed out that Christians have impacted on the history of South Africa in unexpected ways.

"They told me that Gedleyihlekisa was not a proper name, that it was barbaric, and they called me Jacob," said Jacob Zuma, attacking Christians for helping destroy African culture. This was when he was not comparing either himself or the ANC to Christ.

Just think. We could be telling Gedleyihlekisa Zuma jokes. So we have the Christians to thank for Jacob's ladder to the top.

> "For me, it's not so much about the photo, but about the disgusting Satanist style of writing." Amor Vittone, responding to a spurious article about her in local porn title *Loslyf*.

And, say what you like about Christians, but they do try hard. Even at the apparently spiritually barren wasteland of a bikers' rally at a resort between Rawsonville and Worcester, as described by Casper Greeff:

> The brethren gather in great multitude to worship their gods and to sin. Their gods came from the East and were called Suzuki, Yamaha, Kawasaki and Honda. The sins were universal and included fornication, drunkenness and blasphemy. The brethren also gathered in the name of speed and noise.

Amidst all this, the Christian Motorcyclists' Association provides foam cups of instant coffee and the hopes that this will turn the members of the Evil Riders, Pure Venom, Ama Wyn Wyn, Papsakke, Kreefsmokkelaars, the Dropouts, the Vikings and the Squarrows from a road that is hardly paved with good intentions, but which leads to Hell anyway. The slogan of the CMA is 'Riding for the Son' and they have a large banner that assures the flock: "U don't have to end up in hell!!! Jesus allows U-turns."

Even the Evil Riders and Satan's Saints come to the church, says one of its pastors. Casper Greeff watches the crowd yelling "*Wys jou muis*" at a beauty contest and wonders how religion fits in. "It was hard to imagine this mob discussing tracts from the Bible and bowing their heads to pray every Sunday."

We're all God's Chosen People

In the end, the truth is that a great deal of confusion has arisen from the fact that South Africa is full of people who are convinced that God likes them more than anyone else.

> "In South Africa God in his all-wise rule has placed the white race and the non-white race groups with deep racial and other differences." Sauer Commission, reporting on the views of the NP, 1948.

Fortunately, the Lord occasionally emerges from His infinite silence to speak to the chosen. He spoke to H. F. Verwoerd, who said, "We did what God wanted us to do."

Cecil Rhodes was a little more ambivalent about the existence of God (since presumably this would mean admitting that there was actually someone out there who was more important than his lordship), but no less confident about what He would want. "If there be a God," said CJ, "I think He would like me to paint Africa as British-Red as possible."

> "They have persuaded themselves by some wonderful mental process that they are God's chosen people." John Mackenzie, a nineteenth-century missionary, commenting on the Boers.

God also spoke to Brenda Fassie, telling her, "Hey chick, woman, come here, let me show you what you are supposed to be," proving to the doubtful that not only was the holy thumb on the pulse of future music trends, but was not above using slang to get His point across.

Thank God for Brenda.

> "Oh, you mean like a primitive fax machine to God?" Twakkie of *The Most Amazing Show*, on being shown the Paardekraal Monument. His guide said, "I wouldn't call it primitive."

Chapter 8

Getting rogered, and other ways of making money: business

kwaMdidiwenja. 'Dog's arse' in Zulu; the name factory workers gave a textile factory in Hammarsdale, Natal. Quoted by Fred Khumalo.

In January 2006, a landmark ruling took place in South African law. A judge ruled that angry employees could not refer to their boss as an 'arsehole'. "There are few employers," he said, "who would welcome criticism couched in this style and regard it as an invitation to address problems in the workplace."

The law is less clear on whether or not a boss can call an ex-employee an arsehole, like the diamond diver who pulls up in a bakkie outside a pub in Port Nolloth. Caspar Greeff records the outburst with what one must assume is a reasonable degree of accuracy. "You are a fucking arsehole—you and your drugs," yells the man. "I'm going to have a word with your father. You think you're a big *breker* but you're just an arsehole."

"Maria Gemors." Nickname for Maria Ramos, by Transnet workers.

At least the oke in Port Nolloth did not take things as far as the Colyns of Vereeniging may or may not have done. The family, accused of murdering three women workers in their Laundromat, wanted Isabel Mayekana to resign rather than having to fire her. First their lawyer allegedly went to Mayekana and held a gun to her head. "Sign or die," he said. Then they sent her a lawyer's letter demanding R2 million for spreading false rumours, which, given that the Colyns must have known what they were paying the poor woman, seems a little optimistic.

T. L. Janse van Rensburg, the Colyns' attorney, shouted at a reporter that his clients were targeted as part of a "Satanist plot".[1] He said Mayekana was lying. "She's talking the

---

[1] If you have been paying attention, dear reader, you will notice that Satan and his worshipers are apparently very busy in South Africa.

biggest load of nonsense. She's a liar. And she absconded from work like a bad dog." At least Mayekana was one of the lucky ones, escaping the gruesome fate of her colleagues.

"Wendy Lucas-Bullshit." How *Noseweek* described former FNB CEO Wendy Lucas-Bull.

Generally, business in South Africa takes a more subtle approach to HR problems. After Liberty CEO Myles Ruck and his deputy Ian Kirk announced their departures during a single week, Rob Rose of *Business Day* noted that these events "would hardly be a surprise if you'd noted the swarm of senior Liberty staff leaving the building in recent years as if pursued by frothing Thai chickens." Ruck's tenure at Liberty was not popular, and the question, 'Have you been Rucked?' became a common query around the watercooler.

"That grotesque Cardinal Richelieu wannabe." Description of Anglo-American's Michael Spicer, in a letter to *Noseweek*.

"Morally bankrupt plutocrats" is how a letter to *Noseweek* described the powerful businessmen involved in the St. Johns schoolboy brawl débâcle of 2005. Business and conventional morality have never been especially compatible, so it should come as no surprise that the world's foremost expert on psychopaths, a Canadian professor named Robert Hare, has called for potential CEOs and other senior business people to be screened prior to being appointed. The corner office, as it turns out, is just as likely to be occupied by a psychopath as the local jail cell. The ones in business are just better at hiding it.

"I prayed to God this morning, and his name was not Douw Steyn." Ian Levitt, lawyer for Bianca Ferrante, a 'beautician and nail technician' from Pretoria who sued the insurance magnate for R1 million after he allegedly jilted her.

Commenting again on the St. John's scandal, the writer to *Noseweek* observed, "If all schools were successful in turning out only fine upright citizens it would lead to a shortage of the ruthlessly amoral and avaricious liars required for certain senior positions in banking, insurance, politics, and even in the law."

I believe that everyone is born with at least a trace of inherent integrity, so for people to feel comfortable in these positions it's clear that any remnants of morality have to be purged, and if this can be achieved during the school years, so much the better.

Cosatu once sent out a press release noting reports "that several senior SABC staff have resigned from the corporation", but was "disappointed that group CEO Peter Matlare has denied rumours that he too is going to leave".

"Those lying, thieving, double-dealing bastards—this time they've taken on the wrong Jewboy!" 'Flamboyant' Cape Town restaurateur Mark Tarica, reacting to news that the Royal Cape Yacht Club was reneging on a deal with him.

Sol Kerzner was once presenting to the board of a conservative British bank when he suggested that they travel to South Africa to see his properties for themselves. One of them eventually broke the stony silence to thank him for his generosity and enquire whether wives were invited. Upon which Kerzner is alleged to have lost his temper. "Fuck you! I'm offering you a fucking trip to South Africa, where you can stay at Sun City for a week and screw your arses off and you want to bring your fucking wives?"

"Chris Wall is a banker." 1980s graffiti. ANC sympathizer Ball had been forced to resign from Barclays Bank after coming under pressure from the National Party government.

Even packed lunches can be hazardous in the South African office situation. Chwayitha Ngcobo, an accounts clerk at a company in Durban, took a parcel out of her handbag and rubbed the contents in her hands before blowing three times in the direction of her supervisor, Premila Govender. Ngcobo said it was a kiwi fruit she was planning to eat for lunch; Govender said it was witchcraft designed to intimidate her. Alan Gibb, who presided over the hearing, agreed with Govender's version. Ngcobo was found guilty on charges of intimidation, assault and gross negligence and fired.

"I am writing anonymously because I feel very stongly about someone near and dear to me has been mistreated in a business deal by a notorious businessman in Cape Town. I know this businessman socially and am aware of how he boasts of his crooked dealings. It really upset me when I recently learned that my friend was threatened out of a business deal and lost a lot of money. I feel it unfair that he should get away with it again and again because nobody has the balls to expose his shady dealings. He is Dave McKay of Constantia Uitsig. I hope you have the balls." Anonymous letter to *Noseweek*, which thought it a "bit cheeky, your challenge on balls, don't you think, when you yourself clearly have none". "Anyway, Mr. McKay," the editor added, "now you know; someone in your social circle is out to shop and/or defame you."

Wealth without exertion

Thabo Mbeki blamed the British for bringing capitalism to South Africa in his speech on the evils of materialism. This seems rather shortsighted, since as history tells us, our nation has its roots in a colony established and run by the VOC, an organization that would have made the average rapacious modern multinational look like a vaguely leftist NGO run by wussy humanities graduates who sort of want to save the world and couldn't find jobs anywhere else. People droning on about a new era of globalization forget that the VOC epitomized the concept three and a half centuries ago.

Capitalism, then, is in our national DNA. (If you have your doubts about this, chew on the fact that South Africa is probably the only country in the world where teenagers consider chartered accountancy to be a cool career.)

So, when Cecil John Rhodes famously said, "We must find new lands from which we can easily obtain raw materials and at the same time exploit the cheap slave labour that is available from the natives of the colonies. The colonies would also provide a dumping ground for the surplus goods produced in our factories," he was, in a sense, continuing in the spirit if not the letter of the long-defunct Committee of Twelve.

This is held against him to this day. Even former Mandela Rhodes scholars like Adekeye Adebajo suggest that Rhodes is a figure "that Africans should have condemned to the pit-latrine of history," which seems a tad ungrateful all things considered, but there you go.

Rhodes' attitudes were harsh even for his own time. An English observer wrote at the turn of the twentieth century that the political pressure to annex the Transvaal and its lovely gold from the Boers was "nothing more than a continuation of our practice of political burglary."

"[Durban Roodepoort Deep] used them like condoms and dumped them." Congress of SA Trade Unions president Willie Madisha, on the possible retrenchment of thousands of mineworkers, 2006.

Olive Schreiner wrote of "our national English greed for speedy wealth without exertion". She observed that there were basic differences between the way the Boers and the English took things that did not belong to them. The Boers would say, "The damned Kaffir; I'll take his land from him and divide it among my children." The Englishman was different. "When he desires an adjoining Native territory, he sighs, and folds his hands; he says: "It's a very sad thing the way these Natives go on! They believe in witches and kill them … It's my duty to interfere!"

Of course, Schreiner notes, the Englishman says nothing about all the coal mines he has planned, but he kills a couple of thousand people to save a couple of witches "but he has the lands and the mines, and dis-homed and beaten Natives to work for him."

"Apartheid's thuggery ran a spectrum: from the lowbrow violence of the Magnus Malans through the lucrative silkiness of the Randlords." Ronald Suresh Roberts.

A few years later, the Randlord Lionel Phillips, an Englishman who had come from humble beginnings to become one of the most prominent of Johannesburg's Randlords, declared himself unimpressed by communism. "The social pyramid is to be turned upside-down and the dregs of the nation put on top," he sniffed. "Quite a dazzling prospect for the dregs!"

"Hoggenheimer." Anti-Semitic reference to the stereotypical greedy capitalist, popular in cartoons in the Afrikaans press between the world wars.

In the beginning, communism in South Africa was for the most part a whites-only affair. It was only once Afrikaners had managed to get themselves started in business that Rooigevaar and the awful prospect of nationalizing the mines was added to Swartgevaar. As they say, one of the things that makes South Africa unique is that it boasts a communist party with plans for the future.

"If a man wishes to unionize, and disrespect the captains of industry, all he deserves is a public flogging, and a hefty fine." Pinvictor, africans.co.za

The New South Africa's flirtation with socialism was too much for some capitalists. "We can't allow the 'socks and sandals' brigade to determine national policy," Johann Rupert told his company's AGM in 1998:

> We can't allow failed left-wing academics (Afrikaners as well) who are now permeating the civil service and getting into key positions to determine national priorities … The rest of the world perceives that we are totally out of step. We're in cloud-cuckoo-land.

But when communists start investment companies, and capitalist crooks get to be great African patriots, then you know that the old rules no longer apply. As Pieter-Dirk Uys observed, "Scratch a local communist and you'll probably find a capitalist being reborn." Mark Gevisser described this trend as "the quietest and most profound revolution of our time".

"Sometimes, if you wear suits for too long, it changes your ideology." Joe Slovo.

"Anybody who's successful is always a bitch." Susie Jordan.

Take the following encounter, described by American journalist David Goodman. Tumi Modise, a tough black businesswoman who has a lucrative cleaning contract with Eskom, has a disagreement with the NUMSA official based at Megawatt Park. Unaware that she is standing behind him, he tells Modise's workers: "That bitch you work for thinks she's better than you. She is living high while you struggle to feed your families. She is whitey's ass-licker!"

The workers watch, transfixed, waiting to see what will happen.

"Maybe that black bitch thinks she's white, and she wants to return things to the way the were. When you join our union, you can tell her to fuck off!"

Tumi taps him on the shoulder and asks him to discuss the matter in his office. He tells

her that she's an Uncle Tom. "Why don't you show these workers how you lick the baas's arse?" he sneers.

He yells obscenities as he follows her down a corridor. Turning a corner, he finds her waiting for him. Modise, as Goodman notes earlier, is not a small woman.

> "I feel very sorry for people. Especially when I'm walking all over them." Susie Jordan.

"You piece of *rrrrrrubbish*!" she yells as she grabs his tie and begins battering his head 'like a floppy punching bag'. "I'm gonna fuck you up!"

After punching him repeatedly, she yells "Don't you *ever* insult me in front of my employees!"

Ten days later she is hauled before a meeting of Eskom managers and NUMSA representatives. She tells them that she never laid a finger on the man.

She gets away with it.

> "An arrogant little pipskweek (sic)." Archar Head, husband of Storm SA model Michelle Mackintosh, in a letter to the *Sunday Times*. He was referring to Simon Chambers, who ran the financial side of business at Storm UK, and who was concerned about financial irregularities in the South African business. Storm SA was eventually liquidated in May 2005.

Just over the border, in the land of the Number 1 Ladies' Detective Agency, business can also get up close and a little too personal. One of the presenters at Gabz FM radio station was twice kicked in what Krisjan Lemmer described as the "penalty area" by a freelance sub-editor for *Business and Financial Times*. Apparently Charles Kidega was aggrieved by the station's failure to broadcast the magazine's advertisements. Kidega took the only recourse available to freelance subeditors, storming in the Gabz FM offices and taking his frustrations out on poor Jacob Kamodi, who as a result may very well turn out to be the last of his particular line.

Acting programme manager Kenneth Moeng was mystified by the entire incident, since Kidega had not been involved in the original trade exchange contract. "We don't deal with this man when it comes to commercials, I don't know why he came into the picture," said Moeng.

Kidega also asked to be shown which car Kamodi drives, which sounds like the sort of clue that Mma Precious Ramotswe could put to good use. Newspaper reports left the story hanging tantalizingly in the air at this point.

Bending over blackwards

"A necessary process of bending over blackwards." Pieter-Dirk Uys on affirmative action.

"There are few bigger insults to black business people in South Africa today than an invitation to become a front or token for a white company." Pinky Khoabane. "Some white companies, driven by prejudice and steeped in the belief that blacks are hungry for money and basically stupid, will continue to make the advances."

"Supine empowerment mogul." Letter to the *Sunday Times*, referring to Saki Makazoma.

Despite the Patrices and Tokyos and Cyrils of this world, some were not convinced. Mosibudo Mangena, Azapo leader and minister of Science and Technology thought it was all a capitalist plot:

Even though we see a number of black CEs and board members being announced, we are nothing less than glorified *mantshingilanes* [security guards] of the white captains of the industry, who are raking in billions amidst the sea of poverty— employed to sustain and defend the status quo.

The former head of SABC television news, Joe Thlohloe, remarked, "We may have won political power but economic power is still in white hands, so the struggle continues ..."

"You should know, when a politician moves out of government he's moving from retail to wholesale theft." Comment on Moneyweb.

David Bullard suggested that new empowerment criteria should be developed. "A points system will apply and a regular beating and near starvation during childhood will obviously score higher than being able to eat your vegetables and not being allowed to watch *Dallas* on a Tuesday night."

Tom Eaton tried to put it all into perspective. Whites, he argued, should not rely on the government for a living. "Whites do not know racism, which is why they are so hurt by affirmative action (which they read about in *You* magazine while waiting to pick up the kids from dressage classes)."

> Sadly, nobody ever told them that relying on politicians and government policy for job security is like relying on a rottweiler to look after your braai chops while you nip out to get the beers.

> "I don't mind saying that a little less market confidence in the rand might be welcome relief. But the interior calculus in the minds of currency traders and hedge fund treasuries is about as comprehensible, I have come to believe, as the Book of Job." Finance Minister Trevor Manuel, November 2004.

High flyers

One of the more irksome requirements of the high flyer is that they do, well, a lot of flying. Michele Magwood is suspicious of her fellow passengers. When you sit next to a person reading *The Six Psychopathic CEOs* or *Eleven Pathways to Everlasting Enlightenment* or *Seven Ways to Get Sickeningly Rich* you know you are parked next to a Loser.

She advises strongly against talking to people like this.

Another hazard of flying is the food. You would think that the people in business class get a better standard of ration, but apparently not. The Bandit, who reviews breakfasts for the *Sunday Times* Metro section, describes his SAA business-class breakfast, which consists of a glass of "tepid" orange juice, a bowl of "glutinous" yoghurt, "tasteless" fruit, which has been "painstakingly selected for being unripe and therefore less susceptible to the ravages of oxidation".

> The *pièce de résistance*, though, is the visually alarming, shudder-inducing sausage and two blackened button mushrooms with a tomato and onion relish served atop an egg pancake trying to pass itself off as an omelette.

The bland sausage has all the texture and charm of warm liver pâté, the relish is devoid of seasoning and the tasteless, leathery, shrivelled button mushrooms are beyond the pale. The omelette could easily find purpose in a repair kit for athletic shoes.

Later a "jet-lagged-looking" croissant arrives.

Doodgooi—the Afrikaans word used to describe baked products that would be best employed in missile combat—describes the doughy pretender perfectly.

"Plotting the regrowth of a receding airline." Headline of a *Business Times* article on SAA CEO Khaya Ngqula.

The grumpy bear driving a Fisher-Price pushcart

In September 2005, the apparent assassination of Brett Kebble, according to *Business Day* the J. R. Ewing of South African business, brought forth a great selection of business insults. Obviously, Kebble's friends and family praised him as a great visionary. His father said, as fathers do, that Brett had "the intellectual capacity of a giant and the spirit of a warrior". He did add, though, that Brett had been difficult to guide "in terms of the Ten Commandments of life".

His acolytes in the ANCYL added a curiously Eurocentric touch by quoting both Winston Churchill and W. H Auden in their fulsome tribute to the man. Others were less charitable.

Jim Jones, the former editor of *Business Day*, summed up Kebble as a "cheat, manipulator, corrupter, briber, swindler … a carpetbagger whose business methods were unethical and sleazy."

"Farewell to the Great Corruptor." *Sunday Times* editorial.

Brett Kebble, the paper intoned solemnly, "was not a good South African. He was the Great Corruptor, a dirty businessman who had little respect for the law or the codes of good practice. He corrupted politicians and created a parasitical network of politically connected beneficiaries who affectionately called him *umlungu wethu* (our white man)."

"On his death, speculation of a hit was immediately followed by thoughts of the long list of people who would have wanted him dead."

"May no more like you be born."

"That infamous nocturnal aviator." David Bullard.

Kebble, "like so many before him in the parvenu Johannesburg set, believed that social acceptance could be bought by flaunting his wealth, by publicly spreading money around and by buying favour," sniffed Jim Jones.

"The moneyed peasantry, vastly wealthy for a generation and monstrously ignorant of the last millennium, invariably see at as currency, and currency—whether cash or cachet—must be displayed to be of any value."

Tom Eaton once spotted Kebble driving his Mini Cooper in Cape Town: "He looked sombre and huge, like a grumpy bear driving a Fisher-Price pushcart."

Eaton predicted that public opinion would either insist that Kebble was a good guy, or "insinuate that he was a rogue capitalist jostling with puckered lips for position around the sphincter of government."

"The old man should be scrubbing toilets for the remainder of his life for bringing the fat schmuck into this world!" Comment on Moneyweb.

Kebble himself gave as good as he got. When he was asked how he responded to people who suggested that his Art Awards were no more than a scheme to combat all the other negative publicity he was getting, he said, "I usually respond with two words. The first starts with an f."

Describing his business adversaries, Kebble offered this interesting image. "The biggest problem I have is this group of people getting into a huddle trying to monopolize deal flow, not by being the best, not by getting up early and doing their job, not by being clever and smart and building alliances, but by sitting around and drinking huge cases of single-malt Scotch and getting pissed regularly, doing all sorts of strange things to small animals and young girls late at night."

Based on the evidence at hand, it appears that Kebble himself regarded his job as one that involved finding as many ingenious and underhand ways to sidestep the law as he possibly could, but perhaps that is just a technicality.

"History tells us that political favours are not worth the paper they are never written on." John Farquhar.

Other crooks

"A well-known crook about town." Don Mkhwanazi, the former chair of the Central Energy Fund, according to Krisjan Lemmer. Mkhwanazi later sued the *Mail & Guardian* for R3 million.

The evidence to hand suggests that Nigerians were not involved in Kebble's death. Nonethelesss, when you wish to take over a business and the owner of said concern is not an especially willing seller, you could always follow the lead of one Dev Singh and pose as a syndicate of Nigerians who wish to kidnap your rival's daughter. To wit the following SMS:

We are a Nigerian syndicate. We are going to kidnap your sweet little daughter for a R10 million. If you go to the police, we will kill you. We are watching you. Your choice. You can afford it.

A second SMS, sent a couple of months later and clearly hoping to move things along, read, "We are going to cut your daughter to pieces and feed her to the sharks and you are next." Singh's Dainfern home was searched and he was arrested. After attempting to bribe the investigating officer, he was found guilty of intimidation and sentenced to five years' imprisonment, suspended for five years.

"She could not tell the difference between a business plan and a bunch of flowers." Anonymous comment, *Noseweek*, referring to a friend hired by Phillip Dexter to work at the Mpumalanga Economic Growth Agency, where he was acting CEO.

Black Labour, White Guilt

The battle between SA Breweries and Laugh it Off brought the issue of satire and commerce into sharp relief. Laugh It Off was known for printing satirical T-shirts. 'Standard Wank' was one, 'First National Bankie' was another. One of the most popular shirts used the familiar branding of Carling Black Label, favoured beer of mine workers and wannabe subversive hippie slackers, transforming it into 'Black, Labour, White Guilt'.

SAB was not amused. Laugh It Off, they said, was infringing on their trademark. What's more, the parody was "racially inflammatory" and "offensive". The Cape High Court agreed, ruling that the T-shirt bordered on hate speech. LIO's Justin Nurse appealed the decision, but lost. The case went all the way to the Constitutional Court, where Nurse argued that the T-shirt was satirical, and thus protected by the right to freedom of expression.

Lawyers were not optimistic about Nurse's chances. "I put my money on SABMiller, namely because of the racist connotations," said one. "If they would have done it in a more humorous way I think there would have been less problems."

As it turned out, the Constitutional Court judges did see the humour in the Black Labour T-shirt.

"It's probably wise to just let the dust settle," Nurse said after the Constitutional Court ruling. He did print 1,000 limited edition 'Black Labour' T-shirts to be auctioned on the LIO website, with the proceeds to be donated to an anti-alcohol abuse charity.

Tom Eaton thought that SAB's "Gestapo treatment" was "repugnant", though he sought comfort in philosophical reflection. "Big sharks eat little fish," he wrote. "Schoolyard bullies kick chubby six-year-old girls in the shin and grow up to be CEs with anorexic trophy wives. And so the world turns."

But most importantly SABMiller has told me that it is desperately, toe-curlingly, nose-pickingly uncool. In the space of a year they have gone from patriotic cheerleaders and roistering purveyors of bonhomie to faceless slabs of grasping corporate grease, their post-nasal drips plopping on to their patent-leather shoes as they struggle to get their bicycle clips on.

"Louis Luyt may not be a great salesman. But he is consistent. And one thing he has proved time and again: doing business with yourself can be quite as pleasurable as self-abuse." *Noseweek*.

Chapter 9

A voël in the hand:
advertising

"Advertising people use great music, they take lines of great poetry and distort them—if they could get away with it, they would use the crucifixion to advertise nails." Robert Kirby.

In a moment worthy of Nostradamus, the first ever ad on South African television was for Big T burgers. Who else could they have been referring to but the biggest T of all, T-Boz aka Thabo aka President Mbeki?

Since then, there's been Felix Schwartz, the kid with nine lives thanks to Black Cat Peanut Butter, Mum Remembered Melrose, the Wedwo kid, the Simba lion, the Chomp hippos, the Omo tannie who nearly died. United helped you go go go, Cremora was not inside it was on top, that's my Marmite. The Charles Glass society, the Mercedes that fell down the mountain and the BMW that beat the benz. A glass and a half of milk, Raj and Raj, that awful dancing meerkat who needs to see an orthodontist to sort out those weird rodent teeth sooner rather than later.

The Vanish harpy who throws indeterminate substances at innocent shoppers, the McCain woman who hasn't got time to "peel" a pea (who has?), the Harpic perverts who leer at the stains in the toilets of Sandton housewives.

Advertising is ingrained in our culture. The soundtracks to our lives are a collection of jingles and slogans, our memories interspersed with ad breaks. Naturally, this means that many people hate it, and are offended by it every day. Either there is too much advertising during shows like *Survivor* and *Will and Grace*, or too little during *Muvhango* and *Yizo Yizo*.

"22-year-old white girls who live in Sandton and watch *Ally McBeal*." Nat Kekana, chairman of the Parliamentary Portfolio committee investigating transformation in the advertising industry. He was referring to the media planners who decide where advertisers should place their campaigns.

"There is nothing about an advertisement that is not the most hostile assault on the mind and reputation of the target," writes Tom Eaton. "It is a golem, malformed and festering with vile assumption and viler aspersions; and in the space of half a minute it wipes its noxious little arse on everything that elevates the humanity it can never understand." It says:

> I have barged uninvited into your evening's entertainment, and still you watch, because your mind is either malleable or defunct. I will speak for only 30 seconds, because that is all it will take, because your critical faculties have the consistency of porridge. I know you don't want or need what I am selling, but I suspect you may just be stupid enough not to know it yourself; and while you vacillate, I will fellate your greed and your fear.

Zebulon Dread, for his part, hates the way in which sport has become just another excuse for marketers to parade their wares before an audience. Who would pay any attention to sport

> if not for the excessive spending of advertising-hungry corporates who sit and wait for opportunities to increasingly colonize our consumerist tendencies and who gratifyingly add to this nonsensical hype with their only real *raison d'être* being the possibility of our becoming their usable slaves?

"After all, if one does want to be taken seriously as someone of integrity, it's no good dressing up in your best suit, getting your hair cut and then leaving your fly undone with your willy hanging out." Chris Moerdyk suggests that if the newspaper industry wanted to avoid censorship, it could start with the sex ads that clutter the classifieds.

Brazilian? What about Brazilian?

During the 1990s there was the Feminine Hygiene Offensive, when viewers dived behind the sofa every time a soft-focus head-and-shoulders shot of a smiling woman appeared on the screen, and we learned that New Freedom had nothing to do with the rainbow nation. Then there were Acid Indigestion Wars, which pitted ads for Zantac and Maalox against Gaviscon and Eno.

This was followed by the Hair Hostilities. Every ad break was populated by smiling women whose lives were perfect because they had found the right shampoo. Even Jennifer Aniston announced to anyone who was interested, "If this shampoo were a man, I'd marry it."

Given the 20/20 vision of hindsight, what a pity—one is tempted to observe—that she didn't.

The spectres in shampoo ads stride along in slow motion from one photogenic moment to the next, their hair bounces along in a shiny, healthy, non-brittle, vitamin-enriched, 95% less prone to breakage mass, the proud symbol of their status as successful women. This was the decade when haircare products even offered the possibility of erotic bliss: "For the feel you want," sighed an ad for hairspray. "No stiff or sticky feeling." Hmm.

> "Of course the 'before' picture is Photoshopped. Every fucking ad is Photoshopped—otherwise we'd have to pay the model for two pictures—and for another hairdo!" Ad agency, quoted in *Noseweek*.

The brand names floated by in a glorious miasma of narcissism. The Bad Hair Day has become a symbol of the inability of the modern woman to attain perfection on a regular basis.

It should be noted that every one of these ads was an import, so can therefore be understood as a hostile attack by the Americans/ French/ British. (There you go Manto! Forget the submarines: target the supermarket shelves.)

> "I loathe the lifeless nature of advertising." Kitchenboy.

The continued impugning of the IQ of South African women continued into the new millennium, with the Organics ads that ripped off the fake orgasm scene in *When Harry Met Sally* and the Sunsilk chick who tries to suggest a party theme and gets ignored because her hair is flat. "Brazilian," she suggests mournfully, all too aware of her invisibility. "What about Brazilian?"

Then she washes her hair with the aforementioned product and emerges as a new person, the kind of woman who gets to decide on … party themes. Oh, such progress we have made. "Every day, haircare ads are wreaking infinitely more havoc on the feminist project than a million episodes of *Ally McBeal* ever could," Jane Seemore wrote in 1998, and nothing has changed.

> "Branding, you will recall, is what happens when you've told a lie for so long that you start believing it yourself." Tom Eaton.

Creative differences

Advertising is an industry that often seems as much to win awards as sell products. The Loeries are an annual exercise in debauchery and decadence, at which people drink a lot, take as many drugs as they can find, and sit at the awards evenings hoping that it is their name that will be announced when the gold statuettes are handed out. Until recently, the Loeries were held at Sun City. In 2005, they were moved to Margate in an attempt to recreate the local equivalent of Cannes. The citizens of Margate, which is also known as RAUgate, in honour of its designation as a Matric and student piss-up venue of choice, are at least accustomed to extended bouts of wantonness, and know what to expect.

Whether or not an advertising campaign wins awards, and whether or not it is intended to find favour with a bunch of judges rather than a focus group of LSM 8–10 housewives ages 35 to 49, is often a source of considerable controversy.

> "To say that advertising is at the cutting edge of various art forms is bullshit." John Hunt.

As one would expect from an industry which employs people who would generally rather be making movies or drawing graphic novels, advertising is a good source of invective. People have been showering abuse on one another with the gay abandon of Jacob Zuma followers preventing the transmission of HIV after sex.

Take the following response, by one 'Vomitoria', to a press release placed on bizcommunity. com:

> Mutual masturbation session.

What a load of sycophantic claptrap! Let's see who will disappear up whose arsehole first out of this bunch of self-congratulatory posturing pillocks.

Such outbursts are mere trifles, however, compared to the long-running feud between advertising maven John Farquhar and South Africa's most awarded advertising agencies. Farquhar, the editor of industry publication *AdVantage*, is in his seventies, looks a bit like Colonel Sanders before he grew that fashionable little *bokbaardjie*, and drives an ageing Toyota Corolla.

If there were anything hip about Johan Farquhar, it would need replacing.

Contrast Oom John with the average advertising creative. For various reasons, most award-winning creatives are young and male. Give the Id a desk and a salary and you've got yourself somebody who sits and thinks (or is at least supposed to sit and think; usually they're outside getting stoned or inside playing Tetris) of new and interesting ways to sell washing powder to housewives and cheeseburgers to their progeny. And in case anyone might suspect them of homosexual tendencies, some males—to call them men brings a little too much cognitive dissonance into play—put up FHM posters of Homegrown Honeys and stickers that read 'I love my penis' on their walls.

Creatives hate Farquhar even more than they hate the dancing meerkat, even more than they hate their clients.

The war of words started in the 1990s, after South African agencies began to win international advertising awards. Creatives wanted to produce advertising that won awards instead of selling products, Farquhar argued. In 1995, he wrote, "If advertising in South Africa is a reflection of the society in which it operates, then this society is heading for a huge train smash."

Later, he mocked creatives, saying that they suffered from insecurity:

These guys have an ejaculation every time they win an award. They walk around with their egos on their sleeves, desperate for peer approval.

Mike Schalit of the Creative Directors' Forum decided to fight back against Farquhar by encouraging everyone in the ad industry to collect their copies of *AdVantage* and dump them at Primedia, the owner of the magazine.

"If you're a creative agency in this country, then you're seen as a bunch of wankers," Schalit complained.

Nothing much came of the exercise and Farquhar continues to snipe at what he says is the obsession of the industry with winning awards. As with dire shampoo ads, nothing much has changed.

"White women can't market to blacks." John Farquhar.

My wank is my ad campaign

Bank advertising attracts more compound interest than any other category. What a pity it is almost all negative.

"My bank is my vuvuzela." How on earth can that be? Is my bank cheap and plasticky? Does it insinuate itself into sports events? Does it make a constant horrible noise in my ear?" Tom Eaton ponders the imponderable.

When Standard Bank changed its payoff line from "Simpler. Better. Faster." to "Inspired. Motivated. Involved." the latter was of course immediately changed to:

Inspired by Ignorance, Motivated by Money, Involved in Incompetence.

"P'raps this will make Stranded Blank 'simpler, better, faster'! Too much to hope for?" wondered one contributor. Others waxed more lyrical. "What a bunch of tossers—can you imagine the concentration etched on the faces of the SB execs and their admen as they thrashed out this bit of dross."

The marketing community also hated the ads themselves. One visitor to marketingweb. co.za had plenty to say about the TV spots which featured ordinary people talking about the things they needed money for. "Watching these two chavs sitting on the Morkels couch jawing on about the cost of educating their offspring is nauseating."

The thought of these two actually producing a bloodline of little chavlettes is scary and frankly there should be a law against it. ... If sub-70 IQ chavs actually have loving conversations about their bank like this then we are in serious dung.

Standard Bank's baptism of fire was nothing compared to the response to Absa's new brand campaign. The ads featured South Africans declaring "My bank is my rock ... my bank is my shelter, my light". Inevitably, it was roundly mocked. Soon a parody was doing the rounds on the Internet, featuring imager "My bank is my elbow", "My bank is my earbud" and "My bank is my erectile dysfunction". The new payoff line "My bank is Absa" was replaced by "My bank is stoopid".

> "My bank is a rock—more likely my bank are a bunch of rocks." Anonymous, Marketingweb.

Tom Eaton felt that Absa should get credit for not paying an advertising agency:

> Indeed, in the fortnight since the launch of the campaign, it has become abundantly clear that Absa has not only economized by eschewing professional copywriters altogether, but has empowered previously marginalized camps by entrusting its re-branding to a band of rhesus monkeys chained to typewriters and supervised by crack addicts.

How on earth, Eaton wondered, had the copywriters chosen the words they did? "If Absa is trying to lure more middle-class consumers into its mighty vaults, why doesn't it simply cut straight to the chase with metaphors far more familiar and comforting to its target market?" In which case, why not a garden gnome or a dog called Ninja or a collection of SABC3 CDs?

> My bank is my overwhelming sense of failure, my creeping suspicion that I might not be a lesbian after all, my Catholic angst, my Semitic nihilism, my threadbare ubuntu crumbling against the onslaught of mobilized capitalism. My bank is my collection of Krugerrands and the two cyanide capsules I keep for when the revolution comes. My bank is my tendency towards hysterical blindness. My bank—until recently —was Schabir Shaik.

The client bombed it

"An uptight, passive-aggressive, sociopathic, frigid, vegetarian, Nazi hippie's gotta make a living, and so most of them have left education and gone into the world of lucrative indolence known as 'marketing'." Tom Eaton.

Most advertising people like to think that advertising would be great if it weren't for their clients. "Most clients are complete prats," declared an anonymous creative on the Marketingweb site. "I mean, let's face it—only the blandest, dullest, most unimaginative twats would ever consider studying something as mindless as marketing."

It's the one course that requires no personality, intelligence, spark or imagination. Any idiot with half a brain and no soul can do it. And yipee! That's where our clients come from! They're either the quiet grey petrified ones who no one ever misses when they're not around, or they're the idiot bullies who use their tiny bit of power to inflict their stupidity on the world at large, until they get found out as useless and fired. Either way, they're pathetic worms. It's laughable.

The clients responded with a low blow. Why was it better to be a client, one of them wondered? Salaries, for one thing. "Decent salaries from big, healthy international corporations which don't have to retrench half their people whenever the smallest thing goes wrong."

We also get bonuses, 13th cheques, company cars, PAs, and we STILL get to go to all of your parties, shoots, award ceremonies etc. Oh yeah, we go home at 5. You guys?

"So next time your '69 Beetle won't start and you can't get it fixed cause you stuck the little that you earn up your nose, and I drive past you while you're waiting for a lift from an unreliable colleague in the piss-pouring rain, you can warm yourself up with the thought that you're the smart one."

"Life's a pitch and then you die." *Style* magazine.

Chapter 10

From Sultans of Bling to the suburbs: new South African citizens

"Eleven languages *se gat*. We all know money's the only real official language of this country. Especially if it's plastic." Maureen Isaacson.

"The deification of personal wealth," Thabo Mbeki has told the nation, is "the distinguishing feature of the new citizen of the new South Africa."

"Socially garrulous individuals, obscenely materialistic, and conveniently forgetting where they came from." Jon Qwelane on the black political and business elite.

The meaning of freedom, the president adds, "has come to be defined not by the seemingly ethereal and therefore intangible gift of liberty but by the designer labels on the clothes we wear, the cars we drive, the spaciousness of our houses and our yards,[1] their geographic location, the company we keep and what we do as part of that company."

Thus every day and during every hour of our time beyond sleep, the demons embedded in our society that stalk us every minute seem always to beckon each one of us towards a realizable dream and nightmare. With every passing second, they advise, with rhythmic and hypnotic regularity—get rich! Get rich! Get rich!

It is difficult to imagine that once we faced the prospect of socialism. Half of South Africa, it seems, has embraced the tenets of kugeldom: spend, spend, and spend some more.

---

[1] Hogarth in the *Sunday Times* wondered if Mbeki's comments on the "spaciousness of our houses and our yards" applied to Mrs. Mbeki's R8-million mansion in Killarney.

"If you're an aspirational Sultan of Bling and somebody gives you a pile of free money, it would be pointless to waste it on the poor." David Bullard.

Long gone are the days when only certain people were allowed to spend money, as Todd Matshikiza experienced in Braamfontein in 1960. "Get out of here, you peppercorned such an' such," the saleslady in a luggage shop scolded him. "You think you're a white man touching things here an' peacocking around."

"I said, 'Yes missus' an' my forty pounds walked out of the shop with me."

Today there are few business people who would have let that forty pounds walk out of that shop. In fact, marketers lie awake at night thinking up ways to sell things to what have been defined as the 'black diamonds'—rough and unpolished though some of them are.

The president might worry about the excessive public display of wealth, the SACP might dismiss the BEE elite as "excessively compradorist and parasitic" —whatever that means—but the truth is that capitalist consumerism was never so cool.

"Gold cards are the foreplay of capitalist intercourse." John Vlismas.

Bongani Madondo wonders at the amount of gloss "dripping from the Mandela/Sandton Square boutique north of mining and whoring (just look at Oxford between 7pm and 2am) Johannesburg." Madondo is both entranced and appalled by it all.

It is raining gloss ... from the super-valved BMWs, and seldom-used bling-bling cutlery at home ... we are swimming in gloss. And perhaps it is true—sick as the contradiction and metaphor are—that Johannesburg is the home of gold.

"And oh, this bling is contagious, man!"

"I did not join the struggle to be poor." Smuts Ngonyama.

Bongani Madondo on The Daddy's Girl:

Call her anything: 'gangstah-chick'; 'the mob's moll'; 'Zozo' or just 'that woman living off the oily back of a stereotyped Nah-Gerian drug dealer'. Just don't refer to her as a sex worker, cause that's pretty libelous and off kilter.

In fact Ntozozo, as her friends playfully call her, played hard to get. South Africa's 'urbanscapes', or as somebody said, 'urban waste' is teeming with Ntozozos. They are usually black, aged between 19 and 28 (not even an hour older), who are a notch above street hookers and one below what the rich white folk call courtesans.

They are terribly stylish and have cultivated, sinfully expensive taste in clothing and drinks. A-class networkers, they know where all the diplomats, soccer players and politicians hang when their wives are not around.

But it's not soccer players Ntozozos want; they're such a low-ranking lot, mostly keen on teenagers, sies! It is the paparazzi riot of flashes that attracts Ntos.

Not all those dames caption writers are too lazy to name in society page group pics are Ntozozos out to milk an unsuspecting politician or a new black zillionaire. There are some familiar tell-tales to spot Ntozozo among pretenders: colour co-ordination. Check those shoes ... are they a screaming colour? Does she change Louis Vuitton bags more times than a rapper curses?

Class differences

"Bantu education: This has been prohibited so stop begging at traffic lights or showing us where to park. Reserve that for the poor whites who were too lazy to benefit from apartheid." Bitch's Brew, *Sunday World*.

So it is that more than a decade into democracy, South African society is defined more than ever by who has money, who has less money and who has no money at all.

The differences manifest themselves in all sorts of ways. For example, if you order a Johnny Walker Black Label—signature tipple of wannabe empowerment moguls—in a dodgy pub, you will get beaten up, as Abdul Milazi warns. Moreover, if you object to being bought a Carling Black Label,[2] the barman will grab you and threaten you. Then

---

[2] Carling Black Label, currently the country's biggest beer brand and traditionally associated with the black working class, has a fascinating history in South Africa. Alyn Adams recalls, "Only two types of rebellious white people drank Labels—dodgy, moffie, kommie, alternative-word-for-labourer-boetie hippies who self-consciously called it 'zamalek' at the Rainbow, and lazy, long-haired surfers who picked it up in quarts at the same shebeens where they bought their Satanic dagga."

the regulars will make snide and vaguely threatening remarks along the lines of "*Abo top shayela basema suburbs, bayazitshela. Lebari ithe ifuna iBlack Label and nami ngiyizwile*". Which means, roughly, *These wannabes from the suburbs are so full of themselves. The fool says he wants a Black Label, and I heard him too.*

"That's about the time you want to leave with your wallet and a full set of teeth."

"Sex is entertainment for the poor." Nkosazana Dlamini-Zuma.

"Fuck the poor." Bumper sticker, seen on a Rolls Royce in Pretoria.

John Matshikiza gets into a one-sided conversation with an Afrikaans builder who starts chatting to him in a Cape Town bar because he doesn't want to talk to the yuppies, his clients:

The builder and the yuppies hate each other. They come from different clans, different classes, different tribes. He is a simple Afrikaner from Pretoria. They are university types from Joeys and Cape Town who speak a language that is distantly related to English.

So the builder sits next to the only black man in the entire joint. "I came here tonight with these cunts, but I can't stand them," he says. "They've got too much money and they don't know what they're talking about."

"We can't live in a society where these sorts of things happen at this kind of level. There is enough killing in the lower classes, let alone when you get into high-profile people." Roger Kebble after the murder of Brett.

Even TV programmes can divide rich and not-so-rich South Africans from one another. Margie from Edenvale writes to *The Citizen* to defend her favourite TV show:

It sounds to me like you are all rich spoilt brats from Bedfordview with DSTV and all that money can buy you. What about us working class who can't afford all the luxuries? We don't have DSTV. We like *Strictly Come Dancing*, in fact "we love it." ... You've got five fingers, choose one of them. Voila!

Rob Handfield-Jones blames the "downward spiral of grotesque materialism" for the traffic congestion on the M1 between Johannesburg and Pretoria on "It seems," he argues, "that many people have become so greedy, insecure and pathologically status-conscious that they will go to almost any lengths to get one-up over their fellow citizens.

One only has to drive through some of the newer suburbs in Pretoria East. Tiny postage-stamp suburban erven are home to revolting pseudo-mansions ... I could well believe that people ensnared by such palpable ostentation may well feel the need to drive 100km a day in pursuit of a job which pays a few thousand rand extra per month for the purchase of the latest status symbol.

What is the cause of these monstrous daily commutes? Handfield-Jones believes "it stems from our being ever-increasingly bombarded with advertising messages which ask us to mortgage our common sense of the sake of appearances."

"Sandton is attractive to the schmucks of this world—get over it—$s don't buy class." Comment on Moneyweb.

Meanwhile, David Bullard suggests that, ultimately, people flash money around as a result of some Darwinian drive to perpetuate our genetic material. "We buy things we don't need because they are part of our breeding plumage. A flashy car and a diamond-encrusted watch send a signal to the opposite sex that says: 'Please mate with me because I can compensate you financially for my lack of personality.'"

"It's better to be wealthy than it is to be right." Mike Lipkin.

Lin Sampson on The Networker:

The she-networker, who looks like a crocodile in Estée Lauder, enters a room with a smile pasted on her face like a postage stamp.
When the networker enters a room, she doesn't see people, she sees contacts. These social vagabonds view the world as a giant Ferris wheel whirling past, full of social opportunity. All she's got to do is get a foot on it.

The Tao of networking is flattery. Adept at social treachery, the networker's head is full of crusty old shibboleths. "Goodness, you look sexy tonight," she (or more probably he) will say to the plain, middle-aged woman.

They reside in the soft shell of other people's glory.

Networkers used to be called arse-creepers and were scorned. Now they are crowned, their talent applauded.

Learn your AA, BEE, Model C

They walk and talk with a swagger that most people love to hate them. I have even sat through a one-sided debate in a taxi where 'Model Cs' were described by one elderly gentleman as a curse.

The Model C is a product of the new South Africa, that generation of black kids who went to white schools and emerged for the most part with white middle-class values.

Model Cs, explains Mlamuli Ndoda Nxele, are disliked because they "embraced the virtues of white middle-class South Africa." This is why they are seen as "culturally bankrupt". Also known as "uglamour". It is also possible to become an instant Model C. Nowadays, notes Nxele, "natives of even the most remote villages can become Model Cs in an instant. The understanding of the appropriate mannerism, the right pronunciation of words, the nasal accent, one can become an Instant Model C." But don't try a fake Model C accent if you want to impress the people who write the Bitch's Brew column for *Sunday World*: "Stop it; we all know it was before your time."

Model Cs have a nasal accent and speak only English. Lindiwe becomes Lindiiiwe, KwaMashu becomes KwaMaaaashu.

"This is local whitey-talk, somewhere between a kugel on a cellphone and a cat sliding down a blackboard. These kids now call their mother 'the maid' and stay as late as they can after school so they don't have to see too much of the family." John Matshikiza.

South Africa's Paris Hilton—in the spirit of Africanization, let's say she's our Ezulwini Sun—Khanyasile Mbau, is ultimate Model C. In 2006 the 20-year-old explained how she managed to snare a 51-year-old billionaire, Mandla Mthembu. "My granny taught us to adopt a more Western way of life and never allowed us to play outside, while my siblings from my father's second marriage were taught to be more black, and they were raised to be more Zulu."

Mthembu said, "She is extremely intelligent for her age, she brings out the best in me, she brings out the best in me and I thank God and the ancestors for blessing me with her." Mbau, said the *Sunday Times*, had "traded in her sporty French car for three Porsches, two Mercedes-Benzes, a R6-milllion penthouse and a collection of expensive shoes that runs to more than 600 pairs."

> "In our culture it's still such an ugly habit … It's like speaking English. You see them wearing pants with cigarette in hand and they seem to have the notion that they are sophisticated. It seems speaking English and smoking cigarettes go hand in hand with these modern women." Nelson Ntshangase, University of KwaZulu-Natal lecturer, who thinks that an African woman smoking is an "eyesore".

Rainbow kugels

> "Who you are depends on what kind of car your father drives and what model your cellphone is." Black kugel, Wits University, 1998.

As a subset of the Model C, we have the phenomenon of the black kugel, cellphone clamped to ear and Louis Vuitton clutched in hand. Empowerment kugels don't hang out in Soweto; they do lunch in Sandton.

They are but the latest incarnation of a creature with a long and illustrious history in South Africa, as Laurice Taitz explains. The kugel, she reminds us,

> was '80s chic, big hair and even bigger shoulder pads. She dripped gold jewellery given to her when she turned 12 by doting relatives for her Batmitzvah (her Jewish coming of age).
> The butterfly clip holding up the large fringe was a must, as was the "Surprise! It's a car" 18th birthday present. Kugels knew about labels long before designers did. They dated overprotective men named Wayne or Bernard who played first team

rugby, came from wealthy families, had good car sound and said endearing things like: "Hey okes, let's go inside. It's so cold out here my chick's feet are numb." Wayne was usually a commerce student who would meet our lass with all those blonde highlights and sweep her off her feet. She would finish her BA in 'psych' and they would marry and have children named Candice and Jared.

By the late '80s the kingdom of the kugel had expanded to include, not only Jewish princesses, but Greek, Italians and Lebanese ones as well. "Before anyone realized it," notes Taitz, "the '90s had arrived. Apartheid ended, sweeping away the barriers that kept all other potential kugels at bay. With the change in entry-level requirements, the right to be a kugel became a constitutional one.

One letter writer to the *Mail & Guardian* wondered whether it could be true that the Hyde Park kugels, spotted by John Matshikiza mobbing Eleanor Kasrils, were wearing, crimplene, as Matshikiza claimed. "Things in the once-Golden City must be worse than we imagined—our Cape Town kugels would rather go naked in the shopping malls than be seen frocked in the stuff."

"Kugel National Park." Josef Talotta's description of the northern suburbs.

Despite their apparent sense of humour—judging by their fondness for leopard print and bling—kugels do not respond well to criticism. When David Bullard wrote a scathing attack on Sandton Square in an early version of his 'Out to Lunch' column, he was sent piles of hate mail including a specially commissioned cartoon of a kugel hitting him with a handbag. (Years later, the seriousness of the threat is now clear. A fully laden handbag is a formidable weapon, capable of reducing even an All Black to tears.)

"If South Africa is a sinking ship, I want to go down First Class." Alexandra Levin.

The original Jewish kugel used words like 'doll' and 'platz' and inspired Pieter-Dirk Uys to create Nowell Fine. Most of her kind is now to be found in Sydney, Perth or Thornhill, Toronto. But her spirit lives on.

Bongani Madondo on The African Goddess

I used to share a maxi-taxi fare with her. Then she graduated to a beat-up Beetle. Last time I saw her, she was cruising Parkhurst in her jelly-baby-coloured Mini Cooper.

By day she works at a TV production house where she's "the only darkie, y'know?"

At best, the secular Nef never gives a fiddler's fart about style tips that are determined by gay men working in the Western media's glossy magazines and television.

Privately, though, she can be seen shopping for the hottest Prada sandals with bead motifs, as advertised in a recent copy of *Elle*.

Maid in South Africa

"My madam doesn't even know where the toilet paper is kept. I am the hand that has wiped this family's bottoms." Dolly Tlabana, a maid who had worked in Houghton for 27 years.

No true kugel can live without a maid; always one of the standard features of South African middle-class life is the maid. A century ago, Olive Schreiner noted that contact with darker races seemed to have a debilitating influence upon English-speaking South Africans, since even the most "feeble and unrichly brained man or woman" refused to undertake physical labour:

We see a hideous tendency to leave all the work of life to the dark races; for the moment this seems to leave us free for higher efforts, but as time passes surely it will enervate; like a rotten aristocracy we shall die out, and the hands which for generations have made our roads, planted and reaped our fields, built our homes and tended our children, will at last be united to the brains that make the laws and govern the land, and we shall fade away.

Nearly nine decades later, Nowell Fine declared, "You can't even get a decent maid overseas—no man, I'd rather be killed in my bed than have to get up and make it myself."

> "You can't just say, 'do this, do that'. They answer back in just these big sentences." Aunty Merle aka Marc Lottering, on the difficulties of handling maids post-democracy.

The Saints came marching in, and beat other Saints to a pulp

In 2005, a group of St. John's boys assaulted a St. Stithian's boy outside a house in an exclusive Johannesburg suburb. For some reason, the scandal evolved into one of the rare examinations of class in South Africa, something that is usually glossed over, or dealt with in the form of Brakpan jokes. Usually, we ignore the rich; they're just there, living in nice houses, going away on skiing holidays or doing whatever it is that rich people do.

Part of the reason was that *The Star*'s Brendan Templeton was emailed by a St. John's boy who was "perturbed and annoyed" by the quality of the journalism in newspaper's coverage of the affair. Templeton replied:

> Coming as I do from Springs—a dying mining town stuck in a swamp—I don't have any interest whatsoever in the misbehaviour of spoilt, selfish brats from Jo'burg's northern suburbs. However such tripe occasionally finds itself on my daily news radar screen ... I do, however, love getting under the skin of Johannesburg's elite, because most of them are a sorry, scrofulous bunch blinded by pride, greed, fear and money.

Templeton also wrote, "As for the 'men' these institutions are turning out, they hit like girls and they cry like girls—and so do their daddies."

> "Brutal, pampered brats." Letter to the *Saturday Star*, commenting on the St. John's débâcle.

Violence is not restricted to Saints. Toffs, a type generally restricted to the eastern slopes of Table Mountain, are also known to indulge in a spot of fisticuffs when the urge takes hold. Earl Charles Spencer was involved in a savage punch-up with a former best friend, Darius Guppy, who sounds like a character out of *Harry Potter* but is in fact a convicted fraudster. When Guppy found out that Spencer had been making moves on his wife while he was sitting in jail, he kicked and punched him, fractured the latter's cheekbone and injured his ribs and nose. Guppy was something of an enigma to his usually very discreet Constantia community. Locals, noted the newspaper article, "speak of him as a rather menacing, egotistical man with an interest in martial arts and extreme pastimes such as diving with sharks."

Which leads to the rather obvious headline: "Guppy swims with sharks."

Lin Sampson on The Alice Bander

An Alice Bander often says, "Oh, I don't care about money at all." In fact, they care about very little else.

They are fluent in money.

Strangely, unlike the Jewish Princess, the Alice Bander is not that hygienic and often wears dirty knickers and has soiled bra straps … Going into an Alice Bander's room in the morning is rather like an early assault on the Cairo rubbish dumps.

They only have two states of being: very fat or very thin. Nearly all of them have had near-death experiences with anorexia. As a result all their teeth are capped and their breath is often a bit whiffy.

They are sartorial disasters, sticking a puffer jacket that looks like a lavatory cistern cover over a Laura Ashley skirt.

They are terrified of pain—all babies are produced through a knock-out C-section, keeping the more normal channels open for other activities.

Stunning in the suburbs

Lin Sampson once cast aspersions on one of the greatest inventions since sliced bread. "People with duvets," she wrote, "have matching accessories and Laura Ashley wedding dresses, Liebermann pottery and name tiles on the front gate, houses called Costa del Sol, striped awnings and problems with ejaculation."

"White South Africans are very free with their superlatives—they say stunning instead of good, gross instead of bad, and call every second bottle of wine a Grand Cru." Anthony Sher.

Two decades later, Tom Eaton writes of the "mediocrity and self-esteem cult of the middle classes." As for whites, he argues, "their perceived racism is simply a reflection of their cultural affinity for cliché,"

it takes an almost priest-like devotion to banality to have the options provided by money and education, and to still choose to become a sexually frustrated housewife or the CEO of a company that makes doilies.

"Boring people," opines Pinvoctor of Africans.co.za, "fool themselves into thinking bland shit like golf, wine tasting, tile grouting, and Nora Jones passes for exciting—their whole rotten lives are basically lies, and if the truth was revealed to them, they would crumble to dust, like a vampire that has just got a stake in the heart."

John Matshikiza, arriving in South Africa after decades of exile, reflects that he should be able to fit in with a pastiche-Hollywood lifestyle, given that he has lived overseas for most of his life. He pondered on how "the poolside lifestyle of rich white South Africa was merely a pastiche of a pastiche."

Matshikiza soon discovers that suburban life has its challenges. There is the maid and the gardener for instance. "The maid accused the gardener of being a substance abuser with homicidal tendencies. The gardener accused the maid of being an illegal alien from Malawi."

I was beginning to reel under the weight of what had previously been the white man's burden, and discovered that I was not very good at it.

The pool in his northern suburbs garden was to give him plenty of trouble. It was the pool, "and the vicious Barracuda that lurks inside it like a servant of the deep, that eats up most of our physical and intellectual resources." Matshikiza is reduced to uncontrollable weeping, his shoes "ruined by pool acid" and his chest "thick with chlorine fumes".

A field guide to common garden birds

In the suburbs you will find guys called Jason who drive GTIs, work in sales and spend all their spare time in the gym, housewives called Bev and Lorna, PAs called Ronel and Marelize and Riette. There is the oke with money who drives a double cab and rides his KTM scrambler on weekends (look for the KTM sticker on his bumper; one of the more popular ones reads 'Ditch the bitch').

You get your kugels, your African queens, your daddy's girls, your *bokkies* (sweet fresh-faced Afrikaans girls; on most Emirates flights you will be served by a *bokkie*) and your *poppe* (effectively Afrikaans kugels with a weakness for stilettos and blue eye shadow).

One of the most reliably entertaining of suburban types is the Slag, who may or may not be a desperate housewife (but rather fancies herself as one, if she looks like Teri Hatcher). Slags range in age from thirty to fifty and may be distinguished above all by morals that evoke a pair of Decitex 17 pantyhose in their elasticity, artificiality and transparency. Newly divorced slags know that they are at the peak of their sexuality and are determined to make up for all the bonking time lost to married life with rich boring accountants. They will sleep with anything with a penis and a positive attitude.

> "An unspoken rule of slagdom is the more sheer the shirt, the lacier the bra. Also that sequins do maketh the slag." Bernice van Jaarsfeldt.

The more well-heeled areas of South Africa's major urban centres are full of slags; typically they favour areas associated with new rather than old money. Your typical slag will be blonde, her features preserved by years of investment in face creams that cost more than the average monthly car repayment. This despite the fact that she is often a smoker, which as all women know is the worst possible factor for premature ageing, apart from excessive exposure to the sun. All self-respecting slags also drink far too much—usually white wine—and routinely drive drunk.

Since many slags are divorced, certain sacrifices have had to be made. Fortunately, they were able to keep all the chunky gold jewellery they received as birthday and anniversary gifts from their rich, boring accountant ex-husbands.

"Café Vacca Matta: If elitism (quite strange, considering it's located in a cheesy casino) and overpriced food is your thing, this is the place for you." Nadine Botha, *Mail & Guardian* listings.

White noise

What has 500 eyes, 250 noses, 125 teeth and an IQ of one? The front row of a Bles Bridges concert.

Football is a beautiful game to what Tom Eaton defines:

> as a species of which the average specimen prizes doilies, strip-malls, nylon shorts, porcelain harlequins with a single tear on each cheek, welded-chain letterboxes, Africa-shaped clocks and Angelina Jolie.

They probably prize Bles Bridges retrospectives, too.

Lin Sampson attends an arm wrestling competition attended by people with shoulders "like unmade beds ... It is a planet of endomorphs, people with bodies like old-fashioned synagogues, very solid in the middle, rolls of bolshy flesh that expands beyond its restraining clothes, a world where people still listen to rock and roll—and more, can still dance to it". One woman, all of 1.58m tall and 150kg, has arms "the size of well-fed Dachshunds".

Sampson is impressed by their dedication:

> Although arm wrestlers might look like a group of de-institutionalized psychotics and borderline personalities, these are nice people with small incomes that do not stretch to golf clubs or yachts, who give their absolute best to their chosen sport.

"In Brakpan when you divorce your wife, does she still remain your sister?" Joe Parker.

Darren 'Whackhead' Simpson caused an international incident when offending the inhabitants of the Far East one morning. "Did you grow up in Brakpan and now you made it big and you being transferred to the Sandton branch of the Cash Converters and you just can't sleep at night?" he asked listeners of *The Rude Awakening* on Highveld Stereo. The White-Trash Noise CD would help former residents of the East Rand to sleep by playing them familiar sounds.

Excerpts included:

"Where the hell are my toothpaste? I need to brush my one tooth."
"It is your baby Johann, it's just a coincidence he look like Steve Hofmeyr."
and
"Come here I'm gonna give you a snot klap."

The ad also included testimonials from people who said that the White-Trash Noise CD was even better than Klippies at knocking them out. Listeners who ordered that day would get a bonus CD of white-trash sounds including a restraining order and a repossession man.

"The mere term white trash is a demeaning term and the use of such term is irreconcilable with our democratic and constitutional values." Complaint about Whackhead Simpson skit, to the Broadcasting Complaints Commission.

"The East Rand people have a wonderful sense of humour and the only reason why we make fun of them is because they can handle it," Jeremy Mansfield said in response to complaints about the skit. "We do not do anything with the purpose of belittling any section of the community."

Steve Hofmeyr was not impressed. "If they want to refer to this market as white trash they are making a very serious mistake," said Louis van Wyk, Hofmeyr's agent. The joke was ridiculous, he said.

Ultimately, the argument was an economic one: "Steve's Sama award for best sales proves that people like to listen to him."

"Shoppers in South Africa ... tend to sport a uniformly greasy, edgy and vacuous expression typical of veterans of savage colonic irrigation." Justin Cartwright.

Chapter 11

From padkos to Putco:
on the road

"Anyone under the age of 70 who pretends not to be interested in cars is either lying or should be pronounced brain dead." David Bullard.

South Africans love cars.

Here, you are what you drive. This is the land of G-strings and dolphins, Black Man's Wheels and the Worst4x4xfar; blue Cortinas driven by ageing East Rand mullets, Cressidas dutifully patrolling the townships, Tata ma chance, double cabs without ABS doing 180 on the road to Polokwane, SUVs that have never tackled an obstacle any more challenging than the kerb in the Hyde Park shopping centre parking lot.

Entire subcultures—hijacking syndicates, illegal street racers, car guards—have grown up around cars.

"Spartan, unsafe and slow ... the Tazz, more than any car I have ever driven, completely lacked any sense of zip, fun or soul. It handled like a pudding, its steering was vaguer than a politician on television, and it looked completely anonymous." Alexander Parker.

There are South Africans who will live in a shack so that they can afford a car they are proud to park outside the carwash at The Rock on weekends. Corrupt politicians buy Mercedes-Benzes before they invest in Hugo Boss suits and northern suburbs mansions. Even royalty—especially royalty—appreciates a fine piece of machinery. All our kings and queens—gosh, there are so many of them—require top-end SUVs for those dreadful ex-Bantustan roads. King Mswati,[1] of course, owns a Maybach; in a land with so many

---

[1] As we know, King Mswati is not a South African, for which we are very grateful. But he's the only Maybach owner we know.

goats and potholes, an absolute monarch requires the absolute certainty of ABS and comfortable suspension.

Fatalistic types who obsess about One World Government and the apocalypse worry about the arrival of black helicopters, when in fact it's the black X5s they should be looking out for.

> "They do fuck all and people throw money at them. But when I got back to South Africa I realized the market was flooded. Only we call them carguards." Chris Forrest, after watching mimes in Covent Garden and wondering whether he couldn't bring the concept back to South Africa.

We spend half our lives in our cars. And yet it's a dangerous love, this lust for these collections of metal and rubber. We hijack them, and get hijacked for them. We pass on the left, ride up the backside of the car in front, overtake a line of trucks while travelling uphill in a 1300 with aircon with a Volvo travelling in the opposite direction (fortunately, a Volvo driver can always be relied upon to stop in time).

South Africans think that 'the rules of the road' means flashing your hazards when you pass a truck driving illegally in the emergency lane. Yes, this is a place where the owner of a chain of titty bars gets trapped on a busy highway doing 243kph in his Lamborghini, boasts about it on a billboard—and half the country thinks he's a hero.[2]

> "If that bastard kills us all I'm going to fuck him up." Passenger in the back of an unroadworthy vehicle, as reported by Steven Botha.

It should come as no surprise then that South Africans experience the world's highest levels of road rage.[3] When it comes to persistent flashing of headlights and hooting, we're global leaders, though we trail the Brits in rude gestures and verbal abuse. The Greeks and Indians outperform us when it comes to drivers physically leaving their vehicles and threatening other motorists, though we head the scores again on 'threatened with a weapon'.

---

[2] Mind you, it's so difficult not to speed. When former sports and recreation MEC Mondli Gungubele was stopped for doing 182kph, he told the cops that his car tended to speed "when you are not thinking".

[3] This is according to genuine, actual research conducted globally in 2005 by Synovate.

In truth, we are defined as much by our driving styles as our accents or the clothing we wear. As James Clarke reminds readers:

> One hand on wheel, one hand out of window—that's Durban.
>
> One hand on wheel, one hand on horn—that's Soweto.
>
> One hand on wheel, one hand on newspaper, foot solidly on accelerator—that's Sandton.
>
> Both hands on wheel, eyes shut, both feet on brake, quivering in terror—that's Bloemfontein driving in Johannesburg.
>
> Both hands in air, gesturing, both feet on accelerator, head turned to talk to someone in back seat—that's Matubatuba.
>
> One hand on horn, one hand greeting, one ear on cellphone, one ear listening to loud music, foot on accelerator, eyes on female pedestrians, conversation with someone driving vehicle alongside—that's a Diepkloof taxi driver.

Opinions vary as to which drivers are in fact the worst. Tyrone August, a Capetonian, defends Joburg drivers. Capetonians who complain about them ignore the fact that Joburgers can actually drive, he maintains, "even though they often choose to ignore the most basic rules of the road for whatever reason (personality defects, death-wish, boredom etc)."

"Capetonians don't drive their cars, they aim them." Stephen Mulholland.

Bad drivers in Cape Town, on the other hand, drive badly simply because they can't drive properly. August notes the "mysterious belief" that "using an indicator somehow causes the resale value of the car to drop drastically every time it is used."

August quotes a traumatized witness as described in the following letter to a Cape Town newspaper:

> The driver was either high on drugs or blind drunk ... The driver recklessly shot at least three red lights ... before smashing, without braking, into a parked car while trying to squeeze through a gap that existed only in his mind.

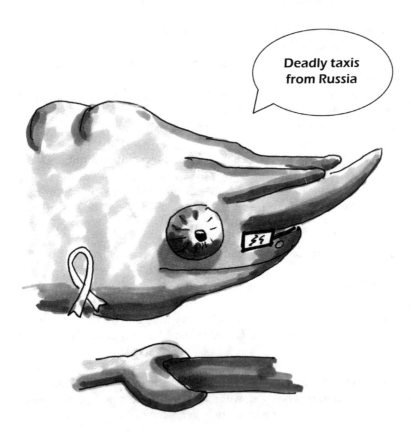

Bankrot maar windgat

Chris Roper lives in Cape Town, and he encounters bad driving every day. Take the time when he was cut off on Voortrekker Road in Bellville by a woman with big hair, driving a Jeep Cherokee. "Nothing unusual in that, you'll say. Happens all the time. Not the big hair so much, but this was Bellville after all."

> What was unusual was the number plate of the Jeep. It read: 4NIC8U2 … It says, Fornicate you too. Isn't that weird? And kind of sad? That some woman can tell me to go fuck myself, and she doesn't even know me?

"And doesn't this tell us a lot about the state of our driving culture?"

So Roper is moved to describe a type known as the Highly Defective Driver. Among his ten points, he lists:

> 6. You impatiently tailgate the car in front of you, even though there's another slow car in front holding him up. "He's just not trying hard enough to get the other car out of the way."

> 8. When you pass a car that's been holding you up for at least thirty seconds, just because the wussie driving is too scared to take the gap between two trucks that are passing on the left, you stare malevolently at the driver so that he'll realize how he's ruined your entire day. Your entire damn life, in fact.

"If you score more than zero out of ten for this, then I'm sorry to have to tell you, you ARE a Highly Defective Driver. If you score more than seven out of ten, you stand a chance of winning this year's coveted BMW Award. No, that's not a prize of a BMW X5,

BMW, according to Roper, stands for "Bastard in a Motor Vehicle".

On the other hand, you know you're from Johannesburg when you have a minimum of five worst taxi stories and the last time you drove your car without swearing at someone was when you took your driving test. You also know you are from Johannesburg when:

It takes you an hour and a half to drive 5km to work in the morning and you think "Wow, good traffic day."

You can get into a four-hour argument about the quickest way out of Sunninghill after work on a Friday, but can't find Boksburg on a map.

The last time you visited Durban, you paid more in accumulated speeding fines than you did for the entire holiday.

You greet the windscreen-washing man at the robot of Glenhove and the onramp to the M1 North by his name.

The four wheels of the Apocalypse

"If George Bush declared war on South Africa, Madiba would say to him, 'These are not weapons of mass destruction. This is a taxi driver.'" David Kau.

"Things fall apart; the centre cannot hold," wrote Thabo Mbeki's favourite poet. W. B. Yeats obviously never encountered a South African minibus taxi. Long after they have fallen apart, you will find them doing 130kph on our highways, sprinting through red robots and mounting pavements like, well, a randy pavement special. Reports of brakes held together with wire and spanners serving as a steering wheel are not exaggerated. When Zapiro illustrated a kiosk selling "taxi spare parts", he produced a drawing of wire, string, glue, masking tape and Scotch tape behind the counter.

Everybody in South Africa either hates taxis, or rides in them, or both. Emails with the subject heading *You know you're in South Africa when ...* always contain at least five points about taxis. The back page of the *Sunday Times* Metro section always asks local celebrities where they live, what car they drive, and what they think of taxi drivers. The morning traffic reports can be relied upon to produce a daily body count. "When taxi operators threaten to cause chaos if their demands are not met the obvious retort is that they are causing chaos anyway," *The Citizen* remarked in an editorial during August 2006.

Q: What do you call a TATA with brakes?
A: Customized.

Taxis of course are not the sole culprits on our roads. "Everyone deals with taxi drivers and their crap," Paul Berkowitz points out.

And everyone in Joburg deals with rude arseholes in BMWs and Mercs, self-important housewives in their husband-bought 4x4s and testosterone-powered young dooses in their Opels.

"I expect and can even understand the bad behaviour of taxi drivers. I keep a safe distance from them, fully expecting them to drive badly. I don't condone it, but I have some inkling of why they do what they do. What is the excuse of the white exec who tailgated me on the M1 today, flashing his lights because I dared to drive at only 10km over the speed limit?"

It should be acknowledged that for all their faults, taxi drivers are resourceful men of talent. "Only a taxi driver can talk on the cellphone, drive the car, sing praises to his car, collect fares from passengers and swear at them—all at the same time," observes Fred Khumalo. Only a South African taxi can transport seventeen adults, six children and a fully grown goat to the Transkei—as one attempted to do before it was impounded in Cape Town for overloading, after the traffic police noticed that the door was not closed properly because the goat's head was poking out.

Hey, he'd been doing fine until they stopped him.

"Purgatory with airbrakes." Gillian Rennie, on bus journeys.

Even though this may not have occurred to many South Africans, taxis are the closest we get to a public transport system. Talking about the London bombings, Chris Forrest reflects, "That shit would never happen here because we don't have public transport." In fact, Riaad Moosa points out, if a suicide bomber did get on board a South African train, he'd take one look and say, "Our work here is done."

When Spoornet renamed its new luxury service 'Premier Classe', the *Mail & Guardian*'s

Krisjan Lemmer had one or two sardonic observations to make. "Ja nee," Lemmer wrote, "that faux continental vowel grafted onto the end just oozes glamour."

> In fact, it's time the parastatal renamed all its services: Le Piquant Sardine for rush-hour urban lines, Le Grande Concussion for mid-morning muggings on empty township lines, and of course Le Mort Invisible, for those flung out of unmonitored Spoornet coaches.

My other personality is a doos

Only plebs are forced to use public transport. The moment South Africans can afford a car, they invest in an item that will devalue by 30% within the first year while they pay the bank lots of lovely interest for the privilege of being allowed to spend around R7 a litre for petrol just get the thing to start.

> "The [Nissan] Tiida is like the pick-up whose looks are borderline, prompting one to drink a few more to improve what you are seeing." Morgan Naidu.

Given that one has to spend all this money anyway, it is considered preferable—as noted earlier—that cars should preferably convey some kind of social status, some kind of intimation of the inner qualities of the driver. Parents in particular must give careful consideration to choosing the correct mode of transport, and that does not only apply to the importance of child locks and adequate safety features, as David Bullard reminds his readers:

> With parenthood comes a whole bunch of responsibilities, but principle among them is not making a total arse of your offspring every time you drop them off at the school gates. Let them be seen by the ten-year-old friends climbing out of Dad's Kia Magentis and they will grow up to be murderers, simple as that.

Bullard also dismisses the Toyota Camry as "the mullet of the automotive world" though it must be pointed out that this observation is not quite correct. The Chevy Lumina or the Ford Ranchero bakkie—even the Subaru Impreza WRX— is more of an automotive mullet, while the Camry is best compared less to a hairstyle than a pair of well-worn Grasshoppers in a fetching shade of baby-vomit green.

"Not for Camry drivers." Slogan, *Maverick* magazine, which touted itself as a publication for people "with brains and money".

Therefore, South Africans extrapolate your personal qualities from the kind of car you drive. Driving a Corolla is apparently proof that you are devoid of personality (though, since they have dominated car sales figures until recently, this would seem to suggest that a great many South Africans possess the emotional sensitivity of a Ukrainian abattoir worker). The decision to purchase a SsangYong or a Mahindra indicates both a lack of aesthetic sensibilities and appreciation for the importance of trade-in value, while, if you are behind the wheel of a Golf GTI or an Audi—we will leave off the BMW-bashing for now—you are almost certainly an arsehole.

Not everyone thinks that our obsession with cars as an external indication of one's internal insecurities is a good thing. 702 radio host and documentary filmmaker Redi Direko admonished the anonymous *Sowetan* columnist behind 'uPhoshozwayo', who mocked Metro FM DJ Wilson B. Nkosi for not driving a nice car. Wondering whether he could not afford a new one or Metro FM were not paying him enough "is indicative of the most impoverished and materialistic state of mind imaginable".

Is a new car the measure of a person's worth? Does the fact that he drives whatever he drives make him less of a human being? So what if he is not being paid enough? How many of our people are not paid enough, are exploited or not recognized, and yet they continue, against all odds to exert their potential? Surely that should count more than what car a person drives?

"To the writer I say, your focus on people's cars is more a reflection of your own inadequacies than Wilson's. You buy the expensive car since clearly it validates your worth as a person."

"Driving a Volvo used to be the preserve of balding men who enjoyed writing long reports and going to long meetings. If you wanted the world to know that you had sex with your wife 1.4 times a month in the missionary position, owning a Volvo was the way to do it." David Bullard.

As a consequence of our national appreciation of the horseless carriage, South Africans also have strong opinions on which cars should be driven by certain kinds of people. This is why it is important, if you are a black man who drives a nice car, to always dress well when you are behind the wheel.

While test-driving the new Porsche Cayman, Charleen Clarke stops at the bank, where she encounters two "Krugersdorp specials". They were rendered distinctive by their hairstyles, one shaved flat, one mullet.

"You check, there is a chick driving that Porsche. What a waste," plateau head remarks to mullet.

Mullet man asks her about the transmission.

"Superb," Clarke tells him. "Way better than the BMW M6 ... The M6's gearbox is a shocker; it's as smooth as a potholed South African road."

"What? That's complete bullshit. The M6's box is way better," announces mullet man, who hasn't actually driven either vehicle. "Typical woman; you know nothing about cars."

"I drive a black Citroen C2—not exactly predator material, more like a bushbaby with a slight cold." Oliver Roberts disagrees with a UK-based feng shui expert who argues that your car is a predatory tiger which should be faced away from the home.

Basic rules for driving in Gauteng

1. Indicators will give away your next move. A real Gauteng motorist never uses them.

2. Under no circumstance should you leave a safe distance between you and the car in front of you, or the space will be filled by two Golfs, a BMW and a Getz, putting you in an even more dangerous situation.

3. The faster you drive through a red light, the smaller the chance you have of getting hit.

4. Never, ever come to a complete stop at a stop sign. No one expects it and it will only result in you being rear-ended.

5. Braking is to be done as hard and late as possible to ensure that your ABS kicks in, giving you a nice, relaxing foot massage as the brake pedal pulsates. For those of you without ABS, it's a chance to stretch your legs.

6. Never pass on the right when you can pass on the left. It's a good way to check if the people entering the highway are awake.

7. Speed limits are arbitrary figures, given only as a guideline. They are especially not applicable in Gauteng during rush hour. That's why it's called 'rush hour'.

8. Just because you're in the right lane and have no room to speed up or move over doesn't mean that the double cab driver flashing his high beams behind you doesn't expect you to move over immediately. For fuck's sake, what are you waiting for?

9. Remember that the goal of every Gauteng driver is to get there first by whatever means necessary.

10. On average, at least three cars can still go through an intersection after the light has turned red. It's people not adhering to this basic principle that cause the big traffic jams during rush hour.

Chapter 12

Affirmative shopping:
crime

Teenager A: "You don't sound scared."
Teenager B: "I'm from Johannesburg."
Scene in a derelict desert hotel in the Australian horror movie *Reeker*.

Crime keeps many South Africans awake at night, and not just because of the gunshots being fired in the street outside.

"It's very big here," Mark Banks says of crime. "You get to drive around Sandton—that's Jo'burg's crime resort. Even without a guide, the hijackers come right up to the window. And the gun held to your head is full of live ammunition. I've only been hijacked five times."

"This is not the picture we expected the visitors to take back to their country. It leaves a scar on the image of not only the city, but also the country. It is shocking," said a witness to an incident in which a busload of German travel agents was robbed at gunpoint in Khayelitsha. The travel agents had been brought to Cape Town as part of an initiative to encourage tourism to South Africa and were left "severely traumatized" according to reports.

It is distressing when robbers are so short-sighted. As a result of their actions, the travel agents would discourage other Germans from visiting South Africa. Thus they were impacting on their long term livelihood for short-term gain. Fewer German tourists to rob, less income in the future. Clearly they do not understand the concept of sustainability.

"What are you still doing there? Do you carry a gun? Isn't everyone leaving?" Johannesburg-born Toronto resident Susan Saffer, to South African resident Josef Talotta.

In South Africa, as we know, criminals are active in every sector of the economy. Now they are even releasing CDs from jail. Kwaito singer Sgonondo, in Johannesburg Central Prison for unspecified crimes, showed up at the launch of his debut CD accompanied by a prison warder. The latter had to go up on stage with him and unlock his handcuffs so that he could perform his hit single *AmaDragon*.

He enjoyed his night of freedom so much that he had to be dragged off stage by a policeman.

> "The slogan 'shop till you drop', in South Africa means 'drop while shopping to avoid being hit by bullets in shopping malls'." Letter to *The Citizen*.

"I know very few black male South Africans my age who were not, at one stage or another, pickpockets or knife-wielding muggers," writes Fred Khumalo, who himself smoked dagga and became involved in pickpocketing as a teenager. Criminal activity, driven by desperation and a lack of other suitable role models, was endemic to township life. Petty crime delivered the extra money needed to entertain girls, Khumalo remembers, and it also gave one a sense of belonging.

Later, Khumalo was himself a victim of the kind of people he'd once associated with, waking one night to find burglars in his bedroom. John Matshikiza also experienced crime first hand. "Violence and violation have transformed themselves into a beast of their own making, operating, like Frankenstein's monster, independently of the mad scientists who brought them into being," he wrote in 2004.

> "In the townships, housing, cars, cellphones and even life itself come cheap." John Matshikiza.

In the mid-1990s, Sy Makaringe reports, the Azanian Youth Organization, Azayo, became frustrated with rising levels of crime in the townships. So they issued a bumper sticker in tsotsitaal, which read: "*Asispini elokishini. Asikhawati udarkie*" which means, "We don't operate in the township. We don't target blacks".

Judging by the experiences of Khumalo, Matshikiza, and others, it doesn't seem like this was a campaign that made much of an impact.

"Cops put up with a lot of shit!" *Daily Sun* headline, reporting on the case of a Bushbuckridge man who attempted to evade arrest by jumping into a pit, then defecating and smearing himself with his own faeces. The Mopani police rinsed him off and arrested him anyway. Captain Manno Sadike explained, "We can't leave a suspect just because he smeared himself with faeces. We are not scared of any smell and will arrest any suspect under any circumstances."

Blue-faced whingers

On a visit to Malawi, Charles Nqakula was introduced to a man described as the Minister of the Navy. Our man inquired why Malawi, a landlocked country, needed a navy.

"Well, why not," replied the Malawian. "Aren't you South Africa's minister of Safety and Security?"

It was one fine winter's day that our Minister of Safety and Security, Charles Nqakula opened his mouth and, very carefully, inserted both neatly shod feet into it.

"They can continue to whinge until they're blue in the face," he said, referring to a couple of DA MPs, "be as negative as they want to, or they can simply leave this country so that all of the peace-loving South Africans, good South African people, who want to make this a successful country, can continue with their work."

Somewhat predictably, howls of outrage greeted remarks that were really quite breathtaking in their insensitivity, not just to the feelings of people who had fallen victim to the crime tsunami, but the increasing frustration of the national mood. Letters from *gatvol* South Africans—blue in the face and otherwise—flooded editors' desks across the country. Ordinary people suggested that the minister should try surviving in South Africa without his bodyguards; Tony Leon said that Nqakula should be fired. "Whenever the issue of crime is raised, you get the sycophantic acolytes who unflinchingly serve at the infallible ANC altar questioning the origins of these accusations of government inefficiency," complained Charles Ash of Bruin-ou.com.

"I think the Minister must learn to be a Leader not a Boss, as he is doing. My car was stolen last year, so how should I stop moaning, because now I have to walk to go to work after my hard work to buy one? This is a bad experience. He must forget about these wrong stats and concentrate on action, and lead South Africa to success. Presently he is too much relaxed." Msindo Nkonyane.

Razor wire is so last season, darling

Many South Africans invest in a guard dog, the purpose of which is to scare off the tsotsis lurking outside. W. H. See argues that such dogs should be entitled to counselling, especially when you consider that they have "bite pressure that makes a Great White Shark look like a clothes peg, and bladders swollen with foul-smelling urine that is routinely discharged against the furniture."

He likens his dog, a Belgian Shepherd, to "an impressionable adolescent who has seen too many Quentin Tarantino movies and thinks entertainment equals gratuitous violence. Put him in with your sheep and they will rapidly become mutton."

"I'm so popular with the security guards at Pick 'n Pay that my criminal white friends have started using me as a decoy." Kagiso Lediga.

Other South Africans employ the services of a security guard. Fred Khumalo advises against forcing the guard—who, you will remember from chapter 2, is likely to be a Zulu—to speak English. "A security guard who is inarticulate in English is a better proposition because he will not wax lyrical about the intricacies of the layout of the house, and the nooks and crannies that the robber will have to negotiate to get to valuable goods.

"Seriously, don't force these security guards to speak impeccable English, otherwise they will spend time asking themselves questions such as 'to be or not to be?' while the robbers are busy helping themselves to the employer's belongings."

You know you are in South Africa when the police are the first on the scene for most major crimes, without being called.

Sometimes, one or two of our criminals get arrested, convicted and sent to jail—even said jail is too soft, as a Togolese national who had spent six years behind bars wrote from Malmesbury New Prison to *You* magazine:

It's time the SA government treated prisoners the Togolese way: no food, no medical attention, no education, no electrical appliances. That's the solution to the overcrowding problem.

Steven Botha might disagree with him. "This is Shit Street, and all the robots are red," he wrote of his experiences in a South African jail.

Take the "purplish" coffee, for instance, which had "what looked like yellow spitballs floating in it, connected by a web of blurry tendrils. It was sufficient to rob even a starving man of his appetite."

"Razor wire and rottweilers are passé. It is time to mutilate." Earl Spencer, brother of Princess Diana, in a controversial interview in *Harpers & Queen*.

Many South Africans are starting to think that jail is too good for our criminals, and that other ways and means must be found to make them mend their ways. Many others sign petitions calling for the reintroduction of the death penalty—how disappointed they must have been to read the recent "Tokyo calls for gallows restoration" headlines, only to discover that Tokyo Sexwale was literally calling for a set of gallows at Pretoria Central Prison to be restored as an historical artifact rather than solving the crime problem—while still others take on a more hands-on approach.

David Bullard suggests a suitable punishment— "a uniquely South African answer to a uniquely South African problem" —for rapists and murderers.

Drop convicted criminals in the Kruger Park about 20km from the nearest camp on a night with no moon. If they survive until morning then they go free.

"The way things are going, the Mafia would be advised to hurry up while there is still something to steal." Phillip van Niekerk.

You know you're in South Africa when ...

... the person in front of you in traffic this morning was hijacked and you got irritated because you missed the traffic light.

... while waiting at the ATM the bank is robbed by armed gunmen, but you'll be damned if you're going to lose your place in the queue.

... you're suspicious of strangers who are nice to you.

... you have more barbed wire around your home than Diepkloof Prison.

... your electric fence could stun an elephant.

... even the police pause momentarily at a red light before driving on late at night, so as to avoid being victims of hijacking.

... the signs at your local intersection read 'Stop' and '! Smash and grab hotspot'.

... every time you find your car parked where you left it you are genuinely surprised.

Chapter 13

The nine circles of hell:
from Home Affairs to Hellkom

"You know you are in South Africa when you can experience kak service in eleven official languages."

A man dies and goes to hell, or so the story goes.

There he finds that there is a different hell for each country. He goes first to the German hell and asks, "What do they do here?" He is told, "First they put you in an electric chair for an hour. Then they lay you on a bed of nails for another hour. Then the German devil comes in and whips you for the rest of the day." The man does not like the sound of that at all, so he moves on. He investigates the American hell as well as the Russian hell and many more. He discovers that they are all more or less the same as the German hell.

Then he comes to the South African hell and finds that there is a very long line of people waiting to get in. Amazed, he asks the person in front of him, "What do they do here?"

"First they put you in an electric chair for an hour," explains the man. "Then they lay you on a bed of nails for another hour. Then the South Africa devil comes in and whips you for the rest of the day."

"But that is exactly the same as all the other hells! Why are there so many people waiting to get in?"

"Because," the man tells him, "there is never any electricity, so the electric chair does not work, someone stole all the nails, and the devil used to be a public servant, so he comes in, punches his time-card, shows his face around for five minutes and then goes back home."

Many South Africans have already, in fact, experienced hell. It is otherwise known as Home Affairs. We know that many transactions are entered into with the help of the persuasive end of the barrel of a gun, but there can't be too many other places on the planet where just getting an identity document requires that one resort to violence.

> Anvaise Anmeri Letopstrepie Opi. Name in an identity document belonging to a young Afrikaans woman who should have known better than to issue instructions for the accent on the 'i' in Anmeri on her application form.

Take poor Kabelo Thibedi. After visiting Home Affairs for the twentieth time to no avail, unable to open a bank account or start a business, the young Sowetan snapped. He produced a toy gun and took a supervisor hostage, demanding his ID book. *Citizen* readers generally don't cheer for young black men who use weapons—even fake ones—to commit crimes, but they hailed him as a national hero.

In fact, Thibedi only did what many of us have only fantasized about.

Thibedi noted that Home Affairs was only helping him because of the gun. "These people, they have bad manners, they don't treat us well here." Thibedi had first applied for an ID book in 2003. "I am sick and tired of these people," he said. "These people in Home Affairs are corrupt, they give our IDs to foreigners, and then they are rude to us."

"I want it today, now, now, now."

> "South Africa couldn't organize a bonk in a brothel." Gwen Gill.

At least Thibedi was still officially alive. For five months, the unfortunate Joseph Mogoe was dead man walking, after Home Affairs declared him deceased. The story incensed one *Sowetan* reader, who wrote, "His would be a fitting story in a disorganized society like Iraq or Zimbabwe, but not here."

"Perhaps your fat-cats are sitting in some high-rise building enjoying their gravy-train ride which, in any event, is fuelled by the efforts of working-class people like Mogoe."

The *Mail & Guardian*'s Krisjan Lemmer was interested to see that "improbably inept" Home Affairs Department, known principally for its "wholesale cocking up of every document in its possession", had taken to advertising itself on television. The campaign focused on the new Department motto: 'Caring, compassionate and responsive'.

"If only they had just opted for 'Competent'."

"As useful as clogged toilets in a dysentery ward." David Isaacson, on some of the South African bureaucrats he has encountered.

Telkom

Hellkom.co.za. Anti-Telkom website.

"I want to talk face to face with Telkom," said Meisie Thulane, a pensioner from a village in Thulane. "I want to tell them that they are killing us, their prices are sick."

Hatred of Telkom is a popular dinner party conversation topic. "Here's why Telkom should be charging us less," writes Renée Bonorchis of *Business Report*. "And it has nothing to do with complex bundles of products, or arpus, warpus or snarfus."

It has to do with the fact that Telkom's service levels are lousy … after a year of agonizingly awful, inefficient, ridiculously bad service, I've got to say something … So here's what I say to Telkom: You have a very pretty share price and very lovely profits. But your service levels are not worth 2c and I'm soon going to rip your phone out of the wall and invite my friends to a phone-stomping party. In fact, maybe we'll braai it.

"Telkom is a fiasco hidden inside a disaster enveloped in a national disgrace wrapped inside Ivy Matsepe-Casaburri," said Robert Kirby. "The first law of the Telkom Mission states: If Telkom fucks up, the customer must hurt."

"Do you work for Telkom? Cos it's taking a long time to get through." Conrad Koch.

After digging to a depth of 100m last year, Russian scientists found traces of copper wiring dating back 1,000 years, and came to the conclusion that their ancestors already had a telephone network one thousand years ago.
So as not to be outdone, in the weeks that followed, American scientists dug 200m, and an article in the US newspapers read: "US scientists have found traces of 2,000-year-old optical fibres, and have concluded that their ancestors already had

advanced high-tech digital telephones 1,000 years earlier than the Russians."
One week later, the South African press reported the following: "After digging as deep as 500m, SA scientists have found absolutely nothing. The government has concluded that 5,000 years ago, their ancestors were already using mobile phones due to cable theft problems."

Spietkops

"Don't knock the Metro police. They're the best that money can buy." SMS to 702's John Robbie show.

Nobody likes traffic cops. They were the butt of Leon Schuster jokes during the 1980s, and now Wayne Minnaar and his merry men are the favourite subject of writers of letters to *The Citizen*—even more popular than Graeme Smith or Jake White. "After the various responses from Wayne Minnaar regarding his bad cops (as in *vrot*), I have come to the conclusion that he is a total idiot and measures the public by his intellect," is a typical example of a *Citizen* Metro Cops missive.

"Please motorists, let the Metro police sleep. We are much safer then," is another.

The situation is no different in Cape Town. "Traffic officials," muses Tyrone August, "seem to be out in full force only when the Stormers are playing at Newlands, or when some pop diva is performing at the Bellville Velodrome."

Or else they prowl around fearlessly in the early hours of the morning on Beach Road on the Atlantic Seaboard (I once got a fine at about 3 or 4am for not displaying a vehicle registration disc. It was, in a reckless act of endangering public safety, still tucked away in the cubbyhole.)

"As long as we define speed as an offence, we will continue to see a perfectly usable police car parked by the side of the road and used as a sofa." Sabelo Ndabazindile.

The National Carrier Bag

SAA, the national airline, is known for taking lots of money from passengers and giving it to its CEOs, which tend either to be rich Americans or local empowerment magnates who express their belief in the spirit of Proudly South African by buying apartments in the South of France. Despite its financial woes, the airline has also been running a charity for years, where valuables belonging to their passengers are redistributed to the underpaid workers lined up along the conveyer belts down below—though perhaps it is Acsa and the baggage handling contractors that must take the credit for what is perhaps South Africa's most successful single ongoing donations programme.

SAA also have a frequent flyer programme, which they have given the rather tongue-in-cheek name of Voyager. Very few Voyager members will ever move from their desks where they sit, listening on the phone to the holding tune while they wait for somebody at the call centre to talk to them—let alone getting onto a plane to fly to a place you would be inclined to visit.

"SAA stands for 'Standards Aren't Applied'." Caroline Hurry.

Caroline Hurry, a journalist with *The Saturday Star* Travel supplement, noted with disbelief that the piles of complaint letters about SAA's appalling service merely "disappointed" SAA management.

"What were they expecting? Hugs and kisses? The Easter Bunny?"

"Truth is, it will take more than sweet-smelling, self-congratulatory advertorials to disguise the noxious exhalations rising from the SAA swamp."

Hurry also wondered whether SAA CEO Khaya Ngqula "gives a continental breakfast. How could the lowing of cattle class possibly have reached his ears over the rat-rat-rat of his helicopter rotors?"

It can't be easy to be an SAA staffer with all this criticism flying around. Sometimes they hit back. When a businessman wrote to *The Saturday Star* to complain that SAA flight attendants were too fat, Mpho wrote back "Mr. Hyett, you have some nerve to call SAA flight attendants 'not physically suited to the job and being too big and fat'. I sincerely hope that you have a fabulous 'cover of *Men's Health*' magazine type of body and look so smouldering that all women and men stare each time you walk by … Before I became your 'flying maid', I was a financial consultant and I probably used to scrutinize your financial accounts and call you each time you were way over your overdraft limit."

Ek'sdom

Jokes about not having electricity stopped becoming funny at the beginning of 2006, when rolling blackouts plagued Cape Town and plunged the city into more chaos than it usually experiences. In the interests of energy efficiency, a Cape Town theatre company, the Independent Armchair Theatre, introduced The Eskom Sessions, which were unplugged.

"POWER STRUGGLE: Efforts to get the Koeberg power station back on line."
Hogarth, *Sunday Times.*

After the problems at Koeberg and the bolt from the blue, people started making cynical remarks about the Prince of Darkness. There was the Eskom logo, tweaked to read "Ek'sdom" and the Koeberg staff identity badge featuring the face of the world's most famous nuclear plant worker, Homer Simpson. Even Guinness got in on the act, playing up the fact that the white heads of its beer would show up in the dark.

"They don't need anyone to sabotage them, they're apparently highly capable of doing the job themselves," Chris Roper reflected in the wake of Alec Erwin's use of the S-word.

"We are tired of prepaid water, prepaid phone, prepaid electricity, prepaid education, prepaid going to the toilet, prepaid everything! We are being robbed."
An Orlando, Soweto community member summing up feelings about services.

The Big Four

The Big Four are not to be confused with the Big Five, though in fairness it should be acknowledged that they do keep a great many elephant, rhino, lion, buffalo and leopard in their vaults. For one thing, tourists do not come to see the Big Four. Where they come from, banks don't charge you for the privilege of keeping your money for you.

Just as South Africans hate government bureaucracy, Telkom, and traffic cops, so they hate their banks. Bank-bashing is a national sport, and South Africans like to fantasize about having banks like the ones overseas. Most of them though, are resigned to their fate. Moans one anonymous poster on the Marketingweb site, "Banks have been ripping their clients in this country for too long, they are all crap—I suppose it is only the degree of crapness that varies!" Another wails:

Where do you go? Stranded? Worst National? Deadbank? PLEASE COME AND SAVE US RICHARD BRANSON. SA banks suck.

At least First National Bank has a sense of humour. Ask an FNB employee why they use a thorn tree in the logo, and chances are they will tell you it is because the place is full of pricks. When Laugh It Off produced a parody of their logo with the name 'First National Bankie' they bought a couple of hundred T-shirts. Standard Bank was not impressed with the T-shirt that mocked them: it featured the words 'Standard Wank', with the familiar flag turned into a hand holding onto an erect penis. Naturally the payoff line 'Simpler. Better. Faster' became 'Harder. Deeper. Longer'.

Markas Ferreira, a concerned member of the South African public, sent the following to the *Sunday Times* in the wake of the new Absa campaign:

> MY bank is not MY friend. MY bank takes MY money. MY bank charges me for taking MY money. MY bank uses MY money to make money for itself, not for me. MY bank charges me for taking MY money back. MY bank charges me for giving MY money to someone else. MY bank charges me if I want to know where MY money is. MY bank charges me when I want to know how much of MY money MY bank holds. MY bank is one of the richest companies in SA because of MY money. MY money doesn't make me rich; MY bank doesn't make me rich; MY money makes MY bank rich. MY bank is not MY friend. I can choose MY friends. MY friends don't rob me at the end of every month.

Krisjan Lemmer noticed that FICA, the Financial Intelligence Centre Act—which can freeze your accounts if you don't rock up at your bank to prove you are who you say you are—is a rude word, not just in all eleven official languages of South Africa, but in Italian too. *Fico* is the Italian for fig. "The feminine form of the word, *fica*, denotes a fig-shaped part of a woman, and is considered a dirty word."

> "Have you done FICA?" the woman in the bank asks Mark Banks.
> "I may have … this morning," he says.

In conclusion, it is worth mentioning the possibility that Home Affairs and its fellow diabolical circles are part of an elaborate nation-building strategy orchestrated by the Presidency. The thinking is that by constructing a mutual enemy within the borders of the country, internal differences of class, politics and culture will pale into insignificance. It's the Rainbow Nation again, people—and it's standing in a queue.

"In our Godless world, it's good to know that people still perform acts of blind faith. Like sending valuables through the Post Office." Krisjan Lemmer, *Mail & Guardian*.

Chapter 14

Human bonsai:
celebrities and TV personalities

In South Africa, it does not take much to become a celebrity or, worse, a "personality". Inscribed on the eternal Moebius strip, that modern media machine, celebrities are known simply for being known. Inform viewers of SABC3 that coming up is *Two and a Half Men* followed by *Will and Grace* and next thing you're subjecting yourself to seaweed wraps and mango facials on *Top Billing* (no fat or ugly people allowed) and giving interviews about your shopping habits to the Clicks Clubcard magazine.

> "Two lipless leprechauns with hard-ons for poverty." Tom Eaton on Bono and Bob Geldof. Global celebrities tend to want to save the world. Fortunately, local celebrities restrict their ambitions to Reach for a Dream parties at their local Wimpy.

Like cattle being dipped in the pesticide of manufactured public opinion, celebrities must file through the TV studios of the land, perching on sofas and answering questions about How they Got Started from Paul Viv or Somizi Mhlongo or Dali Tambo. (The latter was once memorably referred to as The Hoarse Whisperer by Darrel Bristow-Bovey, who also noted that even Tony Sanderson swaddled himself "with a tatty bathrobe of tired old has-beens in the faint hope that they'll make him look good".)

> "What! Why can't you bring pots in from South Africa? What's wrong with South African pots?" 2002 Miss South Africa and part-time rocket scientist Cindy Nel, interviewing a 2003 entrant who had said that she was an entrepreneur and sold pots made in Venda.

Andrew Molefe describes those who call themselves celebrities as "mental midgets", "intellectual dwarfs" and "human bonsai":

Celebrities ... need public adulation like the rest of us need air. They rely on the great unwashed to love and cherish them. If their supply of veneration is cut, they wither and die.

Yet celebrities, no matter how minor, always seem to cause excitement wherever they go. Former radio DJ Ernest Pillay found himself at the centre of a catfight at the Randburg club where, according to the *Sunday World*, he had been "enjoying a veritable feast of delights". Arriving at the club with a woman in tow, he was accosted by one of his other lovers.

"Oh, now you don't know me, but last week at my place you failed to shag me because your penis is too small and you came too quickly," yelled the woman, one Nomandla Kepyi. She also wondered how Pillay's wife was coping with such a small penis, and threatened to reveal all to her.

"He was shouting 'fuck you, fuck you,'" Kepyi explained afterwards. "It got me angry and I shouted back, 'Shut up or else I will cut you and your small-man syndrome down to size.'"

The other woman then apparently ran to join her friends, who started to "caterwaul". "They behaved like township girls who were too excited to be with a celebrity," said Kepyi.

Pillay denied everything. "That stage of ladies fighting for me has passed a long time ago, while I was still a DJ. Now I am a happily married person," he said.

"I know—you're Michael Jackson." Namibian concierge to a South African musician who had asked her "Don't you know who I am?"

"Vuyo on air has the mildly engaging presence of a teddy bear ... Nothing is ever at risk in his bland, smiling voice." John Matshikiza, who found that the "sheer numbing mediocrity" of Vuyo's show triggered road rage.

"Why doesn't Gareth Cliff jump off his name?" Conrad Koch.

Steve Hasselhoffmeyr

"When I listen to Boeremusiek, I think, at least the Nazis had Wagner." Ian Fraser.

Historically, South African music has confused many observers, who do not understand its reason for existence. For instance, Pikes, who posts on Africans.co.za, is mystified by P. J. Powers:

I'm hoping that some day, as I travel along life's path, I'll happen across a wise old man, who will explain to me, for once and for all, how the fuck P. J. Powers managed to cling onto her fame for so long.

Generally, however, the most misunderstood celebrities are Afrikaans pop singers, mainly because nobody can understand why, in fact, they are celebrated. Any culture that can produce outfits like Die Campbells or Thys die Bosveld Klong is, on the surface of it, headed for very deep *kak*, but South Africa has always specialized in miracles, so anything is possible.

"For every person you pass this on to, Jurie Els's singing career shortens by one hour." Viral email.

Steve Hofmeyr is, if nothing else, the most mis-spelled celebrity in South Africa. It's his special combination of enormous success, staggering naffness and ability to father entire tribes that has turned him into the kind of celebrity who becomes his own punchline. "I was driving around town and I saw a *Beeld* poster with the headline '*Die Pous is Dood*'," Darren Simpson recalls. "And I thought, fuck me, who killed Steve Hofmeyr?"

"Chester—he's my BEE partner, but he's kept me as a consultant" says Conrad Koch—suggests playing golf with Steve. "What's his handicap?" asks Koch. Chester quips, "He's an ugly Dutchman with a *kak* haircut."

"A white-bread mullet in a puffer jacket and platform takkies." Tom Eaton on Steve Hofmeyr.

The Art of the South African Insult

One day, academics will write doctoral theses deconstructing the significance of Steve Hofmeyr to Afrikaner culture in particular and South African culture in general. They will give their work titles like *Pampoen: liminality, communitas and gendered identities in sokkiejol treffers* and conclude that Steve, a proxy for the devastating loss of political power, represents a yearning to return to hegemony.

It has of course occurred to many South Africans that Steve is our equivalent of The Hoff. One MarkB, unsung literary hero of the internet, offers the following thoughts on Steve Hofmeyr:

Steve Hofmeyr once sakkied with ten poppies at once.
Steve Hofmeyr braais with his fingers.
Steve Hofmeyr doesn't support the Bulls, the Bulls support Steve Hofmeyr.
When Steve Hofmeyr stares at raw meat it turns to biltong.
Morkels gives Steve Hofmeyr any guarantee he wants.
Steve Hofmeyr repossessed Bob Mugabe's farm.
Not even Chuck Norris gets as many father's day cards as Steve Hofmeyr.
The 'National Party' is actually a term to describe Steve Hofmeyr's birthday celebration.
Steve Hofmeyr cannot count. He doesn't need to.
Steve Hofmeyr is the only man alive to turn down Patricia Lewis.
When Steve Hofmeyr goes to Pick 'n Pay he just picks.

"Apartheid may have been the worst thing in South Africa in the 1970s, but Four Jacks and a Jill were a pretty close second." Pikes, Africans.co.za, who felt that their albums only sold to the "culturally destitute".

The Number 1 Pop Pop

"Everything in life is about money." Amor Vittone.

If Steve Hofmeyr is the undisputed king of uncool in South Africa, then Patricia Lewis and Amor Vittone are his consorts.

"Joost and Amor truly are the Posh and Becks of South Africa," says the editor of *Huisgenoot* and *You*, "not only in the Afrikaans market, but also in the English."

"I think a lot of people see me as a bubbly, kind of out-there kind of chick with probably no substance really," Amor admitted to the *Sunday Times*. "When I was little I always used to visualize how I would sign CDs and perform. I used to see it in my mind. I used to talk it through and pray about it."

"The preceding statements tend to reveal much about Vittone, an individual indentured to the celebrity lifestyle yet also fully in awe of the cross," wrote Sean O'Toole, who interviewed her.

Amor had started an historical celebrity spat when she criticized her chief rival for Number 1 Pop *Pop*, Patricia Lewis, and her SABC2 programme *Blonde Ambisie*. Lewis responded in the most public of all fora, in the pages of *Huisgenoot*.

"Critics accuse both," noted O'Toole, "of a sycophantic obsession with omnipotence in the Afrikaans entertainment market, and have labelled them 'slashers'—for the forward slash inserted between their multiple job titles."

Amor tried to prevent the newspaper from publishing the article, which also revealed that Nelson Mandela is apparently a fan (what can we say; Madiba also said that meeting the Spice Girls was the greatest day of his life) and that she enjoys farting loudly while on magazine shoots, thus ensuring that readers who otherwise had no interest in her made sure they read the article.

> "When is she going to realize that no one cares about her life? She should just get on with her 'singing career' and not subject us to this mindless drivel and attention-seeking." *You* reader, on Amor Vittone.

Patricia, meanwhile, had troubles of her own. "This was not just a catfight with market rival Amor Vittone," reported Jean Barker. "Nor just news that she was pregnant and capable of breeding, just like a human. It was bigger even than her hair. Our Patricia had been in a 'porn' flick."

> "Do bad acting, terrible hair, screechingly bright make-up and lousy taste in music make you a proper porn star?" Jean Barker on Patricia Lewis.

The movie, released in 1996, entitled *Dark desires: The other side of the mirror*, was about a bisexual stripper who seduced rich men in order to blackmail them. Plot keywords apparently included bisexual; blackmail; erotica; lesbian scene; lesbian; mirror; nudity; sex; stripper.

Die Son featured stills from the movie alongside the headline *"Dit is Patricia se boobs"*. As if that wasn't enough, Jurie Els also attacked Patricia, saying that her music had become "cheap and voluptuous".

> "Being called South Africa's Barbie doll, gosh, I take it as a compliment, because she's supposed to be the perfect woman." Patricia Lewis.

What not to wear

One of the major disadvantages of being a celebrity is that gossip columnists comment on the size of your bum. Poor ex-Miss South Africa Claudia Henkel was the subject of some particularly catty remarks by Lesley Mofokeng:

> The big gossip was Claudia Henkel's expanding behind—the famous Jennifer Lopez butt had nothing on what we saw on Friday night. She has become a designer's nightmare, with her thunder thighs and her bulging bod.

Some celebrities are honest about their faults. "I have enough chins to cover the width of the N1, so they must take some away," said Nataniël. He also added that if he undressed on stage, he would wear fishnet stockings and stiletto heels— "people may think that's camp, but just think, they go nicely with the G-string."

One shudders to think what society maven Gwen Gill would say about that. Socialites and celebrities alike lie awake at night fretting about what devastating indictments Gwen will pass upon their outfits. Incidentally, both Amor and Patricia made her list of the worst-dressed women of 2005. Amor is criticized for looking too low-class:

> Anyone who buys Louis Vuitton in anything but the original brown is missing a taste gene. Those denims and whites look so Jerry Springer.

While Patricia hardly fares any better:

> It would be lovely to dress "late teenage" forever, like singer Patricia Lewis, but studded and fringed denims have a shelf life and hers have passed it.

Pop Idols winner, Karen "sadly has as much of a pop idol look as Minister Nkosazana Dlamini-Zuma." Babalwa Mneno also makes the list: "less," says Gwen, "is still less."

> "It's a while since someone looked terrible at the Oscars. This year Charlize, bless her, probably took the worst-dressed award with her poppie-rok fit for Alberton Höerskool's Matric dance, her teased hair and outsized shoulder bow that was large enough to obliterate the view of anyone behind her on the red carpet." Jenny Ridyard.

Gwen even pays attention to what non-celebrities are wearing. Jonny Steinberg might have won lots of awards for his books, but he doesn't impress South Africa's cattiest granny, who pronounces him "South Africa's answer to the British anorak—grey, nerdish and dull."

Society hairdresser David Gilson "obviously reckons he's the hottest dresser in town."

> Sorry bru, you just look like a cross between Dion Chang on a bad day and an overdressed peacock.

Artist Beezy Bailey "uses all that hogwash about 'I'm wearing my grandfather's old suit' to cover up his execrable taste in clothes whose colour resembles that of a used Pampers."

> "Bag lady and brilliant writer Lin Sampson is to stylishness what cricketer André

Nel is to rocket science." Gwen Gill on Lin Sampson.

"Far be it from me to criticize a social columnist who is brave enough to have a Prince Valiant hairstyle and go out wearing a polyester bedspread and gold takkies." Lin Sampson on Gwen Gill.

Jou Maas

Deon Maas, judge on Afrikaans *Idols*, is South Africa's very own Simon Cowell.

"Were your balls cut off?" Maas said to a two-metre-tall guy from Bloemfontein "who spoke like Barry White but sang like Aziz Pahad," according to Charles Leonard, who witnessed the scene. The guy responded by threatening to beat Maas up until the show's executive producer told him to go home because "*jy sing kak*".

"Actually, I'm doing those people [who can't sing] a favour because I'm preventing them from making arseholes of themselves in future," Maas said. "I'm not very in favour of fat people. I also don't like ugly people much."

Maas's victims appeared not to see things this way. "Deon Maas! Fuck him! He's a fucking arsehole! I'll go on with my life!" —a "gel-head" who was "waving his arms and shaking his head left to right like an agitated parakeet". "Look, I'm a churchgoer," said another, "and I don't normally talk like this, but Deon Maas *se gat*."

"Sista, you were paid to entertain people, not rehearse some of your favourite crap." Shwashwi column, *Sunday World*, commenting on a performance by Thandiswa Mzwai.

When news of *Idols* judge Randall Abrahams' marriage leaked out, the *Sunday Times* expressed surprise. "We at the *Sunday Times* are ... flummoxed as to what attracted the new Mrs. Abrahams to one of the biggest mamparas on South African television." Furious at being kept away from proceedings by gun-toting bodyguards, the paper suggested spitefully that perhaps the reason the name of the bride was kept so secret was because she was in fact a groom. "The seemingly classy affair also had an air of kitsch to it," the paper added bitchily. Abrahams thus became the paper's first-ever front page mampara.

"Former *Idols* winner Anke: Further devastating proof of Mara Louw's eye for the ordinary; she's still so Free State." Gwen Gill.

Perhaps it is a sign of the normalization of our society that many South Africans care far more about the outcome of reality shows than they do about elections. In fact, democracy would probably work far better if we stuck Tony, Patricia, Thabo, Phumzile and Jacob on a desert island and let them slug it out for rights to the immunity idol. Call it *Survivor Parliament*. Alternatively, make them belt out Roberta Flack numbers or do the Cha Cha and eliminate them week by week. Whether singing or dancing, the competition would be relatively straightforward, as most participants would have at least one foot in their mouths at any given moment.

"A pretentious ponce with a great voice and nothing much else." Craig Canavan on Chris Chameleon.

Cheerleader and professional socialite Babalwa Mneno intimated that black viewers had failed to vote for her during *Strictly Come Dancing*, causing complaints of racism. "I can give her a couple of clues," said Matebello Motloung, who wrote that she had always liked Mneno's style and elegance. "Unlike the other contestants—black and white—Ms. Mneno looked straight-up trashy."

That cheap-looking silver dress she was wearing looked like she had bought it at some flea market in one of the cities renowned for their sex tourism. As if that's not enough, she had to couple it with those hideous fake goldish-brown locks and green (or was it grey?) contact lenses, making her look worse than a R20-a-night Hillbrow hooker on a bad Friday evening.

"And she expected me, the viewer, to vote for that?! I don't think so."

Later, readers of *The Citizen* complained that the competition had been rigged to ensure that a black couple got through. "We all know that this so-called black economic empowerment is an embarrassment to the blacks of the world, as they are getting to the top not through performance, but through skin colour," opined Anton of Springs, who also declared:

A fish has more personality than Mark.

"I can't decide which constitutes the greater waste of column centimetres: the subject herself or Ryan Fortune's tumescent twitterings." Response to an interview with Caprice Bourret, letter to *Sunday Times* Lifestyle.

Heading

The local edition of *Survivor* involved sending to send a group of people to Panama to see who could outwit, outplay and outlast everyone else. It all seemed rather unnecessary when half the country plays that game every day of their lives, but nobody said the world had to make sense.

The announcement of the tribesmates was greeted with howls of outrage. The Archers Aqua man was there, for goodness' sake! "You must be fucking kidding me!" snorted one fan. "I would seriously consider having a face/chest/ass lift before I next enter." Others just laughed:

Is this what all you marketing boys at M-Net think is a reasonable cross-section of SA society? The selection reads like a play-by-play list of SA C-list celebrities.

Others asked why the ordinary *ou* hadn't been given a chance. "Look at the line-up of entries. None of them are ordinary, plain, meat-braaing, beer-drinking, rugby-watching South Africans. Unfortunately I will not be watching this as it is a waste of time from M-Net."

You can just imagine some of the camera shots ... [Archers] Aqua with his carefully sculpted fringe in his face, giving us his 'Blue Steel' stare before, or during a challenge. FHM rocket-scientist chick bouncing around in her bikini all day, and somehow strangely managing to survive one tribal council after another.

The host, Mark Bayly, also came in for flak. One fan commented that he looked like a "South African *boerseun* yuppie from Sandton that just got attacked by a Chihuahua when he stepped out of his artificially mud-coated 4x4."

Casey B. Dolan "is known for making a complete giggly twit out of herself."
Therese Owen.

In 2005, iconoclastic DJ and one-time TV host Riaan van Heerden told his listeners at Radio Punt to shit on the bonnet of Catherine Myburgh's car, and one of them did.

(This tale raises all sorts of questions. But we won't go there.)

Later, van Heerden's show at the West End Theatre in Pretoria was raided by police. "But they were armed with R4 rifles," van Heerden told a journalist in amazement. "They had their fingers ready on the triggers … maybe they were that, I don't know, I'd try to escape or something. I mean, what the fuck?"

Van Heerden was served with a summons for offensive public advertising for his show *Onbesny*; the poster featured him clutching a microphone to his crotch in the style of an Australian batsman facing Makhaya Ntini. The show included an insert where shots of crowds of Afrikaners bopping to treffers are interspersed with footage of farm animals defecating—all of this to a soundtrack provided by Kurt Darren, Dozi and other singers.

"Besides Susie Jordan or Jani Allan, nothing ages so quickly as society's vision of the future." Darrel Bristow-Bovey.

Therese Owen, social columnist for the *Saturday Star*, offers some sage advice to former TV personality Kedibone: "Now that you're no longer wanted as a continuity presenter on SABC1, go hang out in Sandton and catch yourself a BEE boy. Please leave the music industry to people who actually have talent."

"I had to take cover to escape the saliva of DJ Tira, who gave me a thorough shower trying to tell me about his 30th birthday bash … Maybe the dude is really growing up; if only he would dry up too." Shwashwi, *Sunday World*.

An indignant member of the public responded to Owen's less than kind words about Pam Andrews' new CD (she mocked Andrews for singing about a "pwordy" instead of a "party"). Owen, wrote Vicky Jacobs in an impressively sustained piece of invective, "is vacantly silly, her comments are purposeless and she writes the most idiotic rubbish."

Sies! It is obvious she has no clue what the entertainment scene is all about and therefore ends up talking through her perforated hat ... The only scene I can picture is Therese sitting at her keyboard—ignorant, tactless, clueless, biased and talentless.

"By the way, why don't you go for a makeover? The photograph of yourself used in your column strongly suggests that you do. You look so sad and dejected. Is it because you know the only way you will ever be invited to a 'pwordy' is to make as if you are a journo?"

"A classy pervert." Somozi Mhlongo on drag rival the Baroness.

Ultimately, we the public enjoy a mildly dysfunctional, co-dependent relationship with celebrities. They add colour to the monotony of lives spent starring glassily at Excel spreadsheets, and in turn they need us to feed their insatiable desire for validation. Africans.co.za contributor Trixy Honore points out that there is nothing wrong with finding the lives of celebrities interesting, and that gossiping about them is hardly the stuff of psychopathy: "Most people would agree that believing Renée Zellweger is practically a close personal friend of yours because you've watched *Nurse Betty* five times and seen her interviewed on *Oprah* twice makes you just about as thick as pig shit."

Fact is, celebrities are more interesting than most of your friends and relatives.

Mostly they work as retail sales managers, study some dull degree and shop at Mr. Price. So, damn your dull friends. They just don't provide fodder enough to get any decent gossip going.

"You see that new hairbrush Candice bought at Clicks?"

"Oh, ja, very good value, isn't it?"

"Ja, wonderfully inexpensive."

So, go forth and read *heat* magazine. Speculate with your friends on which celebrity marriage will tank next, now that Gerry has left Alex. Spend your days fantasizing about Khanyisile Mbau's shoe size. It's okay.

They might be human bonsai—but they're our human bonsai.

Chapter 15

The evil black box:
television

"Sometimes the kindest thing one can say about South African TV is that it's in colour." David Barritt.

The guardians of the *volk* during the apartheid years were great worriers. They worried about the Bantu. They worried about White civilization. They were terribly concerned about moral decay and living according to what the Bible said (just those good solid Old Testament bits, mind you—none of that commie New Testament rubbish about loving your neighbour).

And, a lot of the time, they worried about television.

Dr. Verwoerd regarded television in the same light as the atom bomb and poison gas. (For those who are not sure, he thought television was a bad thing.)

Dr. Albert Herzog thought that television was "spiritual dagga ... inside the pill [of TV]." He warned. "There is the bitter poison which will ultimately lead to the downfall of civilizations." TV, according to Dr. Herzog was,

that evil black box; sickly, mawkish, sentimentalistic, and leading to dangerous liberalistic tendencies.

Imagine if Dr. Herzog had had his way beyond 1976. Just think: no *Suburban Bliss*. No Felicia Mabuza-Suttle or Debra Patta. No *Top Billing* or *Big Brother*. No *People of the South* or *Laugh Out Loud*.

Come to think of it, maybe the good Doctor had a point.

"Do not install a TV service. South Africa is not open to Russian- or American-controlled propaganda. That way the people will not be abandoned to the forces of commercialization." Jaap Marais, responding to a suggestion by the *Washington Post* in 1969 that television would modernize South Africa's racial attitudes.

The bottom of the barrel

Local TV producers took Marais' statements to heart. Determined not to abandon South Africans to the forces of commercialization, they made sure that they were responsible for endless dramas and sitcoms that nobody wanted to watch. While Afrikaans productions like *Vyfster* or *Agter Elke Man* were so good that even monolingual rooineks would watch them, local English language productions were just embarrassing. There has been the odd decent show, enough to lull us into listless complacency, but just when the unsuspecting television viewer has relaxed in the assumption that the barrel has been scraped to the point of splintering, we're faced with the awful prospect of Paul Viv or *The Most Amazing Show*.

Yes, an entire generation of South Africans have fond memories of *Liewe Heksie* and *Wielie Walie*; yes, being allowed to stay up past 8 to watch Henry Cele in *Shaka Zulu* was a rite of passage—and yes, a part of us longs for the days of innocence when Christopher Dingle made history by using the F-word on *Midweek* and we had no idea what anyone was going on about. But what about *Louis Motors, Suburban Bliss, Homeland, Oh George!, The Mantis Project, Westgate, The Game, Egoli, Backstage, Scandal, Charlie Jade* ...? The list goes on and on.

> "Strictly for those who relish appalling dialogue and sickly sweet sentimentalism, *Honeytown* must rank as one of the most spine-tinglingly awful productions ever to hit the box." *Cape Times* television guide.

Robert Kirby could not understand why the *Cape Times* had been so flattering. An episode of *Loving* was twenty times better than this, he said. Whether or not *Honeytown* was worse than *Suburban Bliss* ("charmless pre-petrified assemblage of tired clichés") or *Homeland* ("dramatic fanagalo"), he did not mention. At least the set could not have compared to that of *Front Row*, which he described as "Art Gecko".

"Faintly reminiscent of one of those lizards that dash across ponds without foundering." Tom Eaton on Gavin Hood's running style in 1980s rugby drama *The Game*.

The road to hell

In the midst of all of this, 1998's *Avenues* was possibly the worst ever, more agonizing to sit through than even *Shado's* or *Snitch*. *Avenues* plumbed such spectacular depths, it rivalled the Mariana Trench. This was the show that forced the SABC to Bow to the Will of the People and move it from Mondays between *Mad About You* and *Ally McBeal* to barren exile at 9.30 on a Sunday evening.

> "The script is from the sledgehammer school of writing." Yvonne Fontyn on *Known Gods*.

This was the "story about South Africa now" that enjoyed the rare honour of stimulating animated morning bitch sessions on talk radio or reviewers to describe how, having had a couple of stiff drinks, they had managed to sit through an episode without vomiting.

In the interests of democracy, the issue of whether the show belonged on prime time was put to the vote. 8,000 viewers paid cellular rates to demand that the show be moved. 900 viewers pressed '1' for "leave it where it is".

The cast was uniformly wrinkly, featuring several actresses well into their hormone-replacement years. And while the feminist part of one cheered the radical rejection of the sexist, ageist patriarchal notion that women who appeared on television should be as smooth as Simonsberg Low Fat Cream Cheese, it also had to be acknowledged that only the French do wrinkles with style.

There were those that suggested that Jan Groenewald, the creator of the series, should be brutally tortured, thus raising the prospect of Jan becoming the Salman Rushdie of the South. Jan, like Salman, remained unrepentant to the end. Unlike Salman Rushdie, though, Jan is a reminder why freedom of speech isn't all that it's made out to be.

> "Who needs pace when you've got Fiona Ramsay lifting an eyebrow and thinning her lips disparagingly?" Tom Eaton on the excess of dramatic pauses in *Hard Copy*.

Gesuip Opera

You and *Huisgenoot* reported on an *Egoli* concert held in Margate in 1997. More than 60,000 people crammed in front of the stage set up on the beach next to the Wimpy to watch their heroes and heroines.

Minie Booyse of Krugersdorp was overwhelmed by the sight of Kimberley, *Egoli*'s superbitch. "Slut! Slut! You monkeys!" she yelled, spraying cigarette ash. "You common little monkeys!"

"Guess what?" one girl said to her friend. "I've heard Mitch doesn't wear underwear."

"WHAT? Genuine?"

"Genuine."

"Genuine?"

"Genuine."

Minie Booyse waited after most of the audience had left to see Kimberley. She shoved her way to the front and clicked away with her camera. "Now I can show my friends I really did see that bitch."

> "Whenever TV news bulletins advise sensitive viewers to look away I get really offended because I do look and that instantly categorizes me as insensitive."
> Andrew Unsworth.

Tony Weaver was not impressed by the short film *Shooting Pink* by David Golden, flighted on M-Net in November 1998. "Frankly, this kind of shit should be banned," he wrote to the *Mail & Guardian*. "If this is what our young film-makers are turning out, then I despair for the future of local film-making. No doubt there will be wanker art critics who will hail this piece of bloodfest as 'Tarantinoesque', 'ground-breaking' and 'brave'."

> Living in Cape Town, I just think it stinks. David Golden gets an A for technique and an F for script. Eff as in fuck off to Hollywood and don't come back. Ever.

Felicia

Few South African television figures enter the realm of myth. There are those of us who dimly recall Michael de Morgan reading the news or the basset-eyed Kim Shippey talking about sport. Perhaps Charl Pauw and the Shipping News or Graeme Hart, who reported so drolly on the weather of Gordonia for so many years.

But none of them are known simply by one name. That honour belongs alone to Felicia.

Felicia Mabuza-Suttle—known, inevitably, as Felicia Mabuza-Unsubtle—has not been on our TV screens for years. Yet Felicia jokes are still told every day. It is as though every stand-up comedian possesses a Felicia gag (or is that Gag Felicia?) default option, which kicks in whenever they are short of ideas. Even 'Jesus' mentioned Felicia during an interview with Gareth Cliff on 5FM.

"Vel," he said, "the truth is we do still have miracles today, like Felicia being on the TV for so long. Is there a bigger miracle?"

"What's worse than Brenda Fassie on crack? Felicia on e." Anonymous.

"If TV criticism were the armed struggle," Darrel Bristow-Bovey wrote," Felicia would be a designated soft target."

What was it about Felicia that prompted the toes to curl inside the pantoffels? Perhaps it was the strident voice, the ego running rampant across the set, the way Felicia could say "I want to reach out to the minds of our men, the hearts of our women, and the souls of her society" and all that came to mind were long red nails and voodoo rituals involving human sacrifice and the odd chicken. Whatever it was about her, "The greatest risk in reviewing Felicia," noted Bristow-Bovey, "is whiplash from the rapid involuntary recoil and writer's cramp from jotting down all the stupid things she says."

Felicia is now far, far away from our TV screens, running the SA Tourism office in New York. So, if we can't blame Neil Watson's crime expo website for falling tourist numbers, we can always blame her for scaring the Americans away.

Noeleen

Then there is Noeleen.

Noeleen Maholwana-Sangcu may be approaching Feliciaesque status, though she is not quite there yet. Give her time.

For Noeleen is perhaps the ultimate new South African, resembling nothing so much as

a Randburg housewife who likes nice shoes, big hair and blue eye shadow. She frowns a lot to look serious and calls everyone 'darling', but a lot of the time she seems distracted, as if, like South Africans moms everywhere, she is trying to remember whether she was supposed to pick the kids from ballet or kung fu. She tells journalists that her favourite restaurant is Wimpy, and ordinary people can relate to that.

Where Felicia divided the nation, Noeleen unites; where Felicia dwelled with unseemly narcissistic relish on herself and the liposuction she had performed on her bum. Noeleen is human; you could imagine yourself buying Tupperware or Justine cosmetics from her and having a good skinner about what Dawn in the lift club is getting up to after her divorce.

> "Jealousy makes you nasty. And nasty makes you fat. And fat makes you … Noeleen." Corné the Love Captain.

Both Noeleen and Felicia have of course taken inspiration from Oprah. While one might be tempted to sneer that both of them are pale imitations of the original, which is probably truer of Ricki Lake and Rosie O'Donnell.

In any event, Oprah, the self-declared Zulu, is what Tom Eaton describes as "the great critical anaesthetic of our times." A family of Rwandans is reunited for the entertainment of "the carrion-birds of American sentimentalism, that gigantic flock of stringy-necked soccer-moms who gorge daily on the carcass of decency, privacy and decorum."

"To watch an episode of the doyen of emoto-slop," he concludes, "is to be filled with despair for the collective mind of our tribe."

> "Apparently you've got nothing better to do than watch our shitty TV shows." Jeremy Clarkson, referring to the popularity of *Top Gear* in South Africa.

Oprah might be one of the world's richest and most powerful woman thanks to the power of the evil black box (perhaps this is the sort of thing that Dr. Herzog was on about all along), but she cannot compare to our own Riaan Cruywagen, who is cooler than The Hoff and Chuck combined. Riaan has not aged a day since he started reading the Afrikaans news back in the 1970s, and that's not something you can say about Oprah—which is why the following Riaan Cruywagen factoids have done the rounds on the internet:

Riaan Cruywagen is fluent in twenty-seven of the eleven official languages.

Riaan Cruywagen knows the news before it happens.

Riaan Cruywagen knew you would say that.

Riaan Cruywagen had a telekinetic showdown with Johan Stemmet. After draining all Stemmet's powers and rendering him severely retarded, he created *Noot vir Noot* and made Stemmet the host.

Some people believe Riaan Cruywagen wears a toupee—he has, in fact, one perfect hair. The one that covers his entire head—giving it that, 'not quite real' look. Riaan himself is not quite real.

One night during an ad break, Riaan Cruywagen mentioned to the makeup lady that he was 'tired of this apartheid nonsense'. Nelson Mandela was released from prison the next day.

Riaan Cruywagen will never die. Thrice fortnightly, his soul gets transferred to another identical body using various arcane rituals as well as the latest nanotechnology.

After reading *Die Nuus*, Riaan Cruywagen built the pyramids. It took precisely 17 minutes to draw up the plans and then a further six minutes to think them into existence.

Chapter 16

The global village idiot:
South Africans on the rest of the world,
and the rest of the world on South Africans

"I've never met a nice South African." *Spitting Image* sketch, 1980s.

South Africa has a co-dependent relationship with the rest of the world, in the psychological sense rather than the field of bi-lateral trade agreements, though the statement holds true for that, too.

For years, South Africa was the pariah of the world. Then, in the era of the rainbow nation and President Mandela, we got used to being a shining example of hope. Everybody loved us.

> "Over-paid, over-sexed and over here." An assessment of South African construction workers, according to the residents of Saint Helena at a rowdy community meeting in May 2006, who claimed that the presence of imported South African workers could introduce HIV/Aids into their isolated community.

Now we are famous for wild animals, wine, HIV/Aids, crap sports teams and crime, not necessarily in that order. This is confusing for the collective psyche. We crave the admiration and esteem of the rest of the world. We want to be loved; we want tourists and investors to come here and spend their money to build our economy. We want to win at team sports, so that we will feel good about ourselves.[1]

---

[1] Tom Eaton find the "pseudo-enthusiasm and dumb optimism on display whenever ordinary events are inflated into pathetic, insular national triumphs" frankly cringeworthy. "The problem with the lies and distractions of developing countries, especially ours, is that they are so pathetically naïve, so palpably dimwitted."

"I see that we still have our heads so far up the anus of the United States and Europe that we think that these arenas, where our gladiators do battle in the games of the 'colonizers', will give us the power to lift our finger in a collective up-yours." Zebulon Dread. He also referred to the Cricket World Cup as "legal international money laundering".

When we lose, we question our reason for being. But on the other hand, we're also given to showing the middle finger to anyone who says horrible things about us. If you criticize us, whether it's our way of life, our sports teams or our policies on Zimbabwe, then screw you. Only we are allowed to be rude about our own.

For example, when Stephen Lewis, the UN special envoy on Aids, famously stated that South Africa's Aids policies were worthy of a lunatic fringe, Karen Bliksem, the *Sunday Independent* columnist in drag, responded with the supremely low blow of bringing in Dubya:

What are you saying there, Stevie boychik? That George 'Dubya' Bush's theories (and practice) in the field of say, international relations make him unworthy of membership of a lunatic fringe?

Rainbow chickens

South Africans have a particularly fraught relationship with South Africans who leave to live permanently in other countries. It's an interesting mixture of envy and contempt, even a sense of betrayal. A psychotherapist would have a field day.

"They say that when the Jews start packing, it's time to go; when the Portuguese start packing, it's too late already!" Pieter-Dirk Uys, repeating a joke told to him by Helen Suzman.

The early 1990s gave rise to the term 'chicken run', reserved for South Africans who decided to leave as the prospect of black majority rule became a reality. Everyone agreed that emigrants were cowards.

Even Nelson Mandela, speaking in September 1998 in the USA, said. "Those who have not got the courage and the patriotism to remain in their country, let them go! It is good riddance!"

"Can you bring me a bottle of Mrs. Balls chutney?"
"No. You left. So we get to eat the Balls chutney. There'll be no chutney in Putney."
And all they talk about is South Africa. "How's Sandton?" "I'm not telling you."
Mark Banks.

Not that this has stopped anybody. The *Sunday Times* must have made a steady income over the years from all those little immigration seminar ads in the business section, not to mention all the recruitment ads in the careers pages. Hospital wards from Auckland to Abu Dhabi, to Aberdeen, are filled with South African doctors and nurses. The New York doctor who supervised Morgan Spurlock's McDonald's-only experimental diet in *Supersize Me* had a distinct Greenside accent.

South African expats are responsible for spreading biltong and boerewors to the rest of the world. They don't necessarily long for highveld thunderstorms and African sunsets, but they do long for Bokjol CDs and Chocolate Logs, which makes perfect sense: in a branded world, you are what you consume.

Meanwhile, South Africans back home comfort themselves by listing Pratley Putty as a reason to be proudly South African, as though this somehow compensates for 40% unemployment and drug-resistant TB but hey, whatever floats your boat china.

Holidays in hell

Not many people visited South Africa during the apartheid years. P. J. O'Rourke was one of the few who showed up in the late 1980s, but that was mainly because he needed a chapter for his book entitled *Holidays in Hell.* "The world is built on discrimination of the most horrible kind," he wrote at the time. "The problem with South Africans is they admit it."

He drives into Soweto, illegally, and is surprised when nobody attacks him.

I mean, personally, if I'd lived my forty years in Soweto and I saw some unprotected honky cruising down my street on a Saturday afternoon, I would have opened that car like an oyster and deep-fat fried me on the spot.

After apartheid was over, Germans in socks and sandals and pasty-legged Brits wearing shorts in the middle of winter started showing up, and we South Africans got all excited at the prospect of all that lovely foreign currency as well as those top-end cameras and credit cards. In Cape Town, argues Chris Roper, "we're all one happy family, banded together to rip off that common enemy we refer to, simply, as The Tourist."

In contrast to common misconceptions, Roper points out that Cape Town is in fact a real African city, with real African hotels that have air-conditioners that don't work, staff that refuse to serve you, and rooms decked out in that classic African look of cheap linoleum and torpid cockroaches."

"I usually beg from tourists—they're dumber than other people." Dolfie, a street child who begs in Greenmarket Square.

Often, visitors to South Africa are distressingly ignorant. They ask questions like, Are there elephants in the streets? and Do you speak English? Thank goodness for films like *Tsotsi*, which show the real South Africa. "Before *Tsotsi*, citizens of developed countries only suspected that Johannesburg looked like Baghdad-on-the-Niger and crawled with murderous blackamoors," Tom Eaton reminded readers. Now, the world could see that South Africa was full of people with guns who broke into nice middle-class homes and terrorized the inhabitants.

What lessons can the world learn from *Tsotsi*? Certainly, they can appreciate that humanity flowers in the darkest holes. But, perhaps more importantly, they can embrace the eternal truth at heart of the film: Always keep your windows rolled up, and whatever you do, keep your car in gear at robots.

"I would like to say I fell in love with South Africa. But I didn't." Rory Carroll.

Some people love us, and buy up all the best wine farms, Plett villas and Camps Bay

penthouses. Others can take us or, more easily, just leave us. After almost four years in Johannesburg, *Guardian* correspondent Rory Carroll wrote of his feelings about leaving South Africa: predominantly, a sense of detachment. "This never really became home," he wrote.

> Partly it was running to the airport every other week for overseas trips; partly it was being white and European; but mainly it was because South Africa was such a fraught place to live. The anxiety about crime, the crunching on racial eggshells, the juxtaposition of first-world materialism with third-world squalor—it all added up.

Crime, of course, puts a lot of people off. "I could easily see how tourists are recognized and mugged: they are the white ones who walk," the English travel writer John Malathronas said soon after arriving in South Africa. On the advice of the guidebook, he stayed in Pretoria rather than Johannesburg.

> When I decided to go to South Africa, everyone and his guidebook was against the idea. At best I would be robbed upon arrival; at worst I would be ritually sacrificed and my entrails used for witchcraft.

"I'd have to carry an Uzi on my shoulder to walk about and drive a Challenger tank to avoid carjacking."

Fortunately, most foreigners who visit don't pay any attention to any of this. They watch charming performances of happy locals dancing in that charming native way of theirs. Some of them may observe, like Malathronas, that the female Zulu dancers had "buffalo-bearing hips"; he thought some of the hips he saw in KwaZulu-Natal "humanly impossible".

But for the most part, they manage to avoid being eaten while on the game-drive and mugged while in the shopping mall, and at the end of it all, they clutch their carved wooden giraffes under one arm and cradle a Backsberg giftbox in the other as they file onto the plane, and they go home happy.

> "The dikkop looks like a chicken drawn by a toddler and it runs with its long stick-

like legs like a surfer who's pissed inside his wetsuit." John Malathronas, English travel writer, being rude about our local birdlife.

In turn, the opening up of South Africa to the rest of the world meant that we could also put ten days in Thailand (including airfare but excluding drinks and taxes) on the gold card and become annoying tourists in other countries.

Being South African is not a guarantee that the locals will be nice to you even in America. When Fred Khumalo refused a request from a homeless man in Washington DC, the latter said, "Mothafucker's eating big but cain't give no bread to another brother, damn mean nigger!"

Ulan Bator, capital of Mongolia. It's a colder, dustier version of Beaufort West. Robert Houwing, editor of *The Wisden Cricketer* magazine, on the one travel destination he would never visit again.

We also discover that other parts of the world are pretty crappy, too. Michelle Sacks describes a harrowing trip to Machu Picchu, which involves staying in a nasty little tourist trap called Aguas Caliente. The place, she writes, "is a festering pustule of a town built on the backside of the famous Inca ruins, for the express purpose, it would seem, of ripping off the poor sods who have no choice but to be there."

The place is a dump in every sense of the word. It smells, it rots, it teems with unsavoury people and pestilence and, contrary to what its name might suggest (Aguas Caliente being 'hot water') there is in fact, no such luxury.

A gastronomic holocaust

Foreigners have been rude about South Africa for years.

Giles Coren, the English food critic, was not impressed with South African cuisine. Gastronomically, he sniffs, we're "little more than Australia-lite". Apparently, we don't even understand barbecuing. "It's a holocaust over there. The thing they call a braai, we call a cremotorium."

We don't know how to cook seafood either.

All that lovely sealife and they never once managed to cook it short of the point where the carapace welds to the meat like napalm to a pig. Somebody has to stop this South African inhumanity. We may have to boycott the fruit, or stop playing cricket with them. And then hold out for another *Mandela: the Long Walk to Correctly Grilled Crustacea*.

Coren finds the The Codfather in Cape Town guilty of serving maki rolls containing both salmon and tuna. "It's like a mouthful of incest."
And though we have decent meat, we turn it into biltong.

In the developed world, we worked out long ago that the cleverest thing is to eat the meat and turn the skin into shoes. In South Africa, they turn the whole animal into shoes. And then eat the shoes.

Appalled, Coren flees back to England on the first available flight.

"[South African wine] is a sea of somewhat vapid but politically correct mouthwashes." Jancis Robinson, wine critic.

Nuclear waste

Top Gear's Jeremy Clarkson, writing about visiting darkest Africa to test drive the new Jaguar XK, was not sure what to expect:

On the one hand you think you'll spot Peter Gabriel with a bone in his nose, chanting. But on the other hand you suspect you may be hacked to pieces by a machete-wielding mob.

Good to know that Clarkson didn't come to our shores burdened with any preconceived ideas then.
Clarkson enjoyed the scenery and the roads (and, incidentally, the car). But he wasn't impressed with the wine. "You certainly don't go to South Africa for the viniculture," he said. The cellar, he said, "was like being in a nuclear power station."

And what did the finished product taste like? Well pretty much like the stuff that comes from the outlet pipe at Sellafield. I doubt the French would wash their windscreens with it.[2]

Having dismissed South Africa's wine industry in a couple of deftly amusing sentences, Clarkson then moved onto an in-depth analysis of race and class divides that persist.

Yes, apartheid is over but all the black people seem to have got now is the vote, and a carrier bag each. I'm not kidding. Even if you go out into the hinterland, you will find the roadside littered with people who are just sitting there, with a plastic bag, doing nothing.
Occasionally, one will stick out his thumb so that you can give him a lift to a new bit of roadside where he can sit with his bag, doing nothing.

South Africa, he concluded, was great. "You have a taste of Africa without malaria, flies in your eyes or having your genitals cut off by angry locals. Yes, the wine's rubbish ... but it's a small price to pay."

"If anyone catches me trying to buy this wine, will they please shoot me." Former England cricket captain David Gower after a tasting of Meerlust's 1999 Chardonnay.

The locals get angry

Reaction to Clarkson's article was swift and vociferous. There were those who were deeply offended. Clarkson's comments, sniffed one letter writer, "tells you more about the writer's character and fragile ego than a million words." When Clarkson returned to Cape Town, suggested another, he should not bet on leaving the Western Cape with his genitalia intact. Trevor Stacey of Cape Town went further. South Africans should not take Clarkson's comments too seriously, he wrote, because his not liking our wine was a bit like George Bush not liking Scotch whisky because he's used to Budweiser.

---

[2] Compare this to Fred Khumalo's experience of a California Chardonnay in a Washington, DC restaurant. It tasted, he wrote, like "liquefied heartburn".

Jeremy is about a stylish as a Brisbane bricklayer, as exciting as a Datsun's dashboard and his taste in cars suitable for the car park in front of the NG kerk in Pofadder on a Sunday morning. In fact, I suspect he's a closet caravaner.

Then comes the moment when the brass band strikes up *Nkosi Sikilele iAfrika* and okes of all shades get misty eyed.

Let me tell you my brother, in my country we like wines that are in your face. Wines that do a gumboot dance on your tongue before delivering a black power punch to your epiglottis and yelling 'A luta continua!' as they drain down your gullet. For our part, you can keep the namby pampy French stuff whose taste is so subtle you need a search party to find it.

America the bootylicious

Along with the rest of the world, South Africa is one of the colonies of American cultural imperialism. We watch American movies; we listen to American music; our local music is often a remarkably close copy of American music.

"How lovely to trace one's roots back to a country that has five-star hotels, rather than to some stricken West African country where the locals won't pay R500 a head for motivational speeches." Krisjan Lemmer, *Mail & Guardian*, commenting on Oprah's declaration that she went in search of her roots and made the quite remarkable discovery that she is Zulu.

In their love of Chevy Luminas and Rancheros, Country & Western music, fast food and shopping malls, there are some South Africans who are more American than anything else. With its soulless strips dominated by garish signage for used car dealers and its collections of Tuscan McMansions, parts of the West Rand could be mistaken for the Mid West.

When Henry Kissinger visited South Africa, he soon became known as 'Kiss Inja'. Reported by Sy Makaringe. *Inja* is Zulu for 'dog'.

Nonetheless, the love of all things American does not extend to our current government. In fact, our government tries hard to be friends with people that America doesn't like, like Iran and North Korea and Zimbabwe (the reason they haven't bombed Zim is not just because there's no oil; it's because they haven't found it on the map yet). Perhaps this is to be expected, since Ronald Reagan, the president who wanted to start Star Wars for real, never wanted to be too hard on the apartheid government, and most of the current cabinet was educated in the USSR, Cuba or the Eastern Bloc. Hell, the head of news on our national broadcaster has a PhD from Bulgaria, whatever that means.

So America is still a bit suspicious of us, and the feeling is mutual. "Look what Bush is doing. He could invade," Manto once told a journalist who asked why the government prioritized new German-made submarines over Aids drugs.

(Why Manto has anything to worry about is a mystery. "Who's going to invade us?" asks John Vlismas. "We don't need guns; our army is 60% HIV positive. All they've got to do is bite them.")

> "Mr. Sin. Super Mean Super Power. Wipes out World Peace. Pentagon. Helps Polish off Foreign Countries." Laugh It Off T-shirt parody of George W. Bush.

So ja, we might have Manto, and Jacob, and Phumzile, and Charles—and Snuki—but America has Bush and Dick so they don't get to laugh at us.

Gareth Cliff had a couple of observations about President Bush when he interviewed 'Jesus' on national radio. "President Bush says he was really anxious to see the film," he said. "Yes," replied Jesus. "But he was a bit upset when he heard that it was in Aramaic and Latin." President Bush said: "Why make a movie—I can't do the accent—Why make a movie only Arams and Latinos will understand?"

> "Americans have to realize that it's not just the Muslims, even God doesn't like them." John Vlismas, in the wake of Hurricane Katrina.

Tony Blair has taken flak for being Bush's favourite pet after Barney the Scottish terrier. "If you're going to be a *stoepkakker*, Blair, for God's sake try find a better grade of owner," sniffs Robert Kirby. Adds a letter to the *Mail & Guardian*:

Blair is no poodle. He's a brown-nosed Bush pig.

Chris Forrest observed that when Tony Blair made a statement after the London bombings, he said, "We think this is the work of terrorists."
"Fuck me Tony," said Chris, "I thought it was the Girl Guides."

"The Englishman does his own blinking dirty work. The South African white foreman would have no job here. Stroos god!" Todd Matshikiza in London in 1960. Nowadays, of course, Saffers in London are quite happy to do the kind of dirty work they would never dream of taking on back home.

Terrorism in London worries South Africans, because, even though Johannesburg always had a suburb called Windsor, Wimbledon is now a suburb of Pretoria. You know you are a significant ethnic minority when the native-born Londoners start beating you up for wearing Springbok rugby jerseys.

When David Kau performed at the Lyric Theatre in London in 2006, he noticed that there were lots of South Africans in the audience, mostly Indians and coloureds.

But I was surprised as I had expected that, at least, the South Africans would be white! South Africa is a fucked up country, and you never know what to expect.

It's Bruce, bru

"You know you're in South Africa when you can't even go on a business trip to Australia without somebody saying knowingly: Oh, having a look around, are you?" Viral email.

Though we may be drenched in what passes for American culture; though many of us hold a candle for England because some long-lost ancestor came over on a boat and thanksalot we don't qualify for an ancestral visa; though vicious fights break out periodically across the dinner tables of the land over whether Princess Diana was wronged by that useless Prince Charles or just a spoilt, shallow cow—it is really across the Indian Ocean that we look with a mixture of envy and resentment.

"There is more culture in an Aussie billabong than we have in our biggest city."
James Clarke.

The South African rivalry with Australia is to be expected. Like us, they're an ex-British colony, although, unlike us, they can't get over their fetish for old women wearing crowns. They play the same sports as us, at which they beat us soundly and repeatedly. In the family of those nations that once saluted the Union Jack, Australia is the golden-haired, blue-eyed sibling who wins all the sporting and academic awards at school and can do no wrong. Meanwhile, bolshy and resentful, South Africa—the black sheep of the family— loiters in dark alleyways, dragging on a joint and scratching listlessly at a mildly Satanic tattoo.

"But where can we go? Australia? Sis—final proof that there's death after life. Herbert went to look around New Zealand but it was closed." So said Nowell Fine (aka Pieter-Dirk Uys) during the 1980s, before the chicken run began in earnest.

Clive James, who was a moderately famous Australian before Paul Hogan and Steve Irwin came along, did not enjoy his first encounter with South Africans.[3] In the 1960s— at around about the same time J. M. Coetzee was there, wandering about in the fog of existential crisis—Clive arrived in London from Australia. Aside from the horrible weather and miserable accommodation, there were also South Africans to deal with.

He first runs into them on a visit to the local launderette, when he is forced to sit down between a pair of them. He can tell that they are South Africans because "when they talked across me it was like being beaten up". Then he describes how they sat there, "clubbing each other with verbal truncheons of crushed Dutch".

Later the South Africans express their annoyance at a film about a courageous black activist who earns the grudging admiration of the security policeman who has been torturing him.

"Thet's what's rewning Efrica, litting a keffir talk to them like thet," says one (do we really sound like that to Australians? They sound bloody awful to us, mate).

"Thet's right. They mist not be allowed to enswer beck," agrees the other.

God, no wonder everybody hated us.

---

[3] Some of you may recall Clive James from various TV travel series that were the staple of TV1 during the late 1980s and early 1990s. Presumably the SABC got a bulk discount.

"There is a joke that does the round every time South Africa plays Australia at any sport: three tourists, a South African, a Zimbabwean and a Pom, are travelling Australia by car. Guess who's driving? The police." Mark Tomkinson, Bridgetown, Australia.

South Africans attempt to deal with their feelings of inferiority relating to the fact that Australia is clean, safe, enjoys efficient government and—apart from the aboriginals and their version of African time, (which they call Dreamtime)—is what Kempton Park would be like if it were the size of an entire continent, by mocking Australia for not being dangerous enough. John Vlismas mocks the total lack of danger in Australia. "I went to a game park and said, show me a vicious beast." The ranger showed him a wombat.

A wombat is not a beast. It looks like a Care Bear came home drunk and pomped a slipper.

(What is Vlismas on about? Did nobody tell him that Australia has the world's deadliest snakes, spiders, jellyfish, octopus and—oh yes—stingrays? Even the duckbilled platypus has poisonous barbs on its hindlegs.)

South Africans who come back from Australia tell horror stories about how terrifyingly law-abiding the place is. Their speed limit is 100! They enforce it, and they won't take bribes! They punish drunken driving by taking away your licence!

There are no maids!

"The blandness of Australia is epidemic." Zebulon Dread.

South Africans who live in Australia congratulate themselves on moving to a place where the sports teams actually win, and make observations like "Perth is just like Cape Town without the mountain." Perth is also like Cape Town without Khayelitsha and the rest of the Cape Flats, but Australia is officially multicultural, so everyone is too polite to say anything out loud.

Around the mid-'90s, a Grapevine postcard from a company called Pet Hate Products proclaimed:

WE HATE SYDNEY.

On the back was a list of reasons for this outburst of ockerphobia:

Your miserable flu
Your irritating accent
Your pathetic patriotism
Crocodile Dundee
Catastrophic Kylie
Shameless Warne
Boring Bondi
Finding sheep in tall grass satisfying
EMIGRATION SUCKS

That is not to say that South Africans cannot get on with Austarlians. Valiant Swart lost his virginity "to an Australian chick named Josephine". He said, "I think that's a nice name for a girl to lose your virginity to."

"You slimed yet mate?" Young Australian woman, after sex with a South African man, who repeated this anecdote to all his friends, who then told all of their friends, which is how it has ended up in this book.

Also, J. M. Coetzee, who gets listed as a reason to be Proudly South African along with Charlize Theron and the invention of the Kreepy Krauly, has allowed his inner Australian to come out. It took him more than six decades, many depressing books and a Nobel Prize, but he finally took the step of emerging from the closet to smile for the cameras when he received his Australian citizenship.

"I hear you'se a man with suffering and sadness in your heart. You must be if you live in Australia," Lourens Ackerman wrote upon hearing of the smiling. "What's it like there in Adelaide? What kindofaname is that anyway? Sounds like a maid what got fancy. Takes a bath when the madam's away."

"A dopey, hairy-backed Sheila." Former cricketer David Hookes, referring to a

South African woman who had accused Shane Warne of sexual harassment. Hookes later died after being beaten by a bouncer at a Melbourne pub. Nobody was terribly surprised.

Sheep shaggers

Many South Africans find insulting Australians an oddly pleasurable pastime.

Fatima Chohan, chairman of Parliament's Portfolio Committee on Justice and Constitutional Development was involved in a discussion on the proposed criminalization of bestiality under the draft Sexual Offences Amendment. "Of course, in Australia," she said, "this is an offence that would never fly." Hogarth of the *Sunday Times* was mystified by Dean Jones' need to characterize Hasi Amla as a "terrorist" (see chapter 3).

> Perhaps it is because Jones is an Australian, a class of people known to enjoy outdoor pursuits, including cricket, drinking large amounts of beer, the burning of meat on open fires and the rearing of animals for sexual pleasure.
> Australia is a homogenous society. To a man, they all fear people who are not like them. That is, everyone on the planet who is not in the process of getting skin cancer. Ask the Aboriginals. If you can find any.
> Many Australians may take offence at such crude generalizations. But who cares? They're only Australian.

Krisjan Lemmer offered a similar take on the situation. "After all", he commented, "if everyone went around indulging provocative and childish stereotypes,"

> the Oom might be tempted to call Jones a livestock-romancing wife-beating string-vest-wearing racist bigot Australian yahoo from the arse end of nowhere whose gigantic mouth is writing cheques his tiny brain can't cash. And that wouldn't be fair, would it?

None so bland

New Zealand, God's Own country, has not come under quite the same scrutiny as its antipodean neighbour. "For those who have not visited New Zealand, it is ... not known for the physical beauty of its female," writes Kevin McCullum.

> This was a nation of ten-beer-looking women, a country of girls with 'nice personalities' who were beautiful on the inside because they certainly weren't much on the outside. It explained two important things about New Zealand: firstly, why it has a population of only four million people and, secondly, why the men drink so much.

Canadians, in contrast, are not given to the undue expression of excitement, except when it comes to ice hockey. "The Canadians are so boring and bland," complains Johannesburg-born Toronto resident Susan Saffer (yes, really). For the most part, agrees Tom Eaton (who, incidentally, dislikes "aggressively sanctimonious countries such as Belgium and the Netherlands"), they are a restrained lot.

> When they get angry, they go to a symphony and stew in the cheap seats. When they get really angry, for instance, when they encounter racial intolerance or impure maple syrup, they go to a symphony but decline to buy a programme.

> "What do you call people from Holland? Hollanders, perhaps? Yes, but there is an argument that if we can call people who come from Poland Poles, we should as well call those from Holland Holes." Sy Makaringe.

When W. H. See was moved to write about his psychopathic Belgian Shepherd, he noted that the "Belgian" part of the dog's name could be misleading "for those of us who associate Belgians with the dull but essentially harmless little gnomes shuffling under umbrellas on the endless commute between grey office blocks and cramped tenement homes in cold, dismal Brussels."

> However, you begin to get a correct picture if you visualize Belgians as the kind of people who regard peacekeeping in Africa as toasting small Somali children over a fire.

So perhaps it is understandable that Tom Eaton should be moved to declare that one

should not need an excuse to wipe out Belgium, "but one doesn't want to be called a racist when the napalm canisters start raining down on Brussels,"

The Dark Incontinent

"Dead Man's Creek, Mississippi, is laughing at the concept of an African renaissance." Thabo Mbeki, 1998.

Africa has always alternately enchanted, intimidated and just plain depressed South Africans. "The continent of hopelessness," is how Shaun Johnson described it. "Africa excels only at the rate at which it produces people," said Lester Venter, who also predicted the end of the world once Mandela went. "A pathologically diseased, drug-addicted, malnourished patient," suggested prominent businessman Reuel Khoza.

"King Mazawattee the Shagged-Out." Krisjan Lemmer, *Mail & Guardian*, on King Mswati of Swaziland.

"Oxygen thief." Hogarth, *Sunday Times*, also on King Mswati of Swaziland, mampara of the week.

"King Mswati III of Swaziland, the man who changes wives with the regularity of changing his underpants." Jon Qwelane.

While the Asian ex-colonies grow up and become tigers that specialize in producing condoms and consumer electronics, Africa seems to specialize in producing charmers like Uncle Bob and his best friend Sam, Liberia's Charles Taylor, the Lord's Resistance Army's Joseph Kony, just to mention a few items on a long, long list of outrageous scumbags. And just when you thought that cannibalism had gone out of fashion along with Milton Obote and Idi Amin, along comes the claim that Equatorial Guinea's Teodor Obiang "devoured" the brains and testicles of a local police chief. (This has been cited as the reason why American music star Rapper Eve dumped Obiang junior, who is best known as a playboy with a penchant for Bentleys and Camps Bay mansions.)

"Please remember today is: AFRICA DAY! Please pay tribute to our Africa custom by making a complete FUCKUP of something today!" Viral email, 2006.

"We have uranium here and we train our own scientists and engineers. If they create nonsense, we can make our own atomic bombs." 'Yosemite' Sam Nujoma, announcing that Namibia is set to join the nuclear arms race.

Makwerekwere

As official apartheid ideology ground to a halt, half of Africa decided to make their fortune in South Africa. Johannesburg became the New York of Africa, welcoming the huddled masses north of the tropic of Capricorn.

Not everyone was happy about this. Suburban South Africans, who enjoyed the services of Malawian gardeners, seemed less concerned than black South Africans, some of whom took to throwing emigrants off trains or attacking them in the street. Locals who considered a little too dark have long since become accustomed to police harassment on the suspicion that they are *amakwerekwere*.

"Let's Africanize, or else we shall perish as a nation." Professor Malegapuru Makgoba, 1996.

"South Africa is encountering an influx of illegal immigrants who constantly plunge it in a state of crisis and instability," complained a letter to the *Mail & Guardian* in 1997. Not only did these immigrants take jobs from South Africans, they undermined the moral rectitude of the nation, trading in drugs and weapons and ushering in an era of "substance abuse and internecine violence". "What is going to become of South Africans when their lives are guided by hedonism?"

Jon Qwelane went further, saying during his show on 702 that "the constitution should be suspended to enable the South African police to arrest and deport all illegal immigrants, that some should be shot on sight, and put on a conveyor belt to hell."

Though Africans of a bewildering array of nationalities now live in South Africa, and are just as likely to be stockbrokers and surgeons as bricklayers and gardeners, certain stereotypes have become part of the fabric of daily life in Mzansi.

Take Nigerians, for instance. 'Nigerian' now codes for drugdealer/ pimp/ bouncer. These are not proper lines of work with which to be associated, but it must be admitted that Nigerians do have a certain dark glamour about them. Nobody poses as a member of a Burundian syndicate. Nobody lies awake at night worrying about Slovakians. All Malawians are gardeners, Zimbabweans apparently make good bank robbers, Burundians are a bit *dof* and all Nigerians are involved in something suspect.

> "But what is this xenophobia story? Is it because we hate the fucking Nigerians?" *Daily Sun* boss Deon du Plessis in a presumably tongue-in-cheek comment on his newspaper's editorial stance.

Certain areas of Johannesburg have become little corners of Lagos. And Addis Ababa, and Kinshasa, and Yaounde. "The announcement that the Nelson Mandela Challenge match between Bafana Bafana and Nigeria will take place at Ellis Park caused wild celebrations from our Nigerian brothers in Hillbrow and surrounding areas," the *Sunday Times* soccer column commented. "We are worried that we could find ourselves outnumbered in our own backyard."

Africans might all be brothers in theory, but in practice this kind of continent-wide ubuntu is something of an abstract concept.

"I decided to come southward because I'm better off being spat at by my own people," explained Congolese immigrant and Hillbrow resident Jemadari Kilele Vi-Bee-Kil. He also told the journalist who interviewed him, "Frankly speaking, drugs are not an African thing, these things belong to Europe."

How anyone who lives in Hillbrow could come up with a statement like that is perhaps beyond the frontiers of human understanding, but everyone is entitled to his own opinion.

> "You know you're in South Africa when Rwandan refugees start leaving the country because the crime rate is too high." Viral email.

"Women who date Nigerians are considered skanky hos by other South African women," notes *Saturday Star* columnist Misty Blade. "This is partly because Nigerians have such bad reputations as rich gangsters and con artists."

Misty Blade is appalled when her Zimbabwean boyfriend is too afraid to be seen with her in the street, lest he be beaten up by South Africans for going out with a local woman.

Not even her friends are impressed with her choice in men. "All the girls know that Zimbabwean men don't wear deodorant," says Thembi. "Plus Zimbabweans are cruel. They would kill you for a cellphone." In Thembi's opinion, Swazis and Botswanans are culturally similar to South Africans, whereas Zimbabweans and Mozambicans are not.

A Nigerian, a Mozambican and a South African are sitting in a South African pub having a pint of beer. The Nigerian grabs his beer, downs it, throws his glass into the air, draws a handgun and shoots the glass in mid-air. He grins at the other two, puts the gun down on the bar and shouts: "In Nigeria we have so many glasses we never drink out of the same glass twice."

The Mozambican then downs his beer, throws his glass into the air, grabs the gun off the bar, shoots the glass, puts the gun back on the bar and says: "Heela, in Mozambique we have so much sand which makes glass really cheap, so we too, never drink out of the same glass twice."

The South African finishes his beer, puts the glass down on the bar, picks up the gun, shoots both the Nigerian and Mozambican and says to the barman: "In South Africa we have so many Nigerians and Mozambicans that we never have to drink with the same ones twice."

The irony of all of this anti-*makwerekwere* feeling is that many South African exiles were shown the most generous hospitality in their host countries. So much so, that South Africans gained something of a reputation for what John Matshikiza describes as "our dangerous township energy". According to Matshikiza, Julius Nyerere is said to have once illustrated the difference between Tanzanians and South Africans by using the analogy of a helicopter. Put a Tanzanian in there, and he or she would have taken one look at the controls and dials and given up. But a South African would have tinkered around until he or she figured out how to fly the thing. "The problem is, the South African would then fly the helicopter to the nearest shebeen and leave it there."

In turn, white South Africans have discovered the rest of Africa. Now we are the America of Africa, using our money and our capitalist ways to take over the rest of the continent.

In the southern areas of Mozambique, the locals speak English with an Afrikaans accent. As Goda of Africans.co.za observes with some distaste,

> The gorgeous coast is crawling with bulbous, crew-cut South Africans who ride quad bikes over the dunes, get fucked, and treat the people like shit. It's South Africa's own little Mexico.

"And the companies fixing the bombed roads are all South African too—still profiteering from their old malice and the days of the rooigevaar and the swartgevaar rolled into one."

> "The three tenets of life were boredom, booze and bonking." Richard E. Grant, on colonial life in Swaziland.

Zimbobwe

After 1980, ex-Rhodesians were mocked as 'Whenwes'. Later they were known as Zimbos. Now they're routinely referred to as The Crime Problem.

Zimbabwe worries South Africans a lot. Either it's because Zimbabweans are apparently responsible for the latest upsurge in our ongoing national crime wave (both the police and the *Daily Sun* say so, so it must be true), and they're taking jobs away from the locals, or it's because Zimbabwe is a harbinger of things to come. Say "Zimbabwe" to your average white (and, increasingly, Indian and coloured) middle-class South African and you'll send them scuttling off to their nearest emigration seminar.

The implosion of our neighbour north of the Limpopo has held a horrible fascination for us for several years now. This is the country ruled by Uncle Bob aka Mad Bob aka Bob Mugabe and the Wailers (a name stemming from Robert Mugabe's phalanx of escorts riding motorcycles with shrieking sirens). For many white South Africans, Uncle Bob is the new millennial equivalent of Winnie of the 1980s and 1990s: the black person who gave them the most nightmares.

Even Jacob Zuma isn't nearly as scary as Mad Bob.

Krisjan Lemmer was intrigued by the report released by Zimbabwe's Central Statistical Office, which insisted that the country's unemployment rate in 2004 was 9%.

Official sources say next year's report will reveal that Robert Mugabe is 36, likes Pina Coladas and getting caught in the rain, and is looking for a slim, discreet, sexy and fun-loving Swiss bank to share good times with.

Zimbabweans are not supposed to make jokes about their dear leader. In 2005, a man arguing with a friend while on a bus in Harare, declared, "You are just thick-headed like Mugabe." As luck would have it, a CIO agent was travelling on the same bus, and promptly arrested him. The man was later acquitted on a technicality, but it was a close shave all the same.

The inherent dangers of making Mugabe jokes have not stopped our irrepressible Zimbabwean cousins, however. If jokes were revolutions, Uncle Bob would have been deposed long ago. SMS jokes doing the rounds have included:

"Vice-President Joshua Nkomo was 82 when he died. Vice-President Simon Muzenda was also 82 when he died. Mugabe has just turned 82. You never know what good happenings are in store for this nation. It's just a thought."

"Country for sale. Non-runner. One owner since 1980. Offers?"

"The government of Zimbabwe loves its people so much that it has made everyone a millionaire!"

"Our currency is in trouble," said Zimbabwe Reserve Bank governer Gideon Gono in July 2006. "Our people are experiencing incredible hardships and inconveniences associated with too many zeroes."

"It is not the zeroes that are at the core of the Zimbabwean crisis ... Mugabe is the big zero and he must go," retorted Tapiwa Mashakada, finance secretary of the Tsvangirai faction of the MDC.

Commenting on the same issue, MDC secretary-general Tendai Biti said, "It's like an ugly person who looks in the mirror, sees his ugly face, but instead of having plastic surgery, breaks the mirror."

"Hogarth has finally cracked what a 'basket case' country is: one in which you need a basket to carry money when you go to the shop for milk and bread." *Sunday Times.*

Uncle Bob goes to visit a sangoma. "I want some *muti* that will tell me how to ensure my victory over the neo-colonialists and their deluded black lackey filthy columnists who think that because they are a majority they can vote for whom they like."

The sangoma instructs Bob to take off his trousers and underpants, and crouch with a mirror between his knees. Once the President is in position, the sangoma asks what he sees in the mirror.

Bob replies, "I am seeing my arse."

And the nyanga says, "Get used to it, Comrade President!"

Chapter 17

A world in one country:
geography

"South Africa is today one of only two countries on the African continent that are prepared to admit that they are somewhere on the African continent." Gus Silber.

During the bad old days, Satour used to market South Africa as "a world in one country". This slogan, though politically incorrect, still holds true today. For instance, here you can experience the Home Counties in Constantia and Bishopscourt—which is presumably why disgraced toffs and dodgy European aristocrats go there—the American Mid West in Roodepoort, Las Vegas in Emperors Palace, Sun Coast and Grand West, Cape Cod on the mud flats of Knysna, Tuscany in housing estates everywhere, the Scottish highlands (with sun, so a marked improvement) in Dullstroom, Mumbai in Durban and Afghanistan, Liberia and Sierra Leone combined on the west bank of Alexandra Township. They even talk about "short sleeves" and "long sleeves" there, though admittedly this refers to how nice your house is, not the length of your amputation.

So our lightning tour of South Africa begins, in Cape Town. The Motherless City is home of vicious seagulls, homicidal squirrels and midget gangsters otherwise known as street children. Travel east along the coast and you will pass the actual meeting point of the Atlantic and Indian oceans, which is at Capo Agulhas on the southern tip of the African continent and not Cape Point as the marketing people in Cape Town would have you believe. (Two Oceans Marathon, my foot.) In South Africa, even geography can be sacrificed for a quick buck and a line in a brochure.

"These people are oleaginous, slimy hot rods with boiling brains." Lin Sampson, on South Africans who like to tan. People like these can be seen on beaches all around South Africa over December.

We pass Mossel Bay, known for enjoying the world's second-mildest climate and second-ugliest houses (after Stilbaai); then enter the region formerly known as the Garden Route, now buried beneath golf estates and triple-storey Tuscan beach villas. Plett, the spiritual home of kugels before they all left for Perth, is now popular with penniless billionaires and wetland-destroying, polo-playing ponces. On we speed through the Tsitsikama Forest and over the world's most inconveniently located Satanist coven, which is to be found at the Bloukrans River Bridge, a location it shares with the world's highest commercial bungee jump.

We arrive in Port Elizabeth, which, despite the best efforts of the marketers to brand it as the Friendly City, will always be the Windy City. PE is in fact only the *second* windiest city in South Africa, but nobody cares.

> "If he wants to get ugly, no one can get uglier than myself in the Eastern Cape."
> Terry Price, defence lawyer, arguing in court against the state prosecutor.

On we go, past East London, where Mercedes-Benzes are made, through to the Transkei, land of a thousand[1] potholes. Recently, a set was built near the Wild Coast Sun to recreate the anarchy of Sierra Leone for the Leonardo di Caprio movie *Blood Diamond*; one wonders why they didn't just film at Port St. Johns.

Up we motor past seaside resorts where wanton destruction of the most appalling kind has taken place. "If you can imagine hillbillies, without recreational incest, feuding, banjos and moonshine, then South Coast whites are hillbillies," David Basckin points out helpfully. On we drive, past Raugate and 'Toti and the Engen refinery until we reach Durban and turn left toward Gauteng.

Leaving Durbs after a quick tour of the purple Indian palaces of Umhlanga and the dreaming shires of Mount Edgecombe, we pass Pietermaritzburg on the way to the Wimpy at Harrismith. "Half the size of New York cemetery and twice as dead," Tom Sharpe reported an American visitor as saying—of Pietermaritzburg, not the Harrismith Wimpy, which at any given time is quite a happening place. "Like a replete puff-adder coiled and bloated it lay under the African sun and dreamt of its brief days of glory," Sharpe wrote of Pietermaritzburg's "venomous" mediocrity.

---

[1] This is only an expression. The actual figure is closer to several thousand or tens of thousands, depending if one counts each individual pothole, or collates smaller potholes that have merged into larger mega-potholes. Most of them are found on the section on the road between Port Edward and Bizana.

"No sea, no surf, no jobs and no M-Net. The town's only disco is a haunt for the culturally bankrupt to discuss shagging and *babalaas*." Pierre du Toit, writing about Dundee. Dundee is a detour between Pietermaritzburg and Harrismith North, and there is really no need to visit it.

Up through the northern Free State we proceed, the smokestacks of Secunda lighting our way. For years, Secunda and Witbank arm-wrestled for the title of Armpit of the Transvaal; the match ended in a draw. Interestingly, successful South African rock band Prime Circle come from Witbank. As Bill Bryson would say, somebody has to.

We skirt around Johannesburg, city of gold under a thick layer of grime. There was a time when Joburgers had to drive for a couple of hours to indulge in a spot of debauchery, but now the lost city is all around them.

Remembering the advice not to stop near the Rivonia Road offramp, or anywhere along any highway regardless of how desperately we need to pee, we speed past the warehouses and townhouses of Midrand, and onto Pretoria. Pretoria used to be a rather staid sort of place, but now is full of gay clubs and drunk soccer players and even black people make sure their doors are locked when they drive through Sunnyside.

"Pretoria is where shopping malls go to die." John Malathronas.

If we continue north from Pretoria, we will enter Limpopo, which is full of luxury game lodges and dorps where Thabo Mbeki Avenue and Nelson Mandela Drive snake past busts of Hans Strijdom and AWB uniforms lie pressed under the spare set of guest towels in trunks in the main bedrooms of modest bungalows. Some tourists, especially NRA members from Midwestern states, may confuse the Kruger National Park with Orania, in which case they may need to be redirected.

"The people of Mooinooi are like ropes: thick, hairy and twisted." Resident of Mooinooi, North West Province.

You may be mystified by some of the names of the towns in Limpopo. Warmbaths is now Bela-Bela (which, incidently, means 'bubble-bubble' for those of you who were wondering

about its deep political significance[2]); Nylstroom is named for the sacred mountain Modimolle; poor unlucky Naboomspruit was left with 'Mookgophong', which will almost certainly scare British tourists away.

For those of you who are not sure, scaring British tourists away is generally considered to be a bad thing.

Pieter-Dirk Uys as the official Censor of 1980s' South Africa suggested that Kakamas, Holfontein, Nigel and Donkergat be changed on the grounds of the obscenity of their names, but the government has not yet got around to fiddling with those. "Why, even today (despite the dastardly efforts of our evil government), if you're thinking despotic racist regime with jacaranda trees, you automatically think 'Pretoria'," Chris Roper reflects on the change of Pretoria to Tshwane.

> "No wonder they call Bronkhorstspruit Dronkwordstryd." Simnikiwe Xabanisa, after experiencing local bar The Stoep and its Black Bitches (shots of half a black sambuca and half Ströh rum).

If you head back south-southwest from Johannesburg you will cross the Vaal into the Free State. Together with the Karoo, the Free State is between Joburg and Cape Town, Joburg and Plett and Joburg and PE. For years the Free State was known as the Orange Free State, though in truth it was really more of a beigey-brownish colour. "The Orange Free State should not be overlooked as a holiday destination," Gus Silber once observed, "for parts of the province offer magnificent panoramic views of Natal, the Transvaal and the Northern Cape."

> "These Afrikaans towns anyway have an unnatural calm, akin to the atmosphere at an embalmer's workshop." Justin Cartwright.

After the Free State there is the aforementioned Karoo, which differs mainly in that there is more of it, and that it tends toward the greyish-brownish of the spectrum. Not much happens there, although there is a hamlet called Prince Albert; which excited gay British travel writer John Malathronas no end to hear that we boasted a town named after

---

[2] Whether this is in fact a literary reference to *Macbeth* is not clear.

a penile piercing. If you are lucky, you may stay over in Beaufort West, which is of course home to the eloquently named politician, Truman Prince, who, as it happens, is none of those things.

Finally, after dodging the trucks, the buses, the suicidal taxis, the cyclists and the donkey carts, we end up back in Cape Town where, if our luck holds, we will avoid having a rock chucked through our windscreen. Then you can get back onto your plane and fly back to your pebble-dash semi in the first world, where you will store your wooden giraffe in the corner next to the home theatre system.

> Journalist: "So, what do you guys do on Friday nights?"
> Local: "Beat up guys from Joburg."
> *Sunday Times* article describing a road trip from Komatipoort to the Groot Marico.

Jozi and the Fat Cats

Inevitably, most of the column centimetres go to Johannesburg and Cape Town. South Africa's first city and its biggest and richest have long been less than friendly rivals. Cape Town might be the pretty one, the glamorous one, but Joburg has the bucks. Before German chain-store owners and Dutch florists started showing up with euros in their wallets, Cape Town relied on the annual influx of T number plates to put some cash in the city coffers. Aspasia Karras describes Johannesburg an "ageing international playboy with a bulging midriff and peculiar dress sense", suggesting that Johannesburg suffers from a mild inferiority complex in relation to its older, more southerly sister.

> "It is said that Johannesburg has been built up and torn down no less than five times since it first appeared on the highveld in 1886. And each time, it has re-emerged even more ugly than it was before." John Matshikiza

It is Joburg that keeps the wheels of the economy turning while Cape Town, like, kinda does its thing. When cellphones first appeared in 1994, they became known as the Gauteng earring. Now that everyone including bricklayers and beggars have cellphones, these devices no longer have the kind of prestige they once did, but the point is that Joburgers usually get the coolest stuff first.

Joburgers resent the fact that they spend money in Cape Town and get no appreciation. As we all know, customer service in Cape Town is a concept that has failed to make it past the Du Toit's Kloof tunnel. "I can't feel sorry for businesses that are crying because of the losses they say were caused by the electricity blackouts," 'Gatvol Consumer' wrote of Cape Town's "dozy bozos" to *You* magazine. "Usually all they want is money; they care nothing about courtesy to potential customers."

I love Joburg ... sort of

"Aah, City of Gold, I tremble. Has thou lost all irony? All wit? All consciousness? Beware the bling that so becomes you." Adam Levin.

Olive Schreiner called Johannesburg "Hell"; Alan Paton once wrote that no second Johannesburg was needed upon the earth, "One is enough." Most of Johannesburg's residents have a healthily co-dependent relationship with the place, drawn by its energy and repelled by its artificial diamond-hard glitter.

"Johannesburg is a fake city," John Matshikiza writes, "its settlement justified neither by proximity to water nor by the safe embrace of mountains. It's just there, ugly and temporary, a shell on the prairie waiting to sink back into the earth as the gold reserves steadily trickle to zero." Anton Harber finds that Johannesburg is still a "crazy mining town ... a chaotic and wild place where people grovel in the dust to find their gleaming fortunes. Some find it, most don't; others just wait in dark alleys and take it from those who have found it."

Johannesburg, Simon Freeman wrote in the English weekly *The Spectator*, is "Hong Kong stripped of mystique and charm."

"Hillbrow is a vivid, national hallucination." Achal Prabhala.

Johannesburg is widely considered to be the national equivalent of Sodom and Gommorah. Its dark heart, reflects Kefuoe Mokpo, is Hillbrow, "the deceptive queen of harlots throttled by precarious laundry lines dripping from her balconies."

There are many aspects to Johannesburg. There is the CBD itself, forever hovering between death and rebirth like some sort of karmic exercise in town non-planning,

Hillbrow (also known, inevitably, as Hellbrow), older suburbs slipping inexorably into urban decay.

Emeka Nwandiko writes about a die-hard group of Yeoville residents who believe that their suburb, once the hangout of choice for whites who drank Zamalek and found Melville too bourgeois, and now a bona fide slum, can return to a semblance of respectability. The task seems enormous, for they are "ill-equipped soldiers in a war that involves the restoration of culture and art in an area that has been swamped by a consumerist lumpen proletariat that desecrates all it touches."

Then there is Soweto, a place which scares the kind of people who choose to hang out at the Devine Lounge in Rosebank, but which still has an intoxicating allure. The pavements outside The Rock over a weekend put the parking garages at Sandton City to shame.

> "Soweto is Sodom and Gomorrah. The place must be razed to the ground and rebuilt afresh, and not with the present child. These children are poison." Headmaster quoted by Nomavenda Mathiane in the late 1980s. She herself described the typical Soweto teenager as a "Frankenstein monster".

Not that flashing money around is new to Sowetans. Writing in the late 1980s, Nomavenda Mathiane described how, in Soweto, people said that those who lived in Diepkloof "Expensive" and other middle-class suburbs could not afford to live properly because they spent all their money on their bond and flashy appearances. Poor people in the old townships believed that rich people in the new townships labelled their food according to the day of the week.

> "Who would want to be called Miss Diepsloot? *I believe I can naai*." (Sung to the tune of *I believe I can fly*), Trevor Gumbe.

Now, many former Sowetans have long since moved into the suburbs. But, ponders the Bitch's Brew column in the *Sunday World*, it seems that black people still seem to think that apartheid is in operation. How else to explain the fact that blacks choose to live on top of each other in townhouses or on golf estates? "You're in Africa. We have land!"

Signs that black people were still trapped in world with 'whites only' signs included a fear of dogs and the hiding of white girlfriends.

Immorality Act: stop hiding your white women, black men. We know you have them, and they wear sandals, sport matted, dirty hair and make your SLK smell like feet.

Go north, young man, and invest in a two-bedroom, one-bathroom apartment in Fourways

Geography in Johannesburg is unequivocal. North good, South bad. West is also bad, and so is East except for Bedfordview and even then that is pushing things a little close to the Boerewors curtain.

"I've always thought fiscal drag was a weight problem people in Sandton suffer from." Bafana Khumalo.

Sandton is north redux. It was only invented in 1969, and almost immediately became the kind of place where new money went to try to become slightly older money. In fact, in many ways Sandton owes its development to Sandton City, which opened in 1972 when many of the residents of the surrounding suburbs kept horses and rejected streetlights on the grounds that they would ruin the 'country character' of the place.

Within less than fifteen years, Sandton became the preferred habitat of the kugel (see *Sultans of Bling*). The northern suburbs definition of natural childbirth, said *Style* magazine, was an epidural without makeup. Over weekends, a quarter of Sandton heads to the Tuscan villa at Hartebeespoort Dam (which is almost an exact replica of the Tuscan villa they own in Plett, and which is starting to look *so* late '90s) and a quarter to the fishing cottage at Dullstroom; the other half is divided between Sandton City and Fourways. "Dullstroom," writes Mandy Morris, "gives me the social equivalent of food poisoning."

Sandton residents as a rule never venture west of Jan Smuts until it passes the all-important threshold of Hyde Park corner, never cross the N3 unless it involves going to the airport, and never drive south of Lower Park Drive except to get to BCom classes at Wits.

Next door to Sandton is Randburg, which was always viewed as the rather cringe-worthy Dutchman neighbour to rich Jewish and rooinek snobs. "Frankly, Randburg doesn't have a lot to say for itself," Jeremy Thomas observes.

Its town centre is a run-down tumble of taxi ranks and discount dealers and its suburbs are the stuff of a Joburg sitcom: bland, anonymous and the butt of every conceivable caricature of bad taste—human and architectural. Its roads boast names like Hendrik Verwoerd and Hans Schoeman.

"From the outside Randburg looks like a jumped-up platteland dorp that has transferred somewhat uneasily to the big city."

"This city of the plastic fantastic." Achal Prabhala on Johannesburg.

Joburg people are impatient, even pushy. They certainly aren't nice, so it hardly comes as a surprise that it was rated our second least polite city according to rigorous tests conducted by *Reader's Digest*.[3]

P. J. Powers for her part thinks that Joburgers are "incredibly friendly and cosmopolitan … we don't have a mountain or the sea but we have so much more," she says of Joburg. Being in the city gives one a "sense of living and being together," she adds. Joburgers are self-sufficient and "rely on themselves … anyway, the sea is just a short journey away," she adds, presumably thinking about Richard Branson's new supersonic shuttle service to Durban.

"Johannesburg is the kind of town where you run like crazy when someone you've never met says hello to you." Gus Silber.

Joseph Talotta argues that everyone in Joburg has a built-in sense of entitlement. In fact, Johannesburg is Africa's World Class Entitlement City. Talotta has identified the unique way Joburgers express themselves as "Joburg Command Posture". Sentences in this language usually start with "Listen", as in "Listen, I can't make it tonight so let's take a rain check." There are no question marks in Joburg Command Posture, which would indicate either a query or a request for permission, something that would never occur to Joburgers.

"In Joburg-speak the speaker is simply informing you that he or she has taken up a

---

[3] No, the friendliest city was not Port Elizabeth. It was Durban, followed by Pretoria and Cape Town, much to everyone's surprise. PE came fourth, followed by Johannesburg. Bloemfontein was ranked last, almost half as polite as the residents of Durban. Now you can post-rationalize why you have never bothered to visit Bloem.

decision with which you must comply; it's a fait accompli. Furthermore, Joburg Command Posture has traumatized countless New Zealanders and Australians in their own countries."

There are many awful, annoying people in Joburg (see *Sultans of Bling* for more detail) but some of the worst are Emmarentia canoeists, also known as *good ole boy rugger bugger closet homosexual backslappingwankers*. "I am so utterly uninterested in the little in-jokes and self-congratulation of the Emmarentia canoeists," writes Paul Berkowitz.

> Having lived in Emmarentia for ten of the last seventeen years, I have been subject to the superior attitudes of these nobs more times than I care to count. On the occasion that my frisbee has landed in the water, I have had to beg and plead with these guys to return it. When they deign to stop their virtual-time trials and man-on-man courtship rituals, I am subjected to their withering scorn for being a land-based exercise pleb. Well fuck them.

Shot bru!

Several times a year, Terry McAllen wrote way back in 1983, "Durban witnesses the strangest phenomenon, that of a motorized lemming invasion. From every point on the Highveld they converge on the N2 South and pour like boiling oil over the escarpment."

> Once the invasion is complete and Durban creaks and groans, stretched to its maximum and beyond, the beachfront becomes alive with calorie-filled buttocks and boobs bouncing alarmingly beneath skimpy satin running shorts and vests, reminding one of the good old days when the air was clean and sex was dirty.

Ja swaer, those were the days, when the beaches were segregated and people were actually prepared to venture into public in things like satin running shorts. Sadly the Speedo, unlike the latter, has yet to go out of fashion, but Durban remains our most popular holiday destination.

In Johannesburg, the only thing that really counts is money. In Durban, everybody who has money is either a Hulett or works as a brand manager for Unilever. Apart from the Indians and the Zulus, everyone else seems to be blonde and tanned and called Shane.

The Art of the South African Insult

"Growing up in Durban you tended to think all Afrikaners were baddies," admits Philippa Green, a jewellery designer who moved to Cape Town, something that got her an interview in *Style* magazine. In fact, the dismissive attitude toward Afrikaners is one of the reasons why Eric Miyeni hates Durban, which he finds stuffy and racist. Too much Natal English hypocrisy in the gin and tonic, he maintains. Whereas Kaapstad is also racist and Afrikaans, but manages nonetheless to be "stylish".

> "Other than the awards function, beach and football, Durban offers beautiful women and we'll encourage our visitors to consider taking them as their wives." Durban mayor Obed Mlaba, at the launch of the Caf awards, 2005.

"Durban is either hot or fucking hot," residents have been known to observe, which is why homeless people have historically hitched a ride down to the coast every winter. Then there is the first Saturday of July—when marquees mushroom at Greyville and most patrons are too drunk to notice when the horses have passed the winning post—the running of the Durban July.

July day, Nick Paul muses, "sits in the middle of Durban's social calendar like a large, clever, sharp-tongued Berea matron with a fine mind and too much time on her hands. Everyone wants to be in her circle but, after a few hours, everyone leaves feeling stupid, over-indulged and perhaps a little resentful."

> "On July day at least, Durban has its Hooray Henrys. Only here, they're called Howzit Kevins." Nick Paul.

Despite the great weather, many Durbanites leave for Cape Town or Joburg. Jozi resident P. J. Powers thinks that Durban, her home town, is "too parochial".

"You can't stay in Durban if you thrive on energy and have something to prove," maintains Rui Esteves of uber-trendy Vida e Caffé.

"There's something about Durban that stops people reaching their full potential," Nicky Falcow agrees.

"You reach a ceiling in Durban," argues André Guilfoyle, an entrepreneur. "It's a lovely lifestyle but the most they aspire to is blonde highlights."

"What would I want to go back for?" Esteves said, when asked whether he would ever go back to Durban. There is one good thing about Durban though: no bat and ball games on the beaches. ""So you don't get the kind of Bat Nazis you get in Camps Bay, with all their attitude."

> Passengers on a 1Time flight erupted into applause when the captain reprimanded a young man who swore at an air hostess who asked him to switch his cellphone off on a flight from Johannesburg. "On landing in Durban the pilot said, 'Don't speak to a woman like you would to a man. Have a bit of respect and manners,'" one of the passengers told the *Sunday Times*. "It made the guy feel like an idiot when everyone clapped at the captain's comments." The airline said that the passenger could be blacklisted if he was found to have been abusive.
> Must have been a Joburger.

The Mugger City

> "*e'Xpensiv*, the San word for 'Place where the Eurotrash run free'." Possible new name for Cape Town, suggested by Chris Roper.

People have always had plenty to say about Cape Town.

"A poor, niggery, yellow-faced, half-bred sort of place, with an ugly Dutch flavour about it," the celebrated English novelist Anthony Trollope said of Cape Town in the nineteenth century.

"Living in Cape Town is like living with a very beautiful but very stupid woman." Jani Allan a little less than a century later.

Jeremy Cronin has written that Cape Town "is not generally very well liked by many of the new political and professional elite in our country." Perhaps this has something to do with what Cronin describes as "the smugness of its leafy suburbs, secure in the knowledge that the property market will continue to regulate what apartheid administratively held asunder. There is a history of divide and rule."

Asked what he likes best about Cape Town, ex-Durbanite Vaughan Lotter tells *Style* magazine, "Cape Town feels like overseas. It's not Africa. You're basically living in Europe, but in a beautiful sunny place."

That's exactly the point, argue many observers. Cape Town tries to pretend that it has

annexed itself from the rest of Africa. It's racist. P. J. Powers thinks that Capetonians are "too full of themselves" and Cape Town does not have "enough Africa in it".

Tom Eaton resents the implication that Cape Town is a racist city.

> Ask the human flotsam who wash up on our shores from urban wrecks like Port Elizabeth if they have ever been denied anything because of their ethnicity. Ask those refugees from other countries, Central African states such as Gauteng and the Free State, if they have found anything but hospitality.

Chris Roper, a born and bred Capetonian, is also having none of this nonsense. In fact, when he visited Johannesburg, he felt totally out of place as an African. "From the minute you arrive at the international airport, your nose is rubbed in money, progress, money and scandal, those pillars of European society." Johannesburg, he reported, is in fact "a garish European knock-off inhabited by flashy gangstas, self-serving warlords, and drug-addled gunrunners."

> There are big Mercs and BMW X5s everywhere, disgorging clumps of expensively dressed people with their heads attached to their bodies by thick skeins of gold jewellery. People are moved effortlessly through the vast airport, and flights take off and land interminably.

> It's a far cry from the rustic, African simplicity of our cute Cape Town airport, with its holes in the runway and deserted covered parking. And then you take one of the Joburg First World taxis (clean, cheap, no smell of old alcohol), and suddenly you're on the autobahn, long swift roads with big German cars screaming along at high speeds. So different to the slow African pace of our beloved Cape streets, with their aimlessly meandering drivers in old skedonks, and their triple-parked snoek vendors.

The most shocking thing about Joburg, Roper observes with rapt amazement, is that there are no black people there, "only a whole lot of what appear to be Afro-Americans … you'd have to look really hard to spot a young black man wearing our traditional garb of Pep Stores jeans and OK Bazaars T-shirt. It's all Diesel, DKNY and Ralph Lauren."

"Capetonians are too hip," complains a viral emailer, who lives in Port Elizabeth and so has an inferiority complex that dwarfs that of anyone from Egoli (Johannesburg, that is, not the soap opera. Anyone who stars in *Egoli* should of course have a massive inferiority complex, if they don't already.) "They're a bunch of namby-pamby poncey glamour queens who think they live in a magazine."

In fact, the people in Cape Town are just plain weird. All the English-speakers talk about "Keptown" and smoke far too much dagga, while the coloureds spend their cash on tik and the *Daily Voice* and tell you horrible things about your mother. "It's common knowledge," the PE viral man points out, "that the only people in Cape Town who aren't alcoholics, smackies, E-freaks, charlie-junkies, goofballs, acid-heads or nexus-fiends are Archbishop Desmond Tutu and the Tunisian High Commissioner."

> "Stabbed in the chest—must be a Mowbray stingray." Comment on Australian naturalist Steve Irwin's accidental death after being stabbed by a stingray barb, Africans.co.za.

Then there is that mountain. "What is it with their precious mountain?" wonders the man from PE. "The bunch of sanctimonious pricks treat it like it's some kind of national treasure, some gift from the Almighty." Appropriately enough considering developments post-1652, the mountain ensures some kind of weather apartheid, so that some suburbs get sun and wind, and other suburbs get rain and wind.

When it isn't raining, many people like to go to the beach, where they sit and look at the sea. The cold Benguela current brings up rich nutrients all the way from the Antarctic to feed crayfish and hake and prevent anyone except for those in wetsuits from offering themselves as shark bait. The sea simply isn't usable.

"Eleven degrees?" snorts our PE man. "That's a geometry angle, not a fuckin' ocean temperature. What's the point of having beaches if the sea's too cold to go swimming in? More proof that the only reason people go on holiday to Cape Town is to get into traffic jams on the way to the beach and then to pose around with their cellphones on the sand, not to go for a ghoef."

For his part, Tom Eaton hates the beach, and cannot understand why anyone would choose to lie in the sun on "a thin crust of flaked-off human skin, sea-slug droppings and vagrant pee." Clifton Fourth is a "white ghetto of pampered misery"; Muizenberg is a "picturesque septic-tank".

"She was Miss Bulawayo, 1965. She looks like a woman who has been taken apart and badly reassembled. Her face is set with fixed disapproval and her legs look like mottled sausage." Lin Sampson on one of the denizens of Camps Bay beach.

Other parts of Cape Town are also less than salubrious. Cosmo Duff Gordon describes the city's taxi deck, where "the cloying ammoniac tang of stale urine dominates, mingling with the stink of old sweat, melted hair wax and sun-rotted vegetables, to form a noxious olfactory wallpaper."

"The organs of state, Parliament, the Law Courts, Home Affairs, the CBD's skyscrapers, all are just a few hundred feet away; they might as well be on the dark side of the moon." "There's actually bugger-all here," Sultan, owner of a food stall there, grunts in disgust.

In fact, Cape Town is full of noxious vapours, and that isn't just the hot air emanating from Parliament. Not many people know that several PhDs at the University of the Witwatersrand have been earned for the study the air pollution of Cape Town. You'd think they had more than enough of their own pollution to keep them busy, but those Joburg interlopers are obviously trying to make a point.

Pniel Street, Groot Drakenstein is "perhaps marginally better than being in Proes Street, Pretoria". *Noseweek*.

You know you're from Johannesburg when ...

... you consider eye contact an act of overt aggression.

... a postage-stamp-sized patch of grass counts as a garden.

... SA south of the Vaal is still theoretical to you.

... while going under the Caltex Star Stop Bridge on the N1 toward Joburg, you catch the first glimpse of the outline of the city, and you think: aaaah, home.

… the concept of being able to see the sea from your office—while working!—is utterly alien to you.

… you wish you could live in Cape Town or Durban but still earn a Joburg salary.

What are stars?

Acknowledgements

If this were an Oscar speech, you'd be reaching for the remote control. There is a long list of people to thank for contributing in various ways, not all of them involving the contribution of material for the book. But there are many people without whose input this tome would not have reached completion.

Thanks first of all to Chris and Kerrin Cocks and Jane Lewis of 30° South Publishers, who helped pull this project together in a ridiculously short space of time. As South African women of a certain age are given to saying, you guys are stars.

Very special thanks to all of those who are either quoted in this book—or have provoked the quotes used in this book.

Thank you also to André Steyn, Chris Roper, Bernice van Jaarsfeldt, Alex Wright, Francoise Armour, Lusapho Njenge, Anton Labuschagne, Reginald Mndzebele, Cath Boland, Bevan Cullinan, Rudolph Jansen van Rensburg, Molly Hare, Kaye Steyn, Paul Berkowitz, Alison Gasparini, Gert Kruger, Richard Plaistowe, Paul Wessels, Lynne Goosen, Julia Seirlis, Gordon Stevens, Kurt Parker, Matthew Kretszchmar and Vicar of Perth. Thanks to Bobbie Jacobs for giving me the idea of having a 'pet' bergie.

Finally, it would be remiss of me not to mention that much of this book was written on Berocca, Côte d'or Bouchées and a selection of Mozart's piano quartets. The combination of vitamin B, imported chocolate and the Mozart Effect is recommended to anyone facing a deadline.